THE SHAKESPEAREAN MOMENT

THE SHAKESPEAREAN MOMENT

AND ITS PLACE IN THE POETRY OF THE 17TH CENTURY

By

Patrick Cruttwell

COLUMBIA UNIVERSITY PRESS

NEW YORK

1970

PUBLISHED BY
CHATTO AND WINDUS
LONDON
*
PUBLISHED IN UNITED STATES BY
COLUMBIA UNIVERSITY PRESS
NEW YORK
*
PUBLISHED BY
CLARKE, IRWIN & CO. LTD
TORONTO

ISBN 0 231 02082 1

© Patrick Cruttwell 1954

Second printing 1970

PRINTED IN GREAT BRITAIN

To
MY WIFE

NOTE

Parts of this book have appeared as articles published in *Essays in Criticism*, *The Hudson Review*, and *The Journal of the History of Ideas*. Thanks are due to the editors and proprietors for permission to reprint.

CONTENTS

Preface to new impression

Since this book first appeared in 1954, I have reconsidered the opinions it expresses, and to some degree modified them — though I am still convinced of the rightness of the central thesis. Anyone interested will find my reconsiderations in the first chapter, which deals with "The Love Poetry of John Donne", of *Metaphysical Poetry* (Stratford upon Avon Studies II, published by Edward Arnold).

1970   P.C.

Chapter 1

SHAKESPEARE'S SONNETS AND THE 1590's

THE 1590's are the crucial years.   In the Elizabethan *fin-de-siècle* there occurred a change, a shift of thought and feeling, which led directly to the greatest moment in English poetry: the "Shakespearean moment", the opening years of the seventeenth century, in which were written all the supreme Shakespearean dramas.   The 1590's brought about that deep change of sensibility which marks off the later from the earlier Elizabethans, which alters the climate from that of *Arcadia* and *The Faerie Queene* to that which welcomed *Hamlet*, which probably demanded the Shakespearean rewriting of that drama from its crude original blood-and-thunder Kyd, and which found its other great poet in the person of Donne.   To think of the Elizabethan age as a solid, unchanging unity is utterly mislead-ing.   Within it there were two generations and (roughly corresponding to those generations) two mentalities.   In the 1590's the one "handed over" to the other.   Such a statement is, of course, the grossest simplification; in the realms of the mind and the imagination things do not happen as neatly as that.   And in fact, the 1590's are intensely confused, precisely because the "handing over" was then taking place; new and old were deeply entangled, and all generalizations must be loaded with exceptions.   But there *was* an old, and there *was* a new, and the task of criticism is to analyse and distinguish.

Of all the poetry then written, none shows better what was really happening than the Sonnets of Shakespeare.   They deal with far more than the personal events which make up their out-ward material; they show an intensely sensitive awareness of the currents and cross-currents of the age.   They have hardly received the properly critical attention that they deserve; real criticism, it may be, has fought shy of them because of the fatal and futile attraction they have exercised on the noble army of cranks, who are far too busy identifying the young man, the dark lady, the rival poet, and William Shakespeare, to bother about the quality of the poetry.   But the Sonnets are, in their

1

own right, and quite apart from external "problems", poems of great and intriguing interest, as well as of beauty; they are much more subtle and varied than a casual reading reveals. The sweet and unchanging smoothness of their form is extremely deceptive; and it is partly this—the contrast between spirit and form—which makes them, of all the works of the 1590's, the best adapted to help us to a comprehension of the age's development in poetry. For what they show is a blending of new and old, the new *in* the old, and the new growing through the old; they use a form (the sonnet-sequence) which was above all the chosen form of the old, and in that form they say something completely at odds with the old, and destined to conquer it. On the surface they are fashionable and conventional, for the 1590's was the great age of the sonnet-sequence; below the surface, they are radically original.

If the word "fact" be given its proper meaning, our external knowledge concerning the Sonnets is limited to three facts, three dates. The first is the well-known reference, in Francis Meres's *Palladis Tamia*, to Shakespeare's "sugard sonnets among his private friends". The date of this is 1598, in which year Shakespeare was thirty-four. The second is the printing of two of the sonnets (the 138th and 144th) in *The Passionate Pilgrim* in 1599. The third is the publication of the whole in 1609. All else is conjecture, ranging from the rational through the plausible to the certifiable. From Meres's remark it would not be safe to conclude that *all* the Sonnets had been written by 1598, but it does seem reasonable to conclude that a good many of them had been; he would hardly have included them, as he does, in a list of Shakespeare's productions, if there had been only a handful. "Among his private friends" gives the kind of public they were written for, the target they were aimed at: that semi-private manuscript circulation so common in Renaissance literature. The fact that Francis Meres, who was a very obscure scribbler, had heard of them, probably read them himself, shows that this sort of privacy was hardly leak-proof. There is nothing surprising in their having stayed in manuscript for at least eleven years; Donne's love-poetry remained unprinted for nearly forty, but was very widely known. The printing (almost certainly unauthorized) of the two sonnets in *The Passionate Pilgrim* tells us one thing of value. These two happen to be among the most savage of those addressed to the lady,,in a style and with a content one is (rightly) inclined to think of as approaching the mature Shakespearean; we know, then, that he *was* writing in this manner in the 1590's.

The first impression which a quick, unprejudiced reading of these 154 sonnets must give is that they are not a unity. There is no coherent plot or dominant theme; mood and style vary enormously, the changes are often abrupt and the connections obscure. Within this miscellany can be seen some groups which hold together. The first seventeen, for instance, are all addressed to a beautiful young nobleman, urging him to hurry up and marry in order to perpetuate his beauty in off-spring. This is followed by a longer group, still addressed to the young man (or *a* young man—it might not be the same), announcing that it is in the poet's verse that his beauty will stay immortal. There are indications of a separation and a return, a quarrel and a reconcilement; there is a hint that the relation-ship has lasted for three years. The young man, as the sequence proceeds, seems to be looked on as a patron no less than as a lover; a rival poet, more successful than the writer at winning the patron's favour, enters on the scene, together with a good deal of self-depreciation and contempt for his own poetry on the part of the writer. The dark lady makes her appearance; first, it would seem, she was the writer's mistress, then the young man's, and by her fickleness she poisons the relations between them. Running through these stories—we can call them that whether we look on them as fiction or autobiography—are other themes: disgust at the dirty job of being a popular play-wright and actor, bitterness at growing old, envy of other writers more up-to-date, intellectual, and highbrow, anger and disillusion with the state of society, uneasiness about the writer's own place in it, disgust with the whole business of love and sex.

Such are the contents. The first decision which has to be made is how we are to take them: as an exercise in fictional sonnetteering, such as the Elizabethans produced as from an assembly-line, or as personal and closely autobiographical. The probabilities seem overwhelmingly in favour of the latter. For one thing, there is the general "feel" of the poems; then there are the many correspondencies between themes in the Sonnets and in the plays of Shakespeare's middle period: that is, round about 1600. Moreover, if Shakespeare had set out to make an objective sequence with a fictional story, he would surely have made a far better job of it, have produced something more coherent and clearer, something nearer to *Venus and Adonis* and *The Rape of Lucrece*; and it seems unlikely, since he was by the 1590's fully launched as a writer of plays, that his dramatic faculty would have wanted to express itself in another form: it was busy enough in the theatre. The Sonnets he probably looked on as a totally different kind of writing, something outside his professional career, aimed at a different audience. They were, perhaps, part of his early campaign to win recognition in another world from that of the London theatres, in the world of the Court, the aristocracy, and the classical highbrows who tended to despise the popular drama. The two long poems, and *Love's Labour's Lost*, are evidence of this effort; to understand it we must forget our own perception that the supreme glory of the Elizabethan age was the achievement of the London theatres, and remember that in the 1590's and earlier virtually all the forces most likely to impress and attract a young writer, almost all that was socially most glittering and culturally most imposing, regarded those theatres and all they had so far produced with a contempt both social and intellectual. This contempt we are apt to regard with indulgent pity—"how ridiculously wrong they were!"—we forget how biting and humiliating it must have been to a sensitive and struggling contemporary. We are apt also to imagine that it died sooner than it did, that it was confined to the earlier, Sidneyan part of the Elizabethan age and limited to courtly snobs or academic pedants; but Hall's satire will prove that it was still pervasive, still powerful, in the 1590's, and Hall was neither courtier nor pedant. The third satire of his first book (*Virgidemiarum*, published in 1597) expresses the highbrow contempt for the popular drama. That drama, says Hall, is full of rant—"graced with huf-cap termes and thundring threats"; its language is tasteless and incongruous—"termes Italianate, Big-sounding sentences, and words of state"; it is "a goodly *botch-potch*" of clownish gagging and tragedy (a criticism which, as we know from *Hamlet*, Shakespeare himself agreed with); it caters for the low and vulgar, and it is thoroughly mercenary:

4

Shame that the Muses should be bought and sold,
For every peasants Brasse, on each scaffold . . .
Too popular is Tragick Poesie,
Strayning his tip-toes for a farthing fee.

What we, in fact, regard with envious admiration—the power
of the Elizabethan drama to appeal to all levels—a very considerable number of very respectable Elizabethans regarded with
shocked disgust. And Shakespeare's 111th sonnet expresses a
self-loathing agreement with this contempt:

O for my sake doe you with fortune chide,
The guiltie goddesse of my harmfull deeds,
That did not better for my life provide,
Then publick meanes which publick manners breeds.
Thence comes it that my name receives a brand,
And almost thence my nature is subdu'd
To what it workes in, like the Dyers hand,
Pitty me then, and wish I were renu'de . . .

The imagery of staining shows a sense of more than intellectual
degradation, of something which infects his whole being, a
moral contagion. That impression is reinforced by the 110th,
which makes a confession of deviations in love, of seeking (and
finding) unworthy substitutes, and makes it through the image
of the actor's life, the touring, self-exhibiting, posturing clown:

Alas, 'tis true, I have gone here and there,
And made my selfe a motley to the view,
Gor'd mine own thoughts, sold cheap what is most deare,
Made old offences of affections new.
Most true it is, that I have lookt on truth
Asconce and strangely . . .

A moral degradation, it would seem to be felt as: and also a
social one. The 100th sonnet is evidence of that:

Where art thou Muse that thou forgetst so long,
To speake of that which gives thee all thy might?
Spendst thou thy furie on some worthless songe,
Darkning thy powre to lend base *subiects light.*
Returne forgetfull Muse, and straight redeeme,
In gentle *numbers time so idely spent . . .*

Base and *gentle* are epithets which, in Elizabethan English, had associations far more precisely social than they have to-day. The Muse is being urged to return to themes not only artistically more elevating but also socially more elevated. In his mingling of social and literary condemnation, Shakespeare on his own occupation is not so far from Hall.

If, then, the Sonnets derive from an episode in Shakespeare's life in which he made some sort of contact with the world of elegance and aristocracy, the next problem is to find the nature of that experience. The Sonnets, as we said, are not a unity; the experience they present was neither simple nor single, but complex and changing. Although there is no evidence at all that the printed arrangement of the poems was Shakespeare's—no evidence, indeed, that there ever *was* an arrangement—still, one can trace a certain logical development, and the development is from simplicity to complexity.

The early sonnets—that is, to speak more exactly, those which come first in the printed text, though it seems very likely that they were also the earliest—show the simple sensibility of the early Renaissance. There is a vast deal of words to very little matter; the method is that of constant variations on the same theme. The language is smooth and mellifluous,[1] the imagery clear and unsurprising. Ideas are few, simple, and in a sense artificial: marry and beget children so that your beauty may outlive you, your beauty will survive your death in my verse. There is no need to think that these ideas were held insincerely, but they do come from the common stock of Renaissance poetry; they lack the force of a theme which has a particular value. Of these poems one may sometimes feel, what

---

[1] "Smooth", "mellifluous", "honey-tongued", etc., seem to have been the stock-epithets for the contemporary praise of Shakespeare's early writings: for examples—

'Honie-tong'd Shakespeare' (John Weever: *Epigrammes*, 1599).

'Mellifluous & hony-tongued S.' (Meres: *Palladis Tamia*, 1598).

'And S. thou, whose hony-flowing Vaine' (Richard Barnfeild: *Poems in Divers Humors*, 1598).

'O sweet Mr. S.' (Anon.: *Return from Parnassus*, c. 1600)

It is not irrelevant to remember that when Ophelia recalls the unspoiled love of Hamlet, his romantic and chivalrous courtship, she remembers how she "suck'd the Honie of his Musicke Vowes".

one could never feel of the later ones, that some other writer could have produced them.

The love that these early sonnets celebrates is a simple unqualified adoration; neither it nor its object is questioned, criticized, or analysed. The object is a young man who is in no way characterized, or rendered with a sense of individual reality; he seems to be rather the ideal youth of the Renaissance, beautiful, highborn, wilful, and irresistible. He is regarded with a curious sexual ambiguity, as in the 53rd:

> *Describe* Adonis *and the counterfet,*
> *Is poorely immitated after you,*
> *On* Hellens *cheeke all art of beautie set,*
> *And you in* Grecian *tires are painted new.*

The symbols of male and female beauty are taken as interchangeable. The 20th sonnet makes that ambiguity more apparent:

> *A Womans face with natures owne hand painted,*
> *Hast thou the Master Mistris of my passion . . .*
> *And for a woman wert thou first created,*
> *Till nature as she wrought thee fell a dotinge,*
> *And by addition me of thee defeated,*
> *By adding one thing to my purpose nothing.*
> > *But since she prickt thee out for womens pleasure,*
> > *Mine be thy love and thy loves use their treasure.*

There is there, perhaps, a slight feeling of frustration, a sense that this sort of love is hardly satisfying, which comes to the surface in the wry punning jest of "prickt". Primarily, it means "marked thee in the list of males"—as Falstaff tells Shallow ("prick him") to mark down his recruits. But it also had a very current sexual meaning: as a verb, "to copulate", and as a noun, "the male sexual organ"—as in Mercutio's "the bawdy hand of the Dyall is now upon the pricke of Noone". This obscene jest in the 20th sonnet seems the first appearance in the sequence of a feeling and meaning not altogether simple; but in general, these first sonnets are quite at home in the climate of Renaissance "homosexual"[1] feeling, which was in part an

[1] The word is to be taken with no implications of abnormality.

æsthetic affectation, based perhaps on Hellenism, imitation of the Greeks, in part a quite genuine emotion, compounded from love of beauty, worship of noble birth, and an elegiac tenderness for youth. The 37th sonnet sums up the nature of the young man's attractiveness; it opens with a simile which likens Shakespeare to a "decrepit Father" who "takes delight To see his active childe doe deedes of youth", and then lists the qualities of his charm: "beautie, birth, or wealth, or wit." The homosexual feeling that undoubtedly exists in the Sonnets has a certain un-physical remoteness; it is never explicit and aggressive, as it is in Marlowe. But then Marlowe was a tough individual and a *mauvais sujet*, while Shakespeare appears to have been a respectable gentleman. There is, of course, no need to evoke the climate of the Renaissance in order to explain how a middle-aged, middle-class, provincial poet, sensuous and sensitive to his fingertips, conceived a passionate adoration for a young, highborn and courtly Adonis; there is no need, in fact, to go further back than Oscar Wilde and Lord Alfred Douglas. (No *literary* comparison intended.) The insistence that the loved one should get married is certainly curious; one can only explain it on the usual terms, that these first seventeen sonnets were "commissioned". But it does at least demonstrate that the quality of this love was neither physical nor possessive.

As the sequence proceeds, the texture of the poems, though the subject remains the young man, shows a slow thickening, an increasing complexity. They become much more introspective; the interest is often far more on the writer's general state of mind than on the object of his love or even the love itself. In the 29th, for instance ("When in disgrace with Fortune and mens eyes"), the real concentration of intensity falls on the sense of utter failure that fills the writer's being; the conclusion, which affirms that this failure is redeemed by his love, is weak and unconvincing by comparison. This pattern is followed in many sonnets; often, the real weight of the poem, which is thoroughly pessimistic, introspective, and not concerned at all with love, is feebly opposed by the final couplet alone. Of these the most striking is the 66th ("Tir'd with all these, for restfull death I cry"), in which the long piling Hamlet-like list of the world's iniquities utterly overwhelms the protesting little line at the end—"save that to dye, I leave my Love alone." In these poems and many more, an all-inclusive self-examination replaces or reinforces the narrow theme of love; self-disgust, self-contempt, self-reproach are the usual tones of this introspection, and even the rare moments of satisfaction are qualified and brushed aside at once:

> *Sinne of selfe-love possesseth al mine eie,*
> *And all my soule, and al my every part;*
> *And for this sinne there is no remedie,*
> *It is so grounded inward in my heart.*
> *Me thinkes no face so gracious is as mine,*
> *No shape so true, no truth of such account,*
> *And for my selfe mine owne worth do define,*
> *As I all other in all worths surmount.*
> *But when my glasse shewes me my selfe indeed*
> *Beated and chopt with tand antiquitie,*
> *Mine owne selfe love quite contrary I read;*
> *Selfe, so selfe loving were iniquity . . .*
>
> (62)

Bitterness at the thought of age, as here, is one of the points on which this self-hatred is focussed; but another, more particular, and also, it would seem, more deeply felt, is the conviction of failure as a poet. This is hinted at in some of the early sonnets, as for example in the 32nd:

> *If thou survive my well contented daie,*
> *When that churle death my bones with dust shall cover*
> *And shalt by fortune once more re-survay*
> *These poore rude lines of thy deceased Lover;*
> *Compare them with the bett'ring of the time,*
> *And though they be out-stript by every pen,*
> *Reserve them for my love, not for their rime,*
> *Exceeded by the hight of happier men . . .*

—but there seems no great bitterness there: it sounds like polite and conventional modesty, and just where the failure lies is not yet defined. It is defined later, with great and bitter precision, stimulated, it seems, by the coming of the more successful rival. His own verse has got into a rut; it is now old-fashioned and monotonous:

> *Why write I still all one, ever the same,*
> *And keepe invention in a noted weed,*
> *That every word doth almost tel my name,*
> *Shewing their birth, and where they did proceed?*
>
> (76)

The 78th particularizes further; the failure is seen as a lack of artistic grace and a deficiency in learning:

> *In others workes thou doost but mend the stile,*
> *And Arts with thy sweete graces graced be.*
> *But thou art all my art, and doost advance*
> *As high as learning, my rude ignorance.*[1]

What this sense of poetic failure means in Shakespeare's literary career, and in relation to the time when the Sonnets were written, will be looked into later.

The poems, as they proceed, then, move away from a simple and single contemplation and adoration of the young Adonis. They widen in scope, till every interest of the writer's life is brought within their reach: his dreams of social success and bitterness at social failure, the problems and rivalries of his career as an author, his perceptions of the evils and injustices in society, his private anguish at growing old and his private fear of death. The young man is still the centre, but he too is involved in the growing complexity. For now he is looked on with a critical eye, as a fallible individual and not as a symbol that cannot be questioned. The obsequious adoration which some of the sonnets award him—"my soverayne", "your servant", "your slave", "your vassal"—is qualified by hints of rebuke:

> *No more bee greev'd at that which thou hast done,*
> *Roses have thornes, and silver fountaines mud,*
> *Cloudes and eclipses staine both Moone and Sunne,*
> *And loathsome canker lives in sweetest bud.*
>
> (35)

---

[1] It is interesting to see, so early and in Shakespeare himself, a recognition of what was to become the critical commonplace: that he "wanted art" (as Jonson put it) and was unlearned.

A contrast is felt between his outward beauty and inward corruption:

> *O what a Mansion have those vices got*
> *Which for their habitation chose out thee.*
>
> (95)

And now he is looked at through the eyes of others:

> *That tongue that tells the story of thy daies,*
> *(Making lascivious comments on thy sport)*
> *Cannot dispraise, but in a kinde of praise,*
> *Naming thy name, blesses an ill report.*
>
> (95)

He is, as it were, becoming dramatized: seen in the round, seen and felt as a real human being, in the context of society and under the scrutiny of an observant though still loving mind.

When the dark lady makes her delayed but most effective entry (she does not effectively appear till the 127th sonnet[1]—one would almost think that Shakespeare's theatrical cunning had something to do with it), the process we have already traced continues, at a faster tempo and with ever-increasing intensity. These sonnets which deal with the lady (127 to 152) contain most of the greatness and most of the maturity in the whole sequence; they can be taken as a single poem, in the way in which (for instance) Donne's nineteen *Holy Sonnets* are a single poem. The lady is depicted with a familiar equality, a bitter and bawdy ferocity, such as are never accorded to the young man even at his naughtiest. His goings-on are excused and even admired; hers are neither. Her promiscuity is described in language of tough and "un-poetic" realism; and this too the young man never receives:

> *If eyes corrupt by over-partiall lookes,*
> *Be anchord in the baye where all men ride,*
> *Why of eyes falsehood hast thou forged hookes,*
> *Whereto the judgement of my heart is tide?*
> *Why should my heart thinke that a severall plot,*
> *Which my heart knowes the wide worlds common place?*
>
> (137)

---

[1] Sonnets 40–42 hint at her.

The first of these images has an indecent pun on "ride", one of the commonest of Elizabethan verbs for describing male sexual activity (the jestings of the Frenchmen, before Agincourt, about the Dauphin's horse, for example); the last is derived from the contemporary enclosures of common land ("severall plot" meaning "privately-owned piece of land"), and its play with the sexual meaning of the word ("promiscuous") was also a favourite Elizabethan jest. The language, when the lady is the subject, comes much nearer to that of common speech—and of the drama—and much farther from the lyrically "poetical", than when the young man is dealt with.

From this perception that the lady is a whore, come a moral tone far fiercer and deeper, and a self-examination more searching, than anything before. There is not only the famous 129th sonnet on lust, there is also the 146th, which is one of the very few passages in Shakespeare explicitly and traditionally theological, in its conflict between body and soul ("poore soul the centre of my sinfull earth"), its advice to the soul to thrive by denying the body, and its Donne-like ending:

> So shalt thou feede on death, that feedes on men,
> And death once dead, there's no more dying then

—which is very close to the last line of Donne's tenth Holy Sonnet:

> And death shall be noe more; death, thou shalt dye.

Of these sonnets' introspection, the dominant theme is that of a self-divided personality, of a love which exists in spite of the judgment of reason, in spite of a moral perception of its wrongness and of its object's worthlessness, even in spite of the senses' recognition that she is not particularly beautiful. Others do not find her so, and the others are probably right:

> If that be faire whereon my false eyes dote,
> What meanes the world to say it is not so?
> If it be not, then love doth well denote,
> Loves eye is not so true as all mens . . .
>
> (148)

There is an utter disintegration of the personality: senses, wits, and heart are at strife ("but my five wits, nor my five senses can Diswade one foolish heart from serving thee"[1]); the whole self is at odds with the love which it cannot resist ("when I against my selfe with thee pertake")[2]. It is not only self-division; it is also a perverted craving for self-deception, a deception that does not deceive. He asks to be cheated; but of course the mere asking implies that the cheat is already detected:

> If I might teach thee witte better it were,
> Though not to love, yet love to tell me so,
> As testie sick-men when their deaths be neere,
> No newes but health from their Phisitions know.
>
> (140)

Behind this is a conviction that the whole relationship is wrong, is false in itself and founded on falsehood—in the sonnets devoted to the lady, the words "false" and "falsehood" occur nine times, "lie" or "belied" six times—and if all is false, then why should the parts be true? This comes to a climax in what is perhaps the most terrible poem of the whole sequence, the 138th: the most terrible, and also the nakedest, since it confesses things that are not easily confessed:

> When my love sweares that she is made of truth,
> I do beleeve her though I know she lyes,
> That she might thinke me some untuterd youth,
> Unlearned in the worlds false subtilties.
> Thus vainely thinking that she thinkes me young,
> Although she knowes my dayes are past the best,
> Simply I credit her false speaking tongue,
> On both sides thus is simple truth supprest:
> But wherefore sayes she not she is unjust?
> And wherefore say not I that I am old?
> O loves best habit is in seeming trust,
> And age in love, loves not t' have yeares told.
>   Therefore I lye with her, and she with me,
>   And in our faults by lyes we flattered be.

Of this climactic poem the last couplet, with its pun on "lye", is

---

[1] 141.
[2] 149.

the very apex. The pun's grim seriousness is quite in the mature Shakespearean manner, like the remarkable triple pun in *The Winter's Tale*—Leontes raving with jealousy to his son:

> *Goe play (Boy) play: thy Mother playes, and I*
> *Play too; but so disgrac'd a part, whose issue*
> *Will hisse me to my Grave . . .*

—in which *play* means, first, the innocent childish play of the boy; next, the adulterous sexual sport of the wife; finally, the playing of an actor, in the shameful role of the cuckold. The pun in the sonnet forces together the physical union and its context, as it were, its whole surrounding universe, of moral defilement and falsehood. It says, in fact, what the opening of the 129th sonnet says:

> *The expence of Spirit in a waste of shame*
> *Is lust in action . . .*

and it says it with the same union of moral power and physical precision. "The expence of spirit," for the modern reader, has only emotional force; it is in fact a piece of contemporary sexual physiology. From the heart to the sexual organs, was believed to go a vein, bearing in it the "spirit generative". "Expence" means "expenditure": what the phrase refers to is the loss of the "spirit generative" in the act of sex.

This love that is known to be wrong, and is yet persisted in, leads at last to a total reversal of the moral order. Good becomes bad in this love, and bad becomes good: "When all my *best* doth worship thy *defect*"—"that in my minde thy *worst* all *best* exceeds." "Fair" is equivocated against "foul", "bright" against "black":

> *Or mine eyes seeing this, say this is not,*
> *To put faire truth upon so foule a face*
> (137)

—which reminds one of the way in which the witches of *Macbeth* juggle and equivocate "fair" against "foul"; and there too the meaning is that the moral order is reversed. Clearest of all is the final couplet of 150:

14

If thy unworthinesse raisd love in me,
More worthy I to be belov'd of thee

—he has loved her for her unworthiness, this in turn has infected him, has made him unworthy, and hence his unworthiness makes him "worthy" of her. This hell is the exact antithesis of the Baudelairian heaven in *Moesta et Errabunda*—"où tout ce que l'on aime est digne d'être aimé." Substitute *indigne* for *digne*, and Baudelaire's meaning would be identical with Shakespeare's.

The sonnet which follows this (151) shows a slight change of tone, a relaxing of the moral struggle; it reads like a resigned sardonic acceptance of the utter wrongness of the whole business. It admits, in terms unusually religious for Shakespeare, that his love is betraying his soul:

For thou betraying me, I doe betray
My nobler part to my gross bodies treason

but the phrases addressed to her—"gentle cheater", "sweet selfe"—have an air of tired and tolerant affection. Two rogues together, might as well have some fun—the spirit is not unlike that of Villon in the *Ballade de la Grosse Margot*:

Ie suis paillard, la paillarde me suit.
Lequel vault mieux? chascun bien s'entresuit.
L'ung l'aultre vault; c'est a mau chat mau rat.

And the rest of the sonnet carries on in that spirit with an almost cheerful obscenity, with an elaborate and thoroughly Donne-like conceit on male sexuality; the final couplet:

No want of conscience hold it that I call
Her love, for whose deare love I rise and fall

is exactly in the manner of the lines in Donne's nineteenth *Elegie*:

We easly know
By this these Angels from an evil sprite,
Those set our hairs, but these our flesh upright.

We have come a long way from the lyrical idealism of the opening sonnet—

15

From fayrest creatures we desire increase,
That thereby beautie's Rose might never dye

—to reach a poem as complex as this, which in fourteen lines can range from religious solemnity to bawdy mockery. We have come, in fact, from Spenser to Donne.

The way that the Sonnets go is also the way of their age. The 1590's, as said above, was the golden age of sonnetteering; as also of amorous pastoral. They darkened the air; they emerged by their thousands. And if we are honest, we must admit that almost all of them are unbearably tedious; what life they ever had has long since departed. "The sweete sobs of Sheepheardes and Nymphes", "the drery abstracts of my endless cares"—Webbe and Drayton, respectively, describe with an all-too-faithful if unmeant precision the nature and effect of this verse:[1] always sweet, always lachrymose, always unreal. If we read through Spenser's *Amoretti*[2]—it is fairer to choose an example from a true poet than from one of the countless poetasters who practised the *genre*—the final impression is monotony. For, first, there is a desperate narrowness of subject; these sonnets *are* really "all about love", which is not true, as we have seen, of Shakespeare's. Then, within this subject, the number of attitudes is strictly limited, and entirely conventional. The Lady is cruel as a tigress, dealing out death with her eyes; the lover despairing and moribund. The loved one is never analysed and never individualized; she is worshipped with the language of religion—"my sweet saynt", "her temple fayre", "my thoughts lyke sacred Priests". As the moods are few and the tone unchanging, so is the language narrow in scope. "Fair", for example, is an epithet-of-all-work; it occurs some sixty times in these 88 sonnets. The particular and the physical are very far away—the 77th sonnet, for example:

Was it a dreame, or did I see it playne?
A goodly table of pure yvory,
All spred with juncats fit to entertayne

[1] The first of these phrases is from William Webbe's *Discourse of English Poetrie* (1586); the second from the first sonnet of Michael Drayton's *Ideas Mirrour* (1594).

[2] Published in 1595; probably written two or three years earlier.

> *The greatest Prince with pompous roialty;*
> *Mongst which, there in a silver dish did ly*
> *Two golden apples of unvalewd price;*
> *Far passing those which Hercules came by,*
> *Or those which Atalanta did entice . . .*

—we need the explanation which the last lines give us, that this is the lady's breast. The 15th has a similar quality, and a curious anticipation of Donne (he may have remembered it when he wrote *The Sunne Rising*); but the contrast between them enforces the point:

> *Ye tradefull Merchants, that with weary toyle*
> *Do seeke most pretious things to make your gaine,*
> *And both the Indias of their treasure spoile;*
> *What needeth you to seeke so farre in vaine?*
> *For loe, my Love doth in her selfe containe*
> *All this worlds riches that may far be found . . .*

> *Looke, and tomorrow late, tell mee,*
> *Whether both th' India's of spice and Myne*
> *Be where thou leftst them, or lie here with mee . . .*

Spenser's "love" is a far-away abstraction; the rest of the sonnet goes off into conceits which build up the idealized, unindividualized "fair one" (sapphire eyes, ruby lips, pearly teeth, ivory forehead, golden hair, silver hands). Donne has the bedroom reality of "lie here with mee", which two lines later is made even more concrete by "all here in one bed lay". When Spenser does try to give a physical force to his abstract verse, it is clear at once that he is outside his proper range; the hackneyed antithesis of ice and fire ("my Love is lyke to yse, and I to fyre") topples to the ludicrous with "but that I burne much more in boyling sweat".

To look at one such sonnet-sequence is to look at them all; there can never have been, before or since, such a standardized and derivative poetry. Drayton's *Ideas Mirrour* (to take just one more example) has all the elements which we have found in Spenser and could find in a hundred others. The religious language: "receave the incense which I offer here . . . My soules oblations to thy sacred name." The murderous cruelty:

O thou unkindest fayre, most fayrest shee,
In thine eyes tryumph murthering my poore hart . . .

The uncritical adoration:

So may he grace all these in her alone,
Superlative in all comparison.

Smoothness and standardization, abstractness and unreality, utter lack of criticism or analysis: these are the marks of the lyrical verse which, in the last years of the sixteenth century, was brought against something new. At the centre of the new thing were a spreading and a sharpening of the spirit of criticism. That Shakespeare both shared in this spirit and shared in it consciously—was aware of its existence—his Sonnets show more than one sign. There is the line in the 38th—"if my slight Muse doe please these curious daies": "curious" means, exactly, "critical". There is that in the 32nd—"had my friend's Muse grown with this growing age":[1] he is clearly aware of a ferment and development around him. But most explicit is the 130th ("My Mistres eyes are nothing like the Sunne"), which goes one by one through the commonplaces of the conventional lyric and points out, in the name of reality and commonsense, that they are so much nonsense. Not much reading is required in Elizabethan poetastery to find these platitudes, to appreciate just how exact and pointed is the satire of this sonnet. The seventh poem of Thomas Watson's ’ΕΚΑΤΟΜΠΑΘΙΑ or *Passionate Centurie of Love* ("published at the request of certain Gentlemen his very frendes" in 1582), contains in its eighteen lines all but one of the platitudes that Shakespeare makes fun of. Watson on the left, Shakespeare's comments on the right:

Her yellow lockes exceede the beaten goulde	*If haires be wiers, black wiers grow on her head*
Her sparkling eies in heav'n a place deserve	*My Mistres eyes are nothing like the Sunne*

[1] The "friend" is Shakespeare himself: the line is put into the mouth of the beloved.

Her wordes are musicke all of silver sounde	*I love to hear her speake, yet well I know, That musick hath a far more pleasing sound*
On either cheeke a Rose *and* Lillie *lies*	*I have seene Roses damaskt, red and white, But noe such Roses see I in her cheekes*
Her breath is sweet perfume, or hollie flame	*And in some perfumes is there more delight Then in the breath that from my Mistres reekes*
Her lips more red then any Corall *stone*	Currall *is far more red then her lips red*
Her necke more white then aged Swans that mone; Her brest transparent is, like Christall rocke	*If Snow be white, why then her Brests are dunne*

The modern reader, if he feels inclined to dismiss as turgid nonsense the great bulk of Elizabethan sonnetteering and amorous versifying, is in good company. Shakespeare thought the same. What he is here writing is literary satire, and what he is satirizing is something not so remote from some of the sonnets which he himself had written in praise of the young Adonis. There was, in fact, in these years, a tremendous outbreak of satirical writing, and one of the favourite targets of this satire was the amorous sonnetteer. Both the fashion and its antidote arose almost simultaneously.[1]

Donne, Hall, and Marston are the most notable of the verse satirists of the 1590's. Their satires have a good deal in common, though Donne's are by far the best and stand apart from the others not only by their finer quality; but the precise nature of the literary *genre* they all practise—its descent from Roman satire, notably Juvenal and Persius, and its convention of "roughness"—matters a good deal less than the mood which created it and which it expressed. The disillusioned man, the unsparing critic, the embittered railer, the Plain Dealer

[1] Cf. J. B. Leishman's introduction to his edition of the *Three Parnassus Plays* (Nicholson & Watson, 1949).

(Wycherley's character is in the tradition): these are the satirist's poses. He is immensely indignant with everyone and everything; indignation is emphatically the making of *his* verses. Society is utterly rotten; all is degenerate, all is corrupt; and he applies himself with fervent and reforming zeal to the "lashing" of the age. The metaphor of flagellation is extraordinarily frequent (these examples are some of many):

> *Quake, guzzel dogs, that live on putrid slime,*
> *Skud from the lashes of my yerking rhyme.*

> *. . . whilst I securely let him overslip,*
> *Nere yerking him with my satiric whip.*

> *Hold out ye guiltie, and ye galled hides,*
> *And meet my far-fetch'd stripes with waiting sides.*

> *Al these and more, deserve some blood-drawne lines:*
> *But my sixe Cords beene of too loose a twine.*[1]

(None of these satirical zealots appears to have had the common-sense of Swift's observation in the *Tale of a Tub*: "Now, if I know anything of mankind, these gentlemen might very well spare their reproof and correction; for there is not, through all nature, another so callous and insensible a member as the world's posteriors, whether you apply to it the toe or the birch.")

The mood, then, is one of unqualified railing and thorough-going criticism. Directed at what? At everything: this satire does not pick and choose, but assaults in all directions—indiscriminate rage, at times on the edge of hysteria, possesses it. It works in much the same way, though with incomparably less terseness and control, as Shakespeare's 66th sonnet; it makes its indictment by sheer piling-up. This wholesale railing enters Shakespeare's drama from the 1600's onwards; it begins in lightweight style with Jaques—"wee two will raile against our

---

[1] These four quotations are from: Marston's *Scourge of Villanie*, proemium ad librum primum, 1598; ibid., Satire III; Hall's *Virgidemiarum*, conclusion to first three books, 1597; ibid., Book IV, Satire I.

Mistris the world, and *all* our miserie", "Ile raile against *all* the first borne of Egypte"—this being the exact equivalent of the (also lightweight) railing of Donne's second Satire: "Sir; though (I thanke God for it) I do hate Perfectly *all* this towne"— and when it has developed to the depth and ferocity of Hamlet and Timon and Lear, universality is still its keynote and "all" the word which signals it:

> *How weary, stale, flat, and unprofitable*
> *Seemes to me* all *the uses of this world?*

> *Who dares? who dares*
> *In puritie of Manhood stand upright*
> *And say, this mans a Flatterer. If one be,*
> *So are they* all: *for everie grize of Fortune*
> *Is smooth'd by that below. The Learned pate*
> *Duckes to the Golden Foole.* All's *oblique:*
> *There's nothing levell in our cursed Natures*
> *But direct villanie. Therefore be abhorr'd,*
> All *Feasts, Societies, and Throngs of men.*

> *Plague* all,
> *That your Activitie may defeat and quell*
> *The sourse of* all *Erection. There's more Gold,*
> *Do you damne others, and let this damne you,*
> *And ditches grave you* all.

> *And thou* all-*shaking Thunder,*
> *Strike flat the thicke Rotundity o' th' world,*
> *Cracke Natures moulds,* all *germaines spill at once*
> *That makes ingratefull Man.*[1]

The end of this railing—as the two last quotations indicate— was a thoroughgoing hatred of life, of the very source of life; its beginning was an individualist criticism, a questioning of assumptions that had gone unquestioned. The curious cult of Melancholy—itself another fashion of the 1590's—was perhaps its beginning, at least one of its earliest symptoms; for melancholy went with solitariness, it was at once the pride and the

---

[1] *Hamlet*, I, 2; *Timon*, IV, 2; ibid.; *Lear*, III, 2.

curse of the man who went off by himself, to criticize what others accepted. Jaques is a lightweight melancholiac, as also a lightweight critical railer; the melancholy-satirical connection is there also in Marston:

> *Thou musing Mother of faire Wisdom's lore,*
> *Ingenuous Melancholy, I implore*
> *Thy grave assistance; take thy gloomie seate,*
> *Enthrone thee in my bloud, let me intreate*
> *Stay his quick jocund skippes, and force him runne*
> *A sad-paced course, until my whippes are done.*[1]

And just as Shakespeare thought of the age as penetrated with the spirit of criticism ("if my slight Muse can please these curious daies"), so did Hall, in the same spirit and with the same word:

> I well foresee in the timely publication of these my con-cealed Satyres, I am set upon the racke of many mercilesse and peremptorie censures; which sith the calmest and most plausible writer is almost fatally subject unto *in the curiositie of these nicer times*, how may I hope to be exempted upon the occasion of so busy and stirring a subject?[2]

This wholesale railing, which has its place and its force when it is only a part of the whole, as it is in Shakespeare's drama, is more than a little disagreeable—even worse, more than a little incredible—when the satirists present it as a total attitude to life. Shakespeare digested and used it, as he did all things; Donne and Hall went beyond it to better things (great poetry and a Deanery for Donne, silence and a Bishopric for Hall); Marston stayed—to become surely the most tediously forcible-feeble of all Jacobean dramatists. The particular criticisms of the satirists are of greater inherent interest than their universal invectives; and for our purpose the most relevant is their

---

[1] *Scourge of Villanie:* proemium in librum primum.

[2] *Virgidemiarum:* postscript. There is also Samuel Daniel, who talks of "these more curious times" in *Musophilus* (1601). The phrase seems to have been a cliché, as, according to Swift, its modern equivalent was in the early eighteenth century: " 'Tis grown a word of Course for Writers to say, This Critical Age, as Divines say, This Sinful Age." (*Thoughts on Various Subjects.*)

criticism of the amorous sonnetteer. They note and deride exactly what wearies a modern reader. They satirise the adoration of the mistress's perfections:

> *Do not I put my mistress in before,*
> *And piteously her gracious aid implore?*
> *Do not I flatter, call her wondrous fair,*
> *Virtuous, divine, most debonair?*[1]

They deal faithfully with the lover's conscientious misery:

> *For when my ears receiv'd a fearful sound*
> *That he was sick, I went, and there I found*
> *Him laid of love, and newly brought to bed*
> *Of monstrous folly, and a frantic head.*
> *His chamber hang'd about with elegies,*
> *With sad complaints of his love's miseries;*
> *His windows strew'd with sonnets, and the glass*
> *Drawn full of loveknots. I approach'd the ass,*
> *And straight he weeps, and sighs some sonnet out*
> *To his fair love . . .*[2]

And above all, their central point of attack is just that which we have seen was Shakespeare's in the 130th sonnet: insincerity and unreality:

> *Nor list I sonnet of my Mistresse face,*
> *To paint some Blowesse with a borrowed grace.*
>
> *Then poures he forth in patched Sonettings*
> *His love, his lust, and loathsome flatterings . . .*
> *Then can he terme his durtie ill-fac'd bride*
> *Lady and Queene, and virgin deifide:*
> *Be shee all sootie-blacke, or bery-browne,*
> *Shees white as morrows milk, or flaks new blowne.*[3]

Satire implies irony, however crude; and irony implies the ability to see and to feel more than one thing at once, and to

[1] Marston: "The Author in praise of his precedent Poem"—i.e., *Metamorphosis of Pygmalion*, 1598.
[2] Marston: Satire III, 1598.
[3] Hall: *Virgidemiarum*, Book I, Satire I; ibid., Satire VII.

feel one's own self as multiple. The single- and simple-minded cannot achieve it. And hence that sense of a multiple and divided personality, which exists so strongly in those of Shakespeare's sonnets which deal with the lady, is also a vital part, deep and widespread, of the new spirit of the age. Civil war—war inside the individual—is a favourite image, one that Shakespeare carries with him from the Sonnets themselves ("such civill warre is in my love and hate")[1] to the plays which he wrote round the turn of the century, the plays which emerged from the crisis. Brutus uses it, tormented by uncertainty:

> Since Cassius *first did whet me against* Cæsar,
> *I have not slept.*
> *Betweene the acting of a dreadfull thing,*
> *And the first motion, all the* Interim *is*
> *Like a* Phantasma, *or a hideous Dreame;*
> *The* Genius, *and the mortall Instruments*
> *Are then in councell; and the state of man,*
> *Like to a little Kingdome, suffers then*
> *The nature of an Insurrection.*
>
> (II, 1)

Hamlet uses it, describing to Horatio his restless broodings on the ship which is taking him to England:

> *Sir, in my heart there was a kinde of fighting,*
> *That would not let me sleepe. . .* (V, 2)

And—nearest in subject and spirit to the Sonnets—Troilus uses it, shocked and hysterical at Cressida's faithlessness:

> *This she? no, this is* Diomeds Cressida:
> *If beautie have a soule, this is not she:*
> *If soules guide vowes, if vowes are sanctimonies;*
> *If sanctimonie be the gods delight:*
> *If there be rule in unitie it selfe,*
> *This is not she: O madnesse of discourse!*
> *That cause sets up, with, and against thy selfe,*
> *Bi-fold authoritie:*[2] *where reason can revolt*

---

[1] 35.

[2] The Folios' reading is "by foule authoritie." This is the Quarto's: spelling modernized from "by-fould" for the sake of clarity.

> *Without perdition, and losse assume all reason,*
> *Without revolt. This is, and is not* Cressid:
> *Within my soule, there doth conduce a fight*
> *Of this strange nature, that a thing inseperate,*
> *Divides more wider then the skie and earth.*
> (V, 2)

This speech, and the scene it is set in, objectify in terms of drama, and divide among the characters, the elements which in the Sonnets are involved and internal. What Troilus is shocked *out of*, is the lyrical ideal love—"if beautie have a soule", "if vowes be sanctimonies" (the language of the "religion" of love); what he is shocked *into*, is an anarchy of the personality and a chaos of all perceptions. "This is, and is not *Cressid*"— the hysterical denial of reality—has its parallel in the 137th sonnet:

> *Thou blinde fool Love, what doost thou to mine eies,*
> *That they behold, and see not what they see? . . .*
> *Or mine eies seeing this, say this is not . . .*

And in another of the plays written in the early 1600's, *Measure for Measure*, we find the same response to the same kind of situation: a sudden, overbalancing moral shock. Angelo, immediately after Isabella's first visit to him and his first perception of his own desire, asks himself: "What dost thou? or what art thou *Angelo?*"

The collapse of reason's authority, which Troilus feels in himself, is in the 147th sonnet:

> *My reason the Phisition to my love,*
> *Angry that his Prescriptions are not kept,*
> *Hath left me, and I desperate now approve,*
> *Desire is death, which physick did except.*
> *Past cure I am, now reason is past care . . .*

The tough commonsense and astringent bawdy, which in the Sonnets are the means of preserving control (certainly for the poetry, perhaps for the poet), are there in the drama: in the dry mockery of Ulysses—"What hath *she* done Prince, that can soyle our mothers?"—and the rant-reducing bathos of Thersites:

Troilus. *Not the dreadfull spout,*
Which Shipmen doe the Hurricano call,
Constring'd in masse by the almightie Fenne,
Shall dizzie with more clamour Neptunes eare,
In his discent; then shall my prompted sword,
Falling on Diomed.
Thersites. *Heele tickle it for his concupie.*

Only a poetry which is complex in itself, the expression of complex conditions, could thus be turned into drama. The simple poetry and single personality of the lyrical sonnetteers denied them the dramatic quality; few of them were dramatists at all, none was a dramatist of living power. From their verse those elements are absent of which, in the play, Ulysses and Thersites are the spokesmen; and this gives a wider relevance to what was noted in the Sonnets, that as they move from uncritical adoration and mellifluous simplicity, from a poetry, that is, not unlike the poetry of the sonnetteers, so their object is dramatized, "seen in the round".

This difference in literary and personal qualities was reinforced by a social difference, a difference in the kind of acceptance which the writers strove for. The simple, lyrical, undramatic appealed to, and wrote for, the courtly Renaissance world and the taste which grew from it, whose attraction, as we have seen, the young Shakespeare felt strongly; the multiple, critical, dramatic was alien to that world, its true home was the London theatre. For the former world, poetry was an elegant accomplishment, something you pleased your friends with ("among his private friends"). Publication was deprecated; the "common reader" (or common spectator) was outside the circle. "Onely he may show (his writings) to a friend", advises Castiglione's *Courtier*, the Bible of the courtly Renaissance: "let him be circumspect in keeping them close."[1] Even when

---

[1] George Pettie protests against this kind of thing:

Those which mislike that a Gentleman should publish the fruits of his learning, and some curious Gentlemen, who thinke it most commendable in a Gentleman, to cloake his art and skill in everie thing, and to seeme to doe all things of his own mother wit, as it were . . . (*A Petite Pallace*, etc., 1576.)

Pettie's sarcastic repetition of "Gentleman" indicates the snobbish element in the anti-printing convention. A later protest came from

they published, which of course they usually did, eventually, being "obliged", like Thomas Watson, by "request of friends" if not by "hunger", they aimed at a one-level audience and a one-level acceptance. There is, in fact, only one way in which a Spenserian or Sidneyan sonnet can be "taken": if not in that way, it is not taken at all. Thus the multiple personality of the dramatist reflected (both caused, and was caused by) the nature of the public he wrote for; thus Shakespeare's complaint that his nature had been "stained" by his bread-winning at the play-house was true in a way which perhaps he did not know: in his raid on the world of politeness and "gentility" and essential simplicity, he took over with him—he could not help it—the complex ironies of the professional dramatist. The gulf was bridged later, at least in part, when the theatre's creations had achieved a prestige they had never had in the earlier days; it was bridged by men like Jonson and Donne—and Shakespeare him-self: but the Sonnets prove how great had been the effort and the strain, what feelings of shame and unworthiness and "not belonging" a popular dramatist had to overcome if he entered the alien world. He was right, in a sense: right, at least, to feel that he did not "belong". At first: but later, he did.

This multiple personality is a prey to uncertainty; his values are never secure. It is this insecurity that makes the "problem-plays" problematical; there seems in their author (and it spreads to his readers) a radical doubt of his ultimate purpose. The doubt appears in all fields which the dramas touch: in politics for one. In such "political" plays as *Henry VI*, *Julius Cæsar*, *Henry IV*, and *Henry V*—plays which do not have the particular "atmo-sphere" of the problem-plays, whatever their dates—there seems no questioning of the basic Elizabethan political assump-tions, even when these are dissected and discussed in dramatic terms. "Honour" (martial glory) in *Henry IV*, for instance.

Drayton, in the preface to the first eighteen books of *Poly-Olbion* (published in 1612):

> In publishing this my poem, there is this great disadvantage against me, that it cometh out at this time, when verses are wholly deducted to chambers, and nothing esteemed in this lunatic age, but what is kept in cabinets, and must only pass by transcription.

Hotspur, Falstaff, and the Prince divide it dramatically between them: Hotspur giving the one extreme, chivalrous, out-of-date bellicosity, Falstaff supplying the other, cynical earthy realism, and the Prince representing the mean, the reasonable honour which is finally victorious, over the opposition of the first and the temptation of the second. All three views are given with an undistorted calmness; each has its full value. One feels that Shakespeare enjoys and appreciates all of them, without worrying over which is "right". So with the presentation of the "mob" in *Henry VI* and *Julius Cæsar*: the conventional view of it as the irrational unstable many-headed monster—the medieval view, as in Chaucer's *Clerk's Tale*—is vigorously and unambiguously upheld. Each of these plays has a brief episode, identical in tone and feeling—in *Henry VI*, the killing of the man who, in all innocence, has failed to address Cade as "Mortimer", and in *Julius Cæsar* the tearing to pieces of the poet Cinna because he shares his name with one of the conspirators—which exposes with grim farce the brutal irresponsible stupidity of the mob and its leaders. But in *Troilus and Cressida* one wonders, and feels that Shakespeare is wondering. Honour is debated in that play also: Hector, speaking for reason, would have Helen returned and the war ended; Troilus, for honour, would have her retained. But the debate is curiously unconvincing and inconclusive; it ends with a sudden and quite unmotivated conversion of Hector, a lapse from his subtle and sensible arguing:

> *But value dwels not in particular will,*
> *It holds his estimate and dignitie*
> *As well, wherein 'tis precious of it selfe,*
> *As in the prizer: 'Tis mad Idolatrie,*
> *To make the service greater then the God . . .*
>
> (II, 2)

—to a bellicose ranting quite out of character—if the former was "in" it:

> *I am yours,*
> *You valiant off-spring of great Priamus,*
> *I have a roisting challenge sent among'st*
> *The dull and factious nobles of the Greekes,*
> *Will strike amazement to their drowsie spirits . . .*
>
> (Ibid.)

And so with the mob's representative in this play. Thersites is foulmouthed, vile, "low" in every sense; but the heroes he rails at are presented in such a way that one cannot but feel some agreement with his railings. So, later, in *Coriolanus*: there, too, the mob and its leaders receive no quarter—but what of the hero, the mob's enemy? He is surely shown to be just as uncontrollable, just as unpredictable, just as much at the mercy of his emotions and prejudices. The critical spirit has spread, from areas where it had always been permitted to areas hitherto comparatively sacrosanct. The new spirit of the 1590's was becoming incapable of the earlier, idealizing worship of the Queen (in her later years she seems to have been positively unpopular); it was losing that strange poetic adoration of Elizabeth which turns her to a blend of lover's mistress, lay Madonna, and medieval Lady of the tourney. Spenser is of course its supreme representative, as in these lines from *The Shepheardes Calender* (April):

> *Of fair Elisa be your silver song,*
> > *That blessed wight,*
> *The flowre of virgins: may she florish long*
> > *In princely plight!*
> *For she is* Syrinx *daughter without spotte,*
> *Which* Pan *the shepheardes god, of her begotte:*
> > *So sprong her grace*
> > *Of heavenlie race,*
> *No mortall blemish may her blotte . . .*
>
> *Tell me, have ye seene her angelike face,*
> > *Like* Phoebe *fayre?*
> *Her heavenlie haveour, her princely grace,*
> > *Can ye well compare?*
> *The redde rose medled with the white yfere*
> *In either cheeke depeincten lively chere:*
> > *Her modest eye,*
> > *Her majestie,*
> *Where have you seene the like but there?*

These lines show how close was such adoration of Gloriana to the sonnetteers' eulogies on their ladies: the critical scepticism which could no longer swallow the one must inevitably reject the other.

Thus from both ends, from the Queen at the apex to the mob at the base, uncertainty spreads, to embrace the whole world of government and authority. In *Measure for Measure*, Isabella's "drest in a little brief authoritie" and Claudio's "the demygod (Authoritye)" remind one of the 66th sonnet's "art made tonguetide by Authoritie". The note is one of puzzlement rather than a firmbased denunciation: Shakespeare was no revolutionary—indeed, if one had to label his political "position", it would be as that of a natural conservative whom the stress of events, internal and external, had driven to the edge of anarchism. Puzzlement is the note: Claudio, again, is utterly baffled to explain his own condemnation:

> *Whether it be the fault and glimpse of newnes*
> *Or whether that the body publique, be*
> *A horse whereon the Governor doth ride,*
> *Who newly in the Seate, that it may know*
> *He can command; lets it straight feele the Spur:*
> *Whether the Tirranny be in his place,*
> *Or in his Eminence that fills it up*
> *I stagger in . . .*
>
> (I, 2)

"I stagger in": indeed, everyone in the play is baffled by Angelo's behaviour—Angelo included. His own bewilderment ("What dost thou? or what art thou *Angelo?*") we have already noted. The others can only conclude that he is abnormal: it is not only the bawdy Lucio who describes him as inhumanly cold in sex, the Duke also refers to him as one who "scarce confesses that his blood flowes". Yet the Duke admires him too—"a man of stricture and firme abstinence"—and this attitude, half-critical, half-admiring, wholly uncertain, is exactly that of the magnificent 94th sonnet:

> *They that have power to hurt and will doe none,*
> *That do not do the thing, they most do showe,*
> *Who mooving others, are them selves as stone,*
> *Unmooved, colde, and to temptation slowe . . .*

—it might be a description of Angelo (the betrayer of Mariana) before he met Isabella—

They rightly do inherit heavens graces

—is that "rightly" ironic or not? What is the exact tone of the superb line which follows—

They are the lords and owners of their faces

—again, ironic or not? Lytton Strachey, quoting these lines in *Eminent Victorians* (apropos of Cromer in Egypt), decided they were simple condemnation: in them, he thought, Shakespeare described a kind of man "whom he did not like". But they are not by any means so simple: they are balanced between a deep envy, a reluctant admiration, and a suppressed distaste, and their net effect is of utter bewilderment: how *can* there be people who feel so little, attract so greatly, are so perfectly successful—and inflict such pain?

Shakespeare reduces all things—as he had to, being a dramatist, and as he was impelled to, being a born dramatist—to terms of human beings; politics, for him, mean the behaviour of individuals. Between the fields of politics, morals and psychology, he, like his age, made no clear divisions. Hence the uncertainty which we are analysing appears with equal clarity in the latter two, as well as in the first, of these fields. In the speech from *Troilus* already cited (when Troilus has realized Cressida's faithlessness) the inner confusion goes much deeper than the simple, traditional antithesis of reason versus passion, as rendered, for example, in the great lines from Fulke Greville's *Mustapha* (probably written in the 1590's):

> *Oh wearisome Condition of Humanity!*
> *Borne under one Law, to another bound:*
> *Vainely begot, and yet forbidden vanity,*
> *Created sicke, commanded to be sound:*
> *What meaneth Nature by these diverse Lawes?*
> *Passion and Reason, selfe-division cause.*

Greville's simpler mind feels the "self-division" which is a feature of the age; but his values are still secure and his terms orthodox, he is still sure what reason stands for and what it should do, even if it fails to do it. Troilus is not; the "authority" within him (which is, or should be, reason) is "bi-fold", it has become interchangeable with what ought to be its clear-cut opposites, "loss" and "revolt": and that is why the "fight" within him is not merely desperate, but also "strange"—something which he cannot understand. So, too, in Angelo's crisis, the twist of bewilderment is supplied by the fact that moral causes are not having their expected moral effects; on the contrary, the effects are the opposites of what they should be. It is Isabella's goodness that tempts him—"corrupt with vertuous season". The oxymoron which expresses this chaos is repeated again and again, in a circling movement which itself represents the speaker's bewilderment:

> Can it be,
> That Modesty may more betray our Sence
> Then womans lightnesse? . . .
> Dost thou desire her fowly, for those things
> That make her good? . . .
> Oh cunning enemy, that to catch a Saint,
> With Saints dost bait thy booke: most dangerous
> Is that temptation, that doth goad us on
> To sinne, in loving vertue.
>
> (II, 2)

Here again Shakespeare is turning into drama the material of the Sonnets; for this is exactly the moral anarchy we have already seen there, in the complex interplay of "foul" and "fair" and in his "unworthiness" which makes him "worthy" of her.

Maturity and complexity are not attained without losses; the works they beget may win the admiration of posterity, but to their possessors they are apt to come unsought and unwelcomed: matters for regret, even for shame, more than for rejoicing. In the age we are considering, a recurrent feeling is a sad looking back to a past idealized out of all reality, when life and love, society and individuals, were simpler and better. To construct an idealized Middle Ages is no Romantic or Victorian invention; the Middle Ages, indeed, seem to have become "romantic" almost as soon as they came to an end. The Elizabethans were just as prone as later ages to "Gothick" fantasies, and their motive was the same—to express by contrast their sense of the wrongness of their own times. There seems a curious paradox here. Modern research has undoubtedly shown how deeply medieval, in all spheres of life, the Elizabethans still were; but if we think that *they* saw themselves as such, we shall see them wrong. *They* thought they were very different from the men of the Middle Ages: thought it, and regretted it. To this feeling, Drayton's stanzas in *Piers Gaveston* (1593) give a thoroughly representative expression.—

> *His (sc. Edward I's) court a schoole, where artes were daily red,*
> *And yet a campe where armes were exercised,*
> *Vertue and learning here were nourished,*
> *And stratagems by souldiers still devised:*
> > *Heere skilfull schoolmen were his counsaylors,*
> > *Schollers his captaines, captaines* Senators.

> *Here sprang the roote of true gentilitie,*
> *Vertue was clad in gold and crownd with honor,*
> *Honor intitled to Nobilitie,*
> *Admired so of all that looked on her:*
> > *Wisedome, not wealth, possessed wisemens roomes,*
> > *Unfitting base insinuating groomes.*

> *Then Machivels were loth'd as filthie toades,*
> *And good men as rare pearles were richely prized,*
> *The learned were accounted little Gods,*
> *The vilest Atheist as the plague despised:*
> > *Desert then gaynd, that virtues merit craves,*
> > *And artles Pesants scorn'd as basest slaves.*

> *Pride was not then, which all things overwhelms,*
> *Promotion was not purchased with gold,*
> *Men hew'd their honor out of steeled helms:*
> *In those dayes fame with bloud was bought and sold,*
> > *No petti-fogger pol'd the poore for pence,*
> > *These dolts, these dogs, as traytors banisht hence.*

> *Then was the Souldier prodigall of bloud,*
> *His deedes eternizd by the Poets pen:*

Who would not dye to doe his countrey good,
When after death his fame yet liv'd to men?
Then learning liv'd with liberalitie,
And men were crowned with immortalitie.

(lines 61-90)

The contrasts, of course, are directed against his own age; the
same spirit fills the lines of *As You Like It* (*c.* 1599) in which
Orlando sees the faithful old Adam as typical figure of "the
constant service of the antique world, When service sweate for
dutie, not for meade"; and Greene's pamphlet *A Quip for an
Upstart Courtier* (1593) laments in similar strain:

> Then charity flourished in the court, and yong courtiers
> strove to exceede one an other in vertue, not in bravery; they
> rode, not with fans to ward their faces from the winde, but
> with burgant to resist the stroke of a battle-axe; they could
> then better exhort a soldier to armor, then court a lady with
> amorets; they caused the trumpette to sound them pointes of
> warre, not poets to write them wanton eligies of love; they
> soght after honorable fame, but hunted not after fading
> honor.[1]

The attraction of this dream was perhaps intensified by the
fact that the Elizabethan age did still contain, in its outward
trappings at least, some of the elements of medieval chivalry:
contained them, and imagined them embodied in certain of its
own men. In Sidney, of course, and later in Essex:

> The household of Robert Earl of Essex perhaps provides
> the last example of a military service in which a complete
> career could be envisaged within the retinue of a single
> powerful subject. Around the Devereux there clustered
> those gentlemen who still felt that their own knightly rank

---

[1] The same pamphlet complains, in what will strike modern
readers as a comically twentieth century manner, that good old
honest workmanship has vanished from the land:

> Now every trade hath his sleight, to slubber up his work to the
> eie, and to make it good to the sale, howsoever it proves in the
> wearing. The shoomaker cares not if his shoes hold the drawing
> on: The taylor sowes with hot needle and burnt thred. Tush
> pride has banisht conscience, and velvet-breeches honestie.

English craftsmanship, like English beer, is never what it was.

was only strengthened by the fact that they served Lord Essex in a brotherhood of the sword.[1]

If this is so, if Essex really presented to his contemporaries the last enchantments of feudal chivalry, we can understand why he exercised such a fascination over the writers of the age (both Spenser and Shakespeare celebrate him, the former as a "faire branch of honor, flower of chevalrie") and why, when he fell, he fell amid such sympathy for himself and such revulsion against the Queen. He stood for the "good old days": hateful modernity had killed him. He died because he was out-of-date. His fate, and Sidney's, are in significant contrast: Sidney dying, in 1586, universally honoured; Essex in 1601, on the scaffold.

Now, whatever may have been the identity, or the fate, of "Mr. W. H.", there is no doubt that he, the young man of the Sonnets, embodied for Shakespeare this dream of a beautiful past:

> *Thus is his cheeke the map of daies out-worne,*
> *When beauty liv'd and dy'd as flowers do now . . .*
>
> *In him those holy antique houres are seene,*
> *Without all ornament, itself, and true.*
>
> (68)

Not only the past, but more precisely the past of medieval chivalry, the past which Drayton lamented:

> *When in the Chronicle of wasted time,*
> *I see discriptions of the fairest wights,*
> *And beautie making beautifull old rime,*
> *In praise of Ladies dead, and lovely Knights,*
> *Then in the blazon of sweet beauties best,*
> *Of hand, of foote, of lip, of eye, of brow,*
> *I see their antique pen would have exprest*
> *Even such a beautie as you maister now.*
>
> (106)

This world was already, by the end of the sixteenth century, invested with an air of picturesque antiquity—"old rime",

---

[1] David Mathew: *Social Structure in Caroline England* (Oxford, 1948).

"antique Pen"—and it is in this world, and not in the world of to-day, that the young man's beauty is at home. Of that unreal, regretted, lost simplicity, he is almost a symbol, as the dark lady of its opposite: of the complex, tortured reality which has taken its place. Her very beauty is doubtful—it is only on the young man that "beauty" and "beautiful" are lavished with Spenserian confidence. *Her* beauty, if beauty it be, is distinctively, and disturbingly, modern:

> *In the ould age blacke was not counted faire,*
> *Or if it weare it bore not beauties name.*
>
> (127)

She is an individual, and her style of attractiveness is individual. She is flesh and blood—"my Mistres when shee walkes treads on the ground".[1] In this profound and widespread storm, of which she would appear to have been, for Shakespeare, the personal centre, a vast deal of junk, early Renaissance and belated medieval, was cast overboard in the name of reality and commonsense; and among it, that standardized international model of feminine beauty—the golden-haired, fair-skinned, blue-eyed lady of Spenser and Botticelli, the imaginary lady of imaginary knights, whose behaviour was as predictable as her looks. But nowadays women use make-up ("fairing the foule with Arts faulse borrow'd face"[2]), and they wear false hair ("ere beauties dead fleece made another gay"[3]), and such things are the outward and trivial signs of the central fact, that love in these modern days is difficult and treacherous. The feeling was shared by Donne, as *Loves Deity* demonstrates:

> *Sure, they which made him* (sc. Love) *god, meant not so much,*
> *Nor he, in his young godhead practis'd it;*

[1] This is exactly in the spirit and manner, the jaunty knowing commonsensical manner, of Donne's

> *Love's not so pure, and abstract, as they use*
> *To say, which have no Mistresse, but their muse*

—as also of Iago's remark to Roderigo—"the Wine she drinkes is made of grapes."

[2] Sonnet 127.

[3] Sonnet 68.

But when an even flame two hearts did touch,
  His office was indulgently to fit
Actives to passives. Correspondencie
Only his subject was; It cannot bee
Love, till I love her, that loves mee.

Lost innocence, lost simplicity, lost certainty, all symbolized
in a lost and regretted past: these themes, strong both in the
Sonnets and in the age when they were written, are equally
strong in the plays which Shakespeare wrote round the turn of
the century. A great deal of *Hamlet* is a lament for these losses.
Hamlet envies in Fortinbras the simple decisive man of action,
who can *do* things for childish reasons, whose certainty and
simplicity of values Hamlet himself can no longer subscribe to:
for he criticizes even while he envies—it is only "for an egg
shell" that the hero is heroic, he finds honour "in a straw", he
dies "for a fantasy, a trick of fame".   Similarly, Hamlet's
repudiation of Ophelia is a rejection of a simple romantic love
which cannot survive in the stress of what has come later; the
letter he sends her is a savage parody (sane or insane, it does
not matter) of that early uncritical adoration, and incidentally of
the kind of poetry which expressed it ("To the Celestiall, and
my Soules Idoll, the most beautified Ophelia"—"an ill phrase,
a vile phrase", says the critical Polonius); and her description
of him, as he had been before the storm blew up, is a description
of the ideal youth of the Renaissance court, the unspoiled unreal
beauty of Castiglione's Courtier, the Adonis of the Sonnets, in
fact—

That unmatch'd Forme and Feature of blowne youth.

The Sonnets, then, give us the perfect text through which to
see what really happened to the minds of men in this crucial
decade, and especially to the poetry which expressed those
happenings. We may well feel inclined to shrink from the
"subjective" reading of the Sonnets, which sees them as the
record of the crisis (or *a* crisis, at least) in their author's personal
life, when we remember the sentimental extravaganzas such a
reading has so often given rise to—and always will, for the
Frank Harrises and Ivor Browns will always be with us; but it
does seem justifiable to a degree which would not be permissible

in a reading of the plays. Justifiable, but inadequate: for the Sonnets record much else. Perhaps this is always the case with any writer whose life and work are unified: the crisis was all-involving. It was personal and emotional; it was social, and touched its victim's professional career and his attitude towards his career; it involved his art, and drove him, both as a result of it and in order to express it, into a change of style; and it was his own microcosmic reproduction of the change and crisis of the time. It brought him towards a new relationship with his medium, the language, and a new use of it; that use remains, in essentials, permanent—the method of his maturity. The Sonnets are a sort of embryo, in which the essential evolution of the whole of Shakespeare is carried out in miniature. The nature of that evolution, and its affinity to the work of the other great poet of the 1590's, are the subjects of the chapter which follows.

Chapter 2

DONNE AND THE "NEW-FOUND METHODS"

IN the last years, then, of the sixteenth century a new mentality was emerging, critical, dramatic, satirical, complex, and uncertain: with it, and part of it, came a new style in poetry to give it expression. This is the true style of the Shakespearean moment. We can call it "metaphysical" or "mature Shakespearean" as we like: in essentials it is the same style, however varied be the subjects, forms, or purposes which employed it. The first thing to make clear is that Shakespeare himself was well aware that something new was emerging, and aware of its nature. We have seen already that he sensed the ferment about him, and had become dissatisfied with his own work: that he felt it to have become old-fashioned, stereotyped, and monotonous, so that everyone knew what sort of writing to expect from him. In the lives of many artists, such a moment seems to come: the need for a change is felt, before the change itself—the change in the medium employed—can be brought about. The change in Shakespeare does not have, of course, the decisive suddenness that it has in Yeats; Shakespeare is the supreme example of the long and gradual developer, the master of assimilation, who loses nothing however much he gains: but Shakespeare, like Yeats, came to a point when he saw his old style, so perfect within its limits and so perfectly mastered, as having lost its true impetus and personal quality and become a common vehicle which others could (and did) pick up. His complaint in the 78th sonnet—"everie alien Pen hath got my use"—is that of Yeats in *The Cloak*:

> *But the fools caught it,*
> *Wore it in the world's eye,*
> *As though they'd wrought it . . .*

A personal envy and distress, as we have seen, sharpened in Shakespeare (and in Yeats, incidentally) this critical awareness; the 82nd sonnet, which acknowledges that his patron has a perfect right to receive the homage of other writers—

I grant thou wert not married to my Muse,
And therefore may without attaint orelooke
The dedicated words which writers use,
Of their faire Subject, blessing everie booke

—contains also this nagging sense of a loss of touch with the age; his patron is "enforct to seeke *anew* Some *fresher* stamp of the timebettering daies". He saw that his own style was out of touch; he saw, too, the nature of the new:

Why is my verse so barren of new pride?
So far from variation or quicke change?
Why with the time, do I not glance aside
To new-found methods and to compounds strange?

(76)

"New-found methods" and "with the time" make it clear that this is a *new* fashion in verse which he is describing and envying; and the rest forms a perfect, and most perceptive, description of the metaphysical manner: its quick shifts of mood, the surprisingness and complexity of its material. We are too apt to imagine—because we have no "formal" literary criticism from Shakespeare—that he had no critical interest; but this sonnet, and the 130th, and Hamlet's talk with the players, are evidence of a critical activity supremely perceptive, analytical, and sane.

Of the new style, Shakespeare was the pioneer in the theatre; but before him, it seems, in poetry not of the theatre, was Donne. Exact dating, of course, is not to be expected, or attempted, in matters like this: a style does not usually emerge, full-grown, at a given point of time. But it does seem clear that in Shakespeare the new manner is not decisively present, not dominant, till *Hamlet* and *Measure for Measure* and *Troilus*— plays written in the first year or two of the seventeenth century —by which time Donne had already written the *Satires*, the bulk of the *Elegies*, and much of the *Songs and Sonets*.[1] To Donne, accordingly, the focus now shifts.

[1] Jonson's statement to Drummond, that Donne had written all of his best verse before he was 25 (i.e., by 1597) is obviously exaggerated; but it does show that a good deal of it had been written by then.

John Donne was born in 1572. He is thus eight years younger than Shakespeare and Marlowe, and the exact contemporary of Ben Jonson. The point needs to be made; for there still seems a curious reluctance (it originated, presumably, from the accident that almost all his poetry was not published till 1633, two years after his death) to see him for what he is: an Elizabethan. Even when this is recognized in theory, it seems to be rarely felt in critical practice. Spenser and Shakespeare still "go together", for most minds, more easily than Shakespeare and Donne; but Shakespeare, from the end of the sixteenth century, has nothing in common with Spenser and a great deal in common with Donne. That common quality can be put in one word; they are both, to their fingertips, dramatic. There were, of course, differences between them. Differences in the backgrounds they grew from: Donne from a family of Roman Catholic metropolitan gentry, Shakespeare from Protestant provincial yeomen and tradespeople. Differences in mentality: Donne much more explicitly religious, more obviously learned and scholarly. Differences in temperament: Donne volatile and explosive, Shakespeare (one deduces) quieter, more ruminating. Differences in the forms of poetry they wrote: Donne's more "personal", more (apparently) autobiographical. But these differences make more striking the essential similarity of their poetry; only a very profound common factor could unite such different men, and only a civilization which was unified at some very profound level, in spite of its obvious schisms, could produce such a common factor. None such could exist to-day; there is nothing in common between Eliot and Priestley, Auden and Coward.

Donne and Shakespeare, in the 1590's, shared a great range of experience. They lived in the same world, the small world of Elizabethan literary London. There is no evidence that they knew each other, nor is there any need to suppose it; the link is close enough, for Donne and Jonson were friends and mutual admirers, and Jonson and Shakespeare were colleagues and friends. The Inns of Court, where Donne was a student and Shakespeare's plays were produced, the courtly patrons of literature, the Court itself, the popular theatres: these were the meeting-grounds, where the two men's minds received the same stimuli. And of these the most vital was the theatre. We

D

do not need the contemporary evidence (Sir Richard Baker's) that the young Donne was "a great frequenter of plays"; his poems abound in proofs of it. There are (to take a few out of many) the references in *The Calme* to Marlowe's *Tamburlaine* ("like *Bajazet* encag'd, the shepheards scoffe") and to the dust and litter of an emptying theatre; the remark in the second verse-letter to Wotton—

> *Beleeve mee Sir, in my youths giddiest dayes,*
> *When to be like the Court, was a playes praise,*
> *Playes were not so like Courts, as Courts' are like playes . . .*

and the delightful detail in the fifteenth *Elegie*, which describes the two lovers, reconciled after quarrelling, who

> *at maskes and playes*
> *Commend the self same Actors, the same wayes . . .*

From such a basis of youthful experience, the image of the play sank through Donne's mind to deeper levels, till it became for him almost as "natural" a metaphor as it did for Shakespeare, as evocative an expression of his deepest emotions: as natural an image for him, when he contemplates his own dissolution in the sixth of the *Holy Sonnets*—

> *This is my playes last scene . . .*

as it is for Macbeth when he has heard of the death of his wife and broods on the futility of his own self-damnation.

This is the basis of what is dramatic in Donne: a deep and lively experience of the theatre in the years when the English drama was on the edge of its greatest moment—years when it meant more, to men of more than usual sensibility and intellect, than ever before or since. The gulf we have noted, between highbrow and lowbrow, courtly and popular, was beginning to close; for Donne, as for Shakespeare from the 1600's, there was no gulf. The experience of the popular theatre could be yielded to, by a man as intellectual and as learned as Donne, with none of the polite and classical shudders which afflicted and inhibited the Sidneys and the Halls; and because it could be thus freely yielded to, it could in turn yield something of the greatest value, could be decisive in the moulding of Donne's creation. The dramatic way of writing enters and permeates all his work. His love-poetry, at first sight, appears intensely "personal"; so it is, of course, in a sense, as all great art is, in a sense. But we have his own word for it—one of the most revealing things we know from him—that it is not always, not necessarily, personal in the sense of being directly "autobiographical". "I did best," he says, "when I had least of truth to go by." That may be partly discounted (it is the later Donne excusing his earlier self); but however interested his motive for saying it, the saying remains true in its critical bearing. It is a habit of Romantic criticism to look on all love-poetry as directly autobiographical—to "feel" it as such even when it is not known to be so[1]—and of most Romantic love-poetry this may be true. But the Renaissance possessed—inherited largely from the Middle Ages—a whole tradition of love-poetry in which the individually autobiographical was so strictly subservient to the preformed conventional as hardly to exist. The European convention of courtly love was a semi-dramatic system of stylized behaviour and styles prescribed, within which each individual writer produced his own variation. And although Donne rejected the sentimentality and blatant unreality of the last decadent flickers of this tradition (for that is what Elizabethan sonnetteering really is), he did not reject it entirely. He kept its way of writing about the experiences of love in a half-detached, half-experimental manner: kept that, but immensely widened its range of moods and so of expression, never broke from the anchor of reality, and revived the whole thing with the spirit of the truly dramatic—the dramatic of the living theatre.

In his different sphere, he too is a dramatist; and a closer look at his poems will show how the dramatist works. In many poems, he sets the scene and objectifies the persons, "seeing" them as an audience sees the players on a stage. *The Extasie* invokes a hypothetical spectator, *The Apparition* sees the lovers as the entering ghost will see them, *The Sunne Rising* looks in on them as the sun will, shining through the window at the curtained bed in the centre of the room. The angle of address continually changes, shifting from third person to second and *vice versa*. *The Relique* shifts from "thou" in the second stanza

[1] Cf. the earnest researches into the identity of Wordsworth's "Lucy".

to "she" in the poem's last line. *The Funerall* talks of "she" throughout, with dignified melancholy restraint, till, again in the last line, viewpoint and mood both change to emphatic and personal bitterness: "that since *you* would save none of mee, I bury some of *you*." The poems abound in sudden reversals— *coups de théâtre*, in fact, carefully prepared-for moments of shock, like the last words of Othello's tirade—"and stabb'd him, thus." The end of *Loves Deity*, for example, denies what all the rest has been affirming; *Aire and Angells*, with its tone of theological solemnity, prepares us for an "idealistic" comment on women, but ends in fact with a piece of critical cynicism.[1] Such effects, of course, must be prepared for; and Donne's poems are always constructed, they are never a shapeless "flowing", as Romantic love-lyrics tend to be (Burns' or Shelley's, for instance). They have clearly-divided sections, which function exactly like the acts of a play. They have, in fact, a plot: an action in the Aristotelian sense, a beginning, a middle, and an end: they move in a known direction. His favourite triple structure, which appears in so many poems,[2] and which Marvell borrowed for the *Coy Mistress*, may have come from the syllogism of medieval logic, but more fruitful is the comparison with the acts of a play. For the structure moves the poem onward, step by step, with the living movement of a drama, rather than with logic's artificial neatness.

Above all, and throughout, Donne uses language as the dramatist uses it—as Shakespeare uses it. It is not merely— what is obvious—that the ground of his rhythm is the speaking voice and of his vocabulary the living speech: when he is artificial, his artificiality is that of the theatre. He uses the rhetorical tirade, with its balance and repetitions, as in the opening of the sixteenth *Elegie*:

> *By our first strange and fatall interview,*
> *By all desires which thereof did ensue,*
> *By our long starving hopes, by that remorse*
> *Which my words masculine perswasive force*
> *Begot in thee, and by the memory*
> *Of hurts, which spies and rivals threatned me,*

[1] We have seen this sort of "reversal" in Shakespeare's Sonnets.

[2] E.g., *Good-morrow, Sunne Rising, Indifferent, Lovers Infinitenesse, Twicknam Garden, Dream, Valediction of Weeping.*

> *I calmly beg: But by thy fathers wrath,*
> *By all paines, which want and divorcement hath,*
> *I conjure thee, and all the oathes which I*
> *And thou have sworne to seale joynt constancy,*
> *Here I unsweare, and overswear them thus,*
> *Thou shalt not love by wayes so dangerous.*

Put this beside a Shakespearean passage of the same form—
Mercutio's mock-heroic conjuring of Romeo—and the similarity
of movement becomes clear:

> *He heareth not, he stirreth not, he moveth not,*
> *The Ape is dead, and I must conjure him,*
> *I conjure thee by* Rosalines *bright eyes,*
> *By her High forehead, and her Scarlet lip,*
> *By her Fine foote, Straight leg, and Quivering thigh,*
> *And the Demeanes, that there Adjacent lie,*
> *That in thy likenesse thou appeare to us.*

Dramatic, too, is the way in which words are played on and
played with, repeated with a new sense or a new emphasis, not
for the mere fun of it, but to render the sense of a mind in
continually changing action. (And drama means action.) For
example (still from the sixteenth *Elegie*):

> *Here I unsweare, and overswear them thus . . .*
> *Temper, O faire Love, loves impetuous rage . . .*
> *I'll goe, and, by thy kinde leave, leave behinde . . .*
> *Will quickly know thee, and know thee . . .*
>   (the word "know" having first the ordinary,
>   and then the sexual, meaning)
> *If thou stay here. O stay here, for, for thee . . .*

Moods change with lightning speed; the moods of a poem by
Donne are its *dramatis personæ*, its plot is their interplay.
Language is telescoped, syntax wrenched, to keep up with the
action:

> *Dissemble nothing, not a boy, nor change*
> *Thy bodies habite, nor mindes . . .*

in which "not a boy" telescopes to three words "do not disguise
yourself as a boy": a parenthesis, flashing across the mind in
mid-sentence and put down just as it flashed. It works as

Shakespeare's description of the battle in *Cymbeline* works—
quickness of words matching quickness of action:

> *Then beganne*
> *A stop i'th' Chaser; a Retyre: Anon*
> *A Rowt, confusion thicke: forthwith they flye*
> *Chickens, the way which they stoopt Eagles: Slaves*
> *The strides they Victors made . . .*
>
> (V, 3)

Of Donne's love-poetry the true subject is something much
more than simply the experiences of John-Donne-in-love; the
subject is love itself, situations between persons in love or
concerned with love, moods, attitudes, experiences, experiments
in love. The fact that not infrequently these moods, etc., flatly
contradict each other—sometimes within a single poem—
worries Donne no more than the blending of tragic and comic
in the same play, or the same scene, worried an Elizabethan
playwright or his audience—and that is the appropriate comparison. A scene like that of Hamlet, the gravediggers, and the
burial of Ophelia, makes the same kind of effect from the same
methods: the juxtaposing of clashing elements. It is a process
not so much of getting away from the mere self and the
moment's emotion, as of always remembering that the mere
self of this very moment is not everything, but was made what
it is by what was done and felt by a self which was different in
an earlier moment, and will in turn bring about another self in a
later moment: precisely as a playwright must always remember
that each speech in each scene contributes to the movement of
the whole play. And just as a dramatist is not "committed" to
any utterance of any of his characters, so Donne himself is not,
to any of the selves which appear in his love-poetry.

Or to any of the "shes". For the "she" of this poetry, who
varies as the "I" varies, from idealized symbol through loved
wife or mistress to plain whore, may be profitably compared
with the Shakespearean presentation of Cleopatra. The play,
if it must be classified, must be called a tragedy; but its heroine
(like its hero, incidentally) is viewed as often with satirical
irony and cheerful familiarity as with tragic solemnness. In the
first scene, she is a teasing, confident mistress, pretending to be
jealous of Fulvia and insisting that Antony shall "hear the

ambassadors". In the next, Enobarbus, with his bawdy jests, comments on her as a mere whore, interested only in satisfying her lusts: ". . . and the businesse you have broach'd heere cannot be without you, especially that of *Cleopatra's*, which wholly depends on your abode." She teases again in the third scene, with, at its end, a sudden shift to generous resignation and dignified rhetoric:

> *Therefore be deafe to my unpitied Folly,*
> *And all the Gods go with you. Upon your Sword*
> *Sit Lawrell victory, and smooth successe*
> *Be strew'd before your feete.*

In the second scene of Act II, the great speech of Enobarbus presents her as the incomparably glamorous and beautiful Queen—from which, in the fifth scene, she descends to violent and unreasonable childishness when she beats the messenger who tells her of Antony's marriage. Throughout the whole play a counterpoint is kept up, between the memories of her exquisite beauty when young and the fact, which is relentlessly harped on, that now she is an ageing woman. She rises, at the death of Antony, to the heights of tragic lament; she falls therefrom, with a bump, detected by her treasurer in petty cheating.[1] Finally, at her own death, she regains the tragic level—but even there, she dies with a joke:

> *Poore venomous Foole,*
> *Be angry, and dispatch. O couldst thou speake,*
> *That I might heare thee call great Cæsar, Asse,*
> *Unpolicied.*

The whole presentation expands the phrase of Enobarbus: "her infinite variety." And also the phrase of Donne (*The Indifferent*): "Love's sweetest part, Variety." And no one facet of the infinite variety, whether in Donne's poems or in Shakespeare's play, is presented with more emphasis than any of the others; none, in the play, is the "real" Cleopatra; none of the attitudes towards her is the "real" Shakespeare's.

Thus, while it may be of biographical or psychological

---

[1] "I left the room with quiet dignity, but caught my foot on the mat"—the spirit of this episode comes a great deal nearer to Mr. Pooter than it does to the decorum of classical tragedy.

interest to probe for the "real" Donne beneath the selves of his creation, or to throw up one's hands in affected astonishment at the man's contradictions and complexities,[1] such procedures, for criticism, for the understanding of his poetry, are irrelevant and valueless. In his poetry there is no "real" Donne, just as in his plays there is no "real" Shakespeare. There are the poems, and there are the plays; there is the body of the poetry, and the body of the plays; and the patterns we may legitimately try to deduce from these are not the sort of patterns which make up a consistent "character". The multiple, the dramatic personality is as native to Donne as it is to Shakespeare: a fact, of course, which caused the former much distress in his later years, when he aspired to the singleness of the mystical vision. He was aware of his own incurable multiplicity: aware of it, in rebellion latterly against it (that is the real meaning of his self-made division between "Doctor Donne" and "Jack Donne", and his efforts to collect and destroy his earlier poetry), but totally unable to change it, unable, even when trying to repudiate it, *not* to write dramatically, as in the last of the *Holy Sonnets*:

> *Oh, to vex me, contraryes meet in one:*
> *Inconstancy unnaturally hath begott*
> *A constant habit: that when I would not*
> *I change in vowes, and in devotion . . .*

"Contraryes meet in one": the phrase, which describes his character, would be also a perfect description of his poetry, of a play such as *Hamlet* and *Lear*, of the whole new style whose emergence Shakespeare had noted and whose nature he analysed in that phrase of the Sonnets which means the same—"compounds strange."

Donne in this, like Shakespeare, proves his descent from the most genuinely vital and revolutionary part of the Renaissance, the part which is self-regarding, self-wondering, self-doubting, yet all the time self-dramatizing, so much more living and

---

[1] As does Lytton Strachey, for instance, in *Elizabeth and Essex*: 'Human beings no doubt would cease to be human beings unless they were inconsistent; but the inconsistency of the Elizabethans exceeds the limits permitted to man. . . . By what perverse magic were intellectual ingenuity and theological ingenuousness intertwined in John Donne?'

fruitful than the sterile and static "imitation-classic". It is Montaigne whom he brings to mind, Montaigne who works within the framework of the first-person essay as Donne within that of the first-person poem, who also is always aware of the changeableness of his self, who builds up a monologue-drama from his shifting "I's", and who never forgets that the "I" of to-day is neither that of yesterday nor that of to-morrow. "Contraryes meet in one," says Donne of himself; and "Sometimes I give my soule one visage, and sometimes another," says Montaigne of *his* self, ". . . if I speake diversely of my selfe, it is because I looke diversely upon my selfe. *All contrarieties are found in her* (his soul), according to some turne or removing, and in some fashion or other."[1] The ego, as Donne and Montaigne both see it, is a shifting and tricky creature— "ondoyant et divers", in the latter's untranslatable phrase—but just because it is so, it is all the more fascinating, and all the more important it becomes not to ignore its smallest manifestations. Nothing is harder than to pin down what was really new in the Renaissance; so much of it (courtly love or Spenserian allegorizing, for instance) was really the Middle Ages dressed up in new clothes. But this obsessive yet dramatic introspection, this sense of the human entity, body and mind and soul, as ever moving, ever interesting, and ever incongruous with its own past and future—this does seem to have been a genuinely new thing, at least when felt with the intensity and continuousness with which it is felt by Montaigne and Shakespeare and Donne.

Of the new style in verse which gave it expression, there is much that is directly derived from this sense. Something, for example, which might be called "psychological impressionism": a constant interest in, and attempt to render in verse, not merely the results, the final settlement, of states of mind and body and emotion, but the very process by which those states are created; whereas the earlier poetry—Marlowe's or Sidney's or Spenser's —presents, rather, completed units of feeling and thought, but not the shifting from one to the next. The Chorus's line in *Henry V*—

In the quick Forge and working-house of Thought

[1] Book II, chap. I: *Of the Inconstancie of our Actions* (Florio's translation).

expresses perfectly (with the double meaning of "quick", *living* and *swift*) both the interest itself and the kind of poetry it led to: poetry such as Troilus's speech when he is waiting for Cressida:

> *I am giddy; expectation whirles me round,*
> *The imaginary relish is so sweete,*
> *That it inchants my sence: what will it be*
> *When that the watry pallat tastes indeede*
> *Loves thrice repured Nectar? Death I feare me*
> *Swounding distruction, or some joy too fine,*
> *Too subtile, potent, and too sharpe in sweetnesse,*
> *For the capacitie of my ruder powers.*
>
> (III, 2)

What is notable there is the absolute fusion of the physical sensation and the intellectual analysis; the *total* condition of the speaker's being, at this one fleeting moment of his life, is seen with a clairvoyance which no "real" person, in such a moment, could ever achieve. Nothing could be more intellectually precise than the line which analyses his sensations into two pairs of antitheses—"too subtile, potent, and too sharpe in sweetnesse"[1]—nothing more physically precise than the "watry pallat". In these antitheses the purely verbal, decorative oxymora which one finds in Kyd and early Shakespeare[2] are turned to the service of a real analysis, to the expression of a deep-rooted sense of complexity and incongruity.

Incongruities—a taste for incongruities, and a need to express and, if possible, reconcile them—lie at the centre of the new style. The cynical and the idealist, the realistic and the fantastic, the homely and the exotic, the grotesque and the beautiful, the mortality of the graveyard and the sensuality of the living body —these are some of them; and deepest of all is that of love and death. As in all this poetry, its root goes down to crude and physical fact, however far-fetched may seem to be its branches

---

[1] "Subtile, potent"—which should perhaps be printed, as most modern editions print it, "subtle-potent"—reminds one of Donne's creation "scatt'ring bright" in *Aire and Angells*: Donne, like Shakespeare, is forcing together, with all the compression that the language can bear, two perceptions which are contradictory, but cohere, he feels, in the entity he is rendering.

[2] E.g., Romeo's lines quoted on p. 59.

of fantasy; the root is found in the constant equivocation (one of the two or three standard Elizabethan jokes) which uses "kill" to mean male love-making and "die" for the female. Of which, in the key of levity, are Enobarbus's "under a more compelling occasion let women die" and Donne's (with a characteristic twisting reversal):

> *Kill mee as woman, let mee die*
> *As a meere man . . .*
> (*The Dampe*)

But it goes much farther than levity; it is a fruitful source of great and tragic moments, not only of such famous moments in metaphysical verse as the "bracelet of bright haire about the bone" and the tomb of Marvell's coy mistress, but also of Othello's

> *I kist thee, ere I kill'd thee: No way but this,*
> *Killing my selfe, to dye upon a kisse*

—of Cleopatra's

> *The stroke of death is as a Lovers pinch,*
> *Which hurts, and is desir'd*

(in which the equivocation resides in the one word "stroke": a *blow* if you think of death, a *caress* if you think of love)—and of Lear's

> *I wil die bravely, like a smugge Bridegroome.*

The tone of Lear's saying—its queer tightrope effect, almost beyond analysis, with bawdy on one side and heartbreaking pathos on the other[1]—is uniquely of the Shakespearean moment in English poetry; no other age could have come within a mile of it, or would even have attempted it. It has a close parallel, both in subject (love and death again) and in ambiguous strangeness, in lines from Donne's first *Anniversarie* poem:

---

[1] The line has two double-meanings. "Die" has both the literal and the sexual meanings; "bravely" means both "courageously" and "in the dressed-up finery of the wedding-day".

For that first marriage was our funerall:[1]
One woman at one blow, then kill'd us all,
And singly, one by one, they kill us now.
We doe delightfully our selves allow
To that consumption; and profusely blinde,
Wee kill our selves to propagate our kinde . . .

There the commonplace jokes, of women who kill men by sexual demandingness and men who waste their virility on women, and the fragment of contemporary physiological theory, that the performance of the sexual act shortens man's life, are harnessed to a solemn, indeed theological, meaning; and the reader is left, at least the modern reader is apt to be left, in a state of total uncertainty—just how "serious" is Donne being here? and if he is serious, just in what way? Understanding, it may be, can be reached only when one sees that in this kind of poetry "seriousness" and "levity" are meaningless expressions; a fusion is achieved in which both exist, both have full value, and both are essential—if your reading misses one (the modern reader is more apt to miss the levity), you are missing the whole—and the total result is beyond the scope of either. Blake, of course, is not in our period; but the collocation is irresistible, of the first line in the passage from Donne—"for that first marriage was our funerall"—and the last stanza (the very last word, indeed) of Blake's *London*:

> *But most through midnight streets I hear*
> *How the youthful Harlot's curse*
> *Blasts the new-born Infant's tear*
> *And blights with plagues the Marriage-hearse.*

Physical disease and moral contagion, love and death brought together in one word—was Blake the only poet, outside the Shakespearean moment, who was capable of such effects?

As deep, perhaps, and as pervasive, is another Renaissance incongruity: wonder at man's achievements and his marvellous nature, dismay at his final unsatisfactoriness, at the fact that

[1] In one of his sermons, Donne uses the same conceit, reversed:
It [sc. "consolation from the Holy Ghost"] makes my death-bed, a marriage-bed; And my Passing-Bell, an Epithalamion. (Sermon XXXVI, *80 Sermons*.)

contemplation of his marvels does not produce the expected exhilaration. (We are badly out if we imagine that it is only the bomb-obsessed twentieth century which is frightened by man's enterprising inventiveness.)   Donne gives the contrast, in another passage from the first *Anniversarie*:

> *Thus man, this worlds Vice-Emperour, in whom*
> *All faculties, all graces are at home;*
> *And if in other creatures they appeare,*
> *They're but mans Ministers, and Legats there,*
> *To worke on their rebellions, and reduce*
> *Them to Civility, and to mans use:*
> *This man, whom God did wooe, and loth t'attend*
> *Till man came up, did downe to man descend,*
> *This man, so great, that all that is, is his,*
> *Oh what a trifle, and poore thing he is!*

In meaning and spirit and method (a building-up to an anti-climax) that comes very near to Hamlet's tirade:

> What a piece of work is a man! how Noble in Reason? how infinite in faculty? in forme and moving how expresse and admirable? in Action, how like an Angel? in apprehension, how like a God? the beauty of the world, the Parragon of Animals; and yet to me, what is this Quintessence of Dust?
>
> (II, 2)

The feeling was strong in Montaigne, whose constant denigration of man's faculties (as in the Apology for Raimond Sebond) is continually, implicitly, contradicted by his passionate interest in the creature. It may be too simple to see this entirely as the clash between Renaissance bumptiousness and medieval humility; but that was at the base of it. In the simpler climate of the earlier English Renaissance one can see two attitudes, each simple, opposing each other, in regard to such phenomena as the new discoveries. Barclay, in *The Ship of Fooles* (1508), gives the one: plain dismay, medieval suspiciousness of anything new:

> *For nowe of late hath large londe and grounde*
> *Ben founde by maryners and craftie governours,*
> *The whiche londes were never knowne ne founde*
> *Before our tyme by oure predecessours,*

And hereafter shall by our successours
Perchance mo be founde, wherein men dwell
Of whom we never before this same harde telle . . .
Thus is it foly to tende unto the lore
And unsure science of vaine geometry[1]
Syns none can knowe all the worlde perfytly.

Spenser gives its opposite: unqualified exhilaration:

And dayly how through hardy enterprize
Manie great Regions are discovered
Which to late age were never mentioned.
Who ever heard of th' Indian Peru?
Or who in venturous vessell measured
The Amazons huge river now found trew?
Or fruitfullest Virginia who did ever vew?

Yet all these were, when no man did them know,
Yet have from wisest ages hidden beene,
And later times things more unknowne shall showe.
Why then should witlesse manne so much misweene
That no thing is, but that which he hath seene?
What if within the Moones faire shining Sphaere,
What if in everie other Starre unseene
Of other worldes he happily should heare?
He woonder would much more: yet such to some appeare.
(*Faerie Queene:* prologue to Book II)

For the men of the following generations, such as Donne and Shakespeare, neither the simple dismay of Barclay nor the simple exhilaration of Spenser was a possible attitude; one finds in them a subtler blending, more painful but more fruitful. Donne on such things as discoveries is characteristically double-faced and surprising; he uses the discoveries of the new astronomy, not, as one would expect, and as the more settled minds of Bacon and Spenser would have used them, to prove that he is living in a brave new world and a wondrous age, but to prove the opposite, that all is decay and confusion:

[1] i.e., exploration, "earth-measuring".

> *And new Philosophy calls all in doubt,*
> *The Element of fire is quite put out;*
> *The Sun is lost, and th' earth, and no mans wit*
> *Can well direct him where to looke for it.*
> *And freely men confesse that this world's spent,*
> *When in the Planets, and the Firmament*
> *They seeke so many new; then see that this*
> *Is crumbled out againe to his Atomies.*
> *'Tis all in peeces, all cohaerence gone;*
> *All just supply, and all Relation;*
> *Prince, Subject, Father, Sonne, are things forgot . . .*[1]

Yet this is no timid dismay; the very spring and humour of the verse show that Donne is intrigued and excited even by what he claims to be symptoms of decay. A Shakespearean passage will show the same blending on a comparable topic: but here in reverse, as it were, since this—the exchange in *Lear* between Edmund and his father on the subject of astrology—deals with an old thing, not a new discovery, and a thing which the science of the Renaissance was beginning to discredit:

Gloucester. These late Eclipses in the Sun and Moone portend no good to us: though the wisedome of Nature can reason it thus, and thus, yet Nature finds itselfe scourg'd by the sequent effects. Love cooles, friendship falls off, Brothers divide. In Cities, mutinies; in Countries, discord; in Pallaces, Treason; and the Bond crack'd, 'twixt Sonne and Father. This villaine of mine comes under the prediction; there's Son against Father, the King fals from byas of Nature, there's Father against Childe. We have seene the best of our time. Machinations, hollownesse, treacherie, and all ruinous disorders follow us disquietly to our Graves . . .

Bastard. This is the excellent foppery of the world, that when we are sicke in fortune, often the surfets of our own behaviour, we make guilty of our disasters, the Sun, the Moone, and Starres, as if we were villaines on necessitie, Fooles by heavenly compulsion, Knaves, Theeves, and Treachers by Sphericall predominance. Drunkards, Lyars, and Adulterers by an inforc'd obedience of Planatary influence; and all that we are evill in, by a divine thrusting on. An admirable evasion of Whore-master-man . . .

(I, 2)

[1] First *Anniversarie.*

Shakespeare, one imagines, was in intellectual agreement with Edmund; but Edmund is a thorough villain, he is utterly condemned, and in fact Gloucester's analysis of the human condition, his vision of universal anarchy (which is identical with Donne's—"Prince, Subject, Father, Sonne, are things forgot"), is confirmed by the whole play: it is just what happens. So—which side is Shakespeare on? On that of the foolish, duped old man, whose head is crammed with discredited superstitions—but whose vision is true? Or on that of the highly intelligent, up-to-date young rationalist—whose vision is so evilly wrong? On neither, or on both, would appear to be the answer: with a casting-vote (as in Donne) on behalf of the former.

For a poetry which seeks to encompass such complexities and incongruities, expressiveness rather than beauty will be the target; beauty will be a bye-product, the result of successful expression. And a poetry which has no preformed convictions on what are "poetical" subjects and attitudes, will have none either on what is "poetical" language. Hence the new style abandons virtually all those variegated forms of "poetic diction" which the earlier Elizabethans, each in his own way, all submitted to. Of all these dictions—Euphuism, Spenserian archaic, Petrarchan sonnetteering, amorous pastoral, classical metrics, and the tricks of Kyd-cum-Seneca (stichomythia, oxymoron, linking of repeated phrases)—the common element is that they were all constructed to formulae: styles that could be "learned" and passed on, from writer to writer, unchanged. Some of these dictions, such as Euphuism and the Senecan tricks, the Renaissance had invented, but the distinction between the poetry which is shaped to a pre-formed style and the poetry of individual expressiveness goes back a great deal farther: it probably reflects a radical distinction between two types of mind. (The academic and the original?) Medieval poetry shows it unmistakably: in the absolute split, for instance, between the Dunbar of the "aureate" diction and courtly allegory, and the Dunbar of colloquial Scots, of the *Sevin Deidly Synnis* and the *Twa Mariit Wemen and the Wedo*. Wyatt shows it, almost as plainly: his Petrarchan sonnets seem lifeless and dutiful, when put against his songs in the native tradition. No style—this is the guiding principle—that is in any way made to a formula, can have the elasticity which individual expressiveness calls for;

and Thomas Carew, reviewing Donne's achievement in his Elegy on him, saw as Donne's first reform the rejection of all such formulae:

> *The Muses garden with Pedantique weedes*
> *O'rspred, was purg'd by thee; the lazie seeds*
> *Of servile imitation throwne away;*
> *And fresh invention planted . . .*

Carew saw too that for the quality of Donne's poetry "beauty" was not the word, worn down, as it had been, by too much and too indiscriminate invocation. Expression—"masculine expression"—is the word he gives it. Donne, of course, begins with this style; he has nothing of the earlier manner which this made outmoded. But Shakespeare has, and in him can be seen the driving of the new through the old: the process we have seen in the Sonnets, writ larger in the plays.

The young Shakespeare shows, as Coleridge remarked in effect, an extraordinary capacity for responding to any subject that occurs—and a real detachment from all subjects. He writes two long poems—*Venus and Adonis* and *Rape of Lucrece*—which may be described as exercises in elegant classical-mythological pornography; he writes a comedy—*Love's Labour's Lost*—which has the mannered, courtly, fantastic atmosphere of Lyly; he writes a tragedy—*Titus Andronicus*[1]—which is almost a parody of all that is bloodiest and most thunderous in the Kyd-Senecan style of blood-and-thunder; he writes a farce of pure situation—*Comedy of Errors*—in the manner of Plautus; and he writes a piece of sentimental fantasy—*Two Gentlemen of Verona*. And all these subjects he covers, equally and impartially, with a hard smooth enamel of words, a surface which gleams and glitters and seems quite unchanged by what it is covering. It is the poetry of a man quite indifferent (in so far as he is a poet) to his subjects; or, perhaps it would be better to say, a man ready to be interested in any subject, provided only that it gave him an opportunity to develop and exploit his extraordinary interest in, and power over, words: to experi-

---

[1] I cannot see why Shakespeare should not have written this play; it seems to me neither worse than some of his other early writings nor more remote from the work of his maturity.

ment with the styles, and assimilate the dictions, current around him. Words, words, words!—Hamlet's comment would surely have been the mature Shakespeare's on his own early work. Words, in his early verse, dominate matter; and the words seem often chosen with an eye to "beauty" rather than expressiveness. They follow, in fact, a poetic diction; instead of keeping their eye on the subject, they keep it, for the most part, on themselves: on themselves, and on the models they are following and imitating with such astonishing powers of assimilation. Had Shakespeare died at about the time that Marlowe, his exact contemporary, "died swearing" in the Deptford tavern (in 1593), he would seem to us incomparably less of an individual, less of an innovating genius, than Marlowe or even than Kyd; he would seem a very slick, and not very interesting, master of pastiche. That was, in fact, the judgment of at least one of his contemporaries; Greene's famous snarl at the "up-start Crow, beautified with our feathers"[1] had more truth in it than we, who know what came later, are willing to allow.

The above, of course, is an overstatement, a ridiculous simplification. Shakespeare was always a dramatist; words could never be his absolute masters and his permanent interest. Even in his early work, signs of maturity, glimpses of the new style, are constantly appearing. And they tend to appear most often and most unmistakably in the speeches of those characters who, by their functions in the plays they appear in, represent willy-nilly the new spirit. That, as we saw, was critical at root; and these are the critical characters. Faulconbridge in *King John*, Berowne in *Love's Labour's Lost*, Mercutio in *Romeo and Juliet*:[2] they all, in their varied ways, stand apart from the company they keep, commenting, mocking, criticizing. Faulconbridge jeers at the pretences and hypocrisies of prelates and kings; Berowne at the courtiers' Platonic affectations; Mercutio at amorous idealism. And the language of all of them has qualities in common: a springing and swinging rhetoric close to the living speech, and a rich colloquial vocabulary:

[1] In *A Groatsworth of Witte* (published in 1592, the year of Greene's death).

[2] These plays were written *c*. 1594–7.

> *Till this advantage, this vile drawing byas,*
> *This sway of motion, this commoditie,*
> *Makes it take head from all indifferency,*
> *From all direction, purpose, course, intent.*
> *And this same byas, this Commoditie,*
> *This Bawd, this Broker, this all-changing-word,*
> *Clapt on the outward eye of fickle France,*
> *Hath drawne him from his own determin'd ayd . . .*
> (*King John*, II, 1)

> *This wimpled, whyning, purblinde waiward Boy,*
> *This signior Junior, gyant dwarfe, don Cupid,*
> *Regent of Love-rimes, Lord of folded armes,*
> *Th' anointed soveraigne of sighes and groanes:*
> *Liedge of all loyterers and malecontents:*
> *Dread Prince of Plackets, King of Codpeeces,*
> *Sole Emperator and great generall . . .*
> (*Love's Labour's Lost*, III, 1)

> Romeo, *Humours, Madman, Passion, Lover,*
> *Appeare thou in the likenesse of a sigh,*
> *Speake but one rime, and I am satisfied:*
> *Cry but ay me, pronounce but Love and dove,*
> *Speake to my gossip Venus one faire word,*
> *One Nickname for her purblind Sonne and heir,*
> *Young Adam Cupid he that shot so true,*
> *When King Cophetua lov'd the begger Maid . . .*
> (*Romeo and Juliet*, II, 1)

Language such as this breaks through the barriers of poetic diction exactly as the characters who use it break through the conventions which surround them; it is the Romeos, the conformers, who deliver (for example) the Kyd-like verbal oxymora with no self-critical qualms:

> *Why then, O brawling love, O loving hate;*
> *O any thing, of nothing first created;*
> *O heavie lightnesse, serious vanity,*
> *Mishapen Chaos of welseeming formes,*
> *Feather of lead, bright smoake, cold fire, sicke healtb,*
> *Still waking sleepe, that is not what it is.*
> (I, 1)

Poetic diction, then, goes overboard whenever the new spirit finds its expression. That is the essential thing: all the changes of style can be thought of as parts of this. We find, for example, a far greater concentration; the progress one notes in Shakespeare's development—a steady decrease in the proportion of words to matter—is also the progress from Spenser to Donne. The metaphysical conceit brings in nothing essentially new; it concentrates something old. It takes the long-drawn-out (often poem-long) conceit of the early Renaissance, and reduces it to a line, or a phrase, or a single word. The old style delights in comparisons long, elaborate, worked-out to the last button, such as that sonnet-long likening of the lover to a storm-tossed ship, which descends from Petrarch through Wyatt and Surrey to Spenser and Drayton; it revels in such space-wasting tricks as the parallelisms of Euphuism, saying the same thing again and again, with a different "illustration" each time. For such amusements the new spirit—what with the pressure of much more to say and the drive of the dramatic necessity to say it quickly—had, literally, no time. Of this whole process Shakespeare's 35th sonnet provides a complete example in miniature:

> *No more bee greev'd at that which thou hast done,*
> *Roses have thornes, and silver fountaines mud,*
> *Cloudes and eclipses staine both Moone and Sunne,*
> *And loathsome canker lives in sweetest bud.*
> *All men make faults, and even I in this,*
> *Authorizing thy trespas with compare,*
> *My selfe corrupting salving thy amisse,*
> *Excusing their sins more then thy sins are;*[1]
> *For to thy sensuall fault I bring in sence,*
> *Thy adverse party is thy Advocate,*
> *And gainst my selfe a lawfull plea commence,*
> *Such civill war is in my love and hate,*
> > *That I an accessary needs must be,*
> > *To that sweet theefe which sourely robs from me.*

[1] The text of this line seems corrupt. "Excusing their sins more then their sins are" is the reading of the first edition. The emendation, which is that usually adopted, can be interpreted: "Excusing thy sins to myself on the plea that *their* sins (i.e., the sins of thy accusers) are greater than thine."

The first quatrain is purely and conventionally Euphuistic: one point made four times by means of proverbial *setentiae*.[1] But the rest is very different: terse, subtle, complex to the point of obscurity, magisterially imposing its meaning on to its syntax, as in the eighth line, punning in the organic, not decorative way ("sensuall fault . . . bring in sence"), finding its imagery not in the "poetical" of roses and fountains, but in the world of law-courts and politics. And the abandonment of the poetical diction corresponds to the complex fullness of what has to be said.

Syntax and rhythm alike, in the new style, become more complex. The rhythmical change is obvious; in itself it needs no comment. But not so clear, perhaps, is that the change in rhythm is there to serve a change in the shape of the sentences. They go together, inevitably; if the sentence-structure is involved, if it breaks and turns and alters in mid-career to match a change in thought or an after-thought, then the rhythm must do the same; conversely, simple syntax means simple rhythm. Marlowe, for instance, presents a virtually unvaried series of straightforward syntactical units, each unit (phrase, clause, or sentence) neatly cut to the also unvarying length and beat of the line; if the sign / be taken as the ending of these units, it will always occur at the end of a line:

> *If all the pens that ever poets held, /*
> *Had fed the feeling of their maisters thoughts, /*
> *And every sweetnes that inspir'd their harts, /*
> *Their minds and muses on admyred theames: /*
> *If all the heavenly Quintessence they still /*
> *From their immortall flowers of Poesy,*
> *Wherein as in a mirrour we perceive /*
> *The highest reaches of a humaine wit: /*
> *If these had made one Poems period /*
> *And all combin'd in Beauties worthinesse, /*

[1] Cf. the 26th sonnet of Spenser's *Amoretti*:

> *Sweet is the Rose, but growes upon a brere;*
> *Sweet is the Junipeer, but sharpe his bough;*
> *Sweet is the Eglantine, but pricketh nere;*
> *Sweet is the Firbloome, but his braunches rough . . .*

But the difference is that Spenser's sonnet continues throughout in the same strain.

Yet should ther hover in their restlesse heads, /
One thought, one grace, one woonder at the least, /
Which into words no vertue can digest.
                              (*Tamburlaine* I, V, 2)

The "end-stopped" line thus forms a regular pattern in syntax as much as in rhythm; and of this kind of verse the extreme opposite, in both respects, is the mature Shakespearean—the series of starts and false starts, for instance, parentheses and repetitions, which, in *The Winter's Tale*, conveys the quality of Leontes' hysterical jealousy:

Thou want'st a rough pash and the shoots that I have
To be full like me: yet they say we are
Almost as like as Egges; Women say so,
(That will say any thing.) But were they false
As o're-dy'd Blacks, as Wind, as Waters; false
As Dice are to be wish'd, by one that fixes
No borne 'twixt his and mine; yet were it true,
To say this Boy were like me.

                                              (I, 2)

This too, as much as the abandoning of such tricks as Euphuism, is the abandonment of a preformed pattern in favour of freedom —freedom to meet and deal with each individual situation as it comes up, in the language that best expresses it; the writer who began as (among many other things) a singularly faithful imitator of Marlowe, ends as the master of a radically different kind of verse. Marlowe himself might have gone the same way, if he had survived through the years of crisis; one wonders if he too would have responded to the ferment of those years, which no lively mind or sensitive spirit—and he was both—went through unchanged. The end of *Dr. Faustus*, with its total break from the steady iambic beat ("See, see where Christ's blood streames i' the firmament") and the vivid clashings of its moods, leaves little doubt of the answer. But the Daniels and Draytons and Fulke Grevilles survived and wrote on, unchanged; worthy and honourable writers, but irredeemably limited—and outside their limits was the capacity to change their tune with the changing age.

Perhaps they did not want to change; perhaps they could not;

perhaps they were simply unaware of the need to change. It is always a nice point to determine just how "aware" writers were, at the time, of the essential changes in their age or, indeed, in their own writings; changes and processes which are (or seem) so clear and undeniable to later critics may have been invisible to those who made them or were involved in them. There is always the danger of being too dogmatic and too simplifying, of ascribing to the writers one looks at from so far away a greater self-knowledge than in fact they had, or a kind of self-knowledge they did not have at all. More than most ages, the Elizabethan encourages such errors; for it produced less than most ages do of conscious literary criticism concerning its own creation. Produced it, at least, in a form available to posterity; one suspects that in truth the Elizabethans indulged in a great deal of it, but largely oral—a spate of tavern-talk. What remain, in writing, available and useful, are scraps and fragments: Jonson talking to Drummond, those bits of Shakespeare we have noted, and so on—but not much else. But there is at least one contemporary witness—himself a poet—who felt at the time the connection between the old kind of rhythm, a smooth mellifluousness, and the old kind of mentality, a preference for simple and agreeable contents and an aversion from complexity and toughness. This witness is Hall, in the postscript to *Virgidemiarum*:

> It is not for every one to rellish a true and naturall Satyre, being of it selfe besides the native and inbred bitternes and tartnes of particulers, both hard of conceipt, and harsh of stile, and therefore cannot but be unpleasing both to the unskilfull, and over Musicall eare, the one being affected with onely a shallow and easie matter, the other with a smoth and currant disposition: so that I well foresee in the timely publication of these my concealed Satyres, I am set upon the racke of many mercilesse and peremptorie censures; which sith the calmest and most plausible writer is almost fatally subject unto in the curiositie of these nicer times, how may I hope to be exempted upon the occasion of so busy and stirring a subject?

"A shallow and easie matter", "a smoth and currant disposition": Hall sees them both as approved by the kind of taste which disapproved of both their opposites, such verse as is "hard of conceipt and harsh of stile". A good deal later, one finds the same combination in the taste of that worthy *laudator temporis acti*, Izaak Walton (whose extreme longevity tends to blind one to the fact that he was born an Elizabethan); when the milkmaid sings "that smooth song which was made by Kitt Marlowe, now at least fifty years ago", and her mother replies with its answer, "which was made by Sir Walter Raleigh in his younger days", Walton-Piscator comments:

> They were oldfashioned poetry, but choicely good; I think much better than the strong lines that are now in fashion in this critical age.

The "smoothness" is set against "the strong lines" (more "expressive" than "beautiful") which suit a "critical age". It is amusing to see how ancient and enduring—and unchanging—this quarrel is; Walton and Hall anticipate, each from his own side, the Tennyson-Palgrave rejection of the metaphysicals' "harshness" and the later taste which has reinstated that and deprecated Spenserian smoothness. Both sides would claim—do claim, in fact—that their taste is *the* taste, that what they like is *the* true tradition of English verse; is it but flabby compromise to suggest that there is no such thing as the Great Tradition—that there are, and always have been, at least two of them?

At any rate it will perhaps be granted that Hall's observations show the writers of the 1590's both as well aware of this quarrel's existence and as seeing and expressing it in terms not essentially dissimilar from those in which we see it to-day. It was not so much the subjects that changed in the 1590's, as the way they were dealt with; the change was in men's minds, and hence, among the writers, in their use of the medium—in their language. Presumably this is always true, in all the arts. Art has no new subjects; self-conscious attempts to present it with such seem to lead invariably to disaster, or at best to rare and sterile successes. Originality in art is not newness of subject; nor does oldness of subject prove unoriginality. It is this, incidentally, that makes so depressingly futile that Quest Endless for sources-and-derivations, which in many academic circles is thought to be criticism; for to prove that a writer has used the same subject as another writer proves nothing except—that he has used it. The revolution which Donne brought about in the

writing of love-poetry was as genuine a revolution as there ever
has been in any kind of writing, as complete a change of spirit;
but a very quick look at the actual contents of his poems will show
that he takes over virtually all the themes of the earlier manner.
The well-worn comparison between the beloved and the sun is
in Drayton:

> *The glorious sunne went blushing to his bed,*
> *When my soules sunne from her fayre Cabynet,*
> *Her golden beames had now discovered,*
> *Lightning the world, eclipsed by his set,*
> *(Ideas Mirrour, Sonnet 25)*

in Dowland's song:

> *But my Sun's heavenlie Eies*
> *View not your weeping,*

and in Donne's *Nocturnall* and *Second Anniversarie*:

> *But I am None; nor will my Sunne renew.*
> *You lovers, for whose sake the lesser Sunne*
> *At this time to the Goat is run . . .*

> *Since both this lower world's, and the Sunnes Sunne,*
> *The Lustre, and the Vigor of this All,*
> *Did set; 'twere blasphemie to say, did fall . . .*

The lady's homicidal cruelty is another such commonplace
which continues—in Drayton and Spenser no more than in
Donne and Marvell:

> *O thou unkindest fayre, most fayrest shee,*
> *In thine eyes tryumph murthering my poore hart . . .*
> *(Ideas Mirrour, 40)*

> *But when I feele the bitter balefull smart*
> *Which her fayre eyes unwares doe worke in mee,*
> *That death out of theyre shiny beames doe dart . . .*
> *(Amoretti, 24)*

> *When by thy scorne O Murderesse I am dead . . .*
> *(The Apparition)*

O then let me in time compound,
And parly with those conquering Eyes;
Ere they have try'd their force to wound . . .
        (The Picture of Little T.C.)

And the argument that such cruelty goes ill with beauty,
which ought to be merciful, is in Spenser as in Donne, and in
both with divine parallels:

But mercy doth with beautie best agree,
As in theyre Maker ye them best may see.
        (Amoretti, 53)

No, no; but as in my idolatrie
I said to all my prophane mistresses,
Beauty, of pity, foulnesse onely is
A signe of rigour: so I say to thee,
To wicked spirits are horrid shapes assign'd,
This beauteous forme assures a pitious minde.
        (Holy Sonnets, 13)

Such examples could be multiplied almost indefinitely; the
identity of subject-matter needs no more proving. Not so easy
to analyse are the differences in everything else, which make
that identity of no importance. A sense of humour and irony,
all-pervading in the new manner, totally absent in the old,
is one of these differences: sometimes, as it were, potential rather
than actual. The conventional hyperbole is there, it may be unqualified in itself, but there is always the chance that irony may
question and qualify it,[1] and the knowledge that that possibility
exists alters its tone. It becomes more acceptable, more credible,
when offered as a part, no longer as a total; and it was in this
way, presumably—by guarding and disinfecting it with irony
—that poets who belonged entirely to the new spirit were able
to accept it and use it themselves. It continues, indeed—this is
one of the oddities of seventeenth century poetry—right through
the century; the whole debased coinage of cruel, chaste, worshipped Lady and heartbroken, adoring, faithful Lover, remains in

---

[1] As it does, for example, in the lines quoted from Marvell's
Picture of Little T.C.: the language of amorous adoration is applied
to a little girl. He plays the same trick in the opening lines of the
Coy Mistress, which parody by inflation the same kind of language.

currency even among writers who quite clearly can scarcely have believed a word of it. Suckling and Dryden, for instance: but both of them save their honours and preserve at least a shred of credibility by writing also some verses of flippant impropriety in praise of promiscuousness. So, of course, does Donne: so do not the Spensers and the Draytons.

Shakespeare in his sphere, the drama, seems to have done much the same as Donne and the poets who followed him, with such elements of the old style as the rhetoric of Kyd and Marlowe and the patterns of Euphuism; he goes on using them even after, long after, he had plainly "seen through" them. Irony and parody put them in their proper place—what had become, for him, their only proper place, since they were no longer adequate for more serious purposes. Pistol parodies the rhetoric of *Tamburlaine*, with its facile exploitation of the resonant-exotic:

> *I speake of* Africa *and golden joyes.*

Hamlet parodies the blood-and-thunder rhetoric of Kyd:

> Begin, Murderer. Pox, leave thy damnable Faces, and begin. Come, the croaking Raven doth bellow for Revenge

—and also (as we have seen, in the letter to Ophelia) he parodies the rhapsodies of amorous poetastery. Falstaff parodies the formalized sentence and moralized botany of Euphuism:

> For though the Camomile, the more it is troden, the faster it growes; yet Youth, the more it is wasted, the sooner it weares.

And Claudius parodies the pedantic antitheses of the Senecan manner:

> . . . *Have we, as 'twere, with a defeated joy,*
> *With one Auspicious, and one Dropping eye,*
> *With mirth in Funerall, and with Dirge in Marriage,*
> *In equall Scale weighing Delight and Dole,*
> *Taken to Wife. . .*

Each of these usages is a miracle of multiple effects; for Shakespeare is making both a literary-critical point, and through that point, a dramatic one. The theatrical absurdity of Pistol;

the dilemmas of Hamlet, between the crude obligation of bloody revenge and his own maturer sensibility, and between his immature courtship of Ophelia and his later perception of its unreality; the mockery of Falstaff, who is posing as the king lecturing his erring son and who imitates, in so doing, the lay-sermons which *Euphues* abounds in and which now, become out-of-date, invest the whole speech with a pompous Polonius-like absurdity; and the wary hypocrisy of Claudius, delivering a "set speech" to an audience whose approval he is far from sure of: all these dramatic points are made, and well made, through the ironic use of dictions which had become, or were becoming, old-fashioned and discredited. Such effects presuppose, of course, an astonishing awareness of language not only in Shakespeare but also in his audience—an audience presumably so experienced in poetic drama that it picked up such signals at once. They confirm yet again what one always feels of Shakespeare, that he never forgot, never quite gave up, anything, and never failed to make some use of everything.

In another respect, another point of style where a general change was brought about, one sees the same power in Shakespeare, of always changing and always assimilating. This is in the use of classical mythology. That, of course—an immensely lavish outpouring of gods and goddesses, nymphs and fauns and so forth—is one of the major phenomena of Renaissance poetry; and its rejection, its virtually total rejection, is one of the most obvious innovations of the love-poetry of Donne. Carew notes it, in that *Elegie* previously cited: notes it, and prophesies (correctly) that Donne's example will not be followed for long:

> *But thou art gone, and thy strict lawes will be*
> *Too hard for Libertines in Poetrie.*
> *They will repeale the goodly exil'd traine*
> *Of gods and goddesses, which in thy just raigne*
> *Were banish'd nobler Poems, now, with these*
> *The silenc'd tales o' th' Metamorphoses*
> *Shall stuffe their lines, and swell the windy Page.*

Donne, presumably, found it necessary to banish "the goodly train of gods and goddesses" because they too had become a poetic diction, a sort of versifiers' vademecum used indiscriminately and unvaryingly by all; they could no longer serve the purposes of those who would write directly and honestly, as complicated individuals.

The kind of use which early Elizabethan poetry made of classical myth and story can be seen, at its very finest, in Marlowe's lines on Helen:

> *I wil be* Paris, *and for love of thee,*
> *Insteede of* Troy *shal* Wertenberge *be sackt,*
> *And I wil combate with weake* Menelaus,
> *And weare thy colours on my plumed crest:*
> *Yea I wil wound* Achillis *on the heele,*
> *And then returne to* Helen *for a kisse.*
> *O thou art fairer then the evening aire,*
> *Clad in the beauty of a thousand starres,*
> *Brighter art thou then flaming* Jupiter,
> *When he appeard to haplesse* Semele,
> *More lovely then the monarke of the skie*
> *In wanton* Arethusaes *azurde armes,*
> *And none but thou shalt be my paramour.*

The wonderful beauty of these lines has a static quality, more lyrical than dramatic. The Hellenic world is used as a kind of shorthand, to provide readymade terms of reference whereby an image of ideal beauty may be created: the beauty of Helen is suggested merely by saying that she is even more beautiful than those fixed standards. Shakespeare also, in his early writings, followed this way; the duet in the last act of *The Merchant of Venice* uses it exactly:

> *In such a night*
> Troylus *me thinkes mounted the* Troian *walls,*
> *And sigh'd his soule toward the* Grecian *tents*
> *Where* Cressid *lay that night.*
> *In such a night*
> *Did* Thisbie *fearefully ore-trip the dewe,*
> *And saw the* Lyons *shadowe ere himselfe,*
> *And ranne dismayed away.*
> *In such a night*
> *Stood* Dido *with a* Willow *in her hand*
> *Upon the wilde sea bankes, and waft her* Love
> *To come againe to* Carthage.

69

> *In such a night*
> Medea *gathered the inchanted hearbs*
> *That did renew old* Eson.
> *In such a night*
> Did Jessica *steale from the wealthy Jewe* . . .

Both passages lose little, if anything, when torn from their contexts; they are perfect anthology-pieces, and one feels that in part they were written as such. But what, in contrast, the mature Shakespeare made of his classical dictionary may be seen from the lines in *The Winter's Tale* (the scene of the sheep-shearing feast):

> *Apprehend*
> *Nothing but jollity: the Goddes themselves*
> *(Humbling their Deities to love) have taken*
> *The shapes of Beasts upon them. Jupiter,*
> *Became a Bull, and bellow'd: the greene Neptune*
> *A Ram, and bleated: and the Fire-rob'd-God*
> *Golden Apollo, a poore humble Swaine,*
> *As I seeme now. Their transformations,*
> *Were never for a peece of beauty, rarer* . . .

These lines, torn from their roots, may seem less beautiful, are certainly less quoted and quotable, than the passages from *Faustus* and *The Merchant of Venice*. They lose because they *are* rooted, in the scene and play they occur in: spoken, as they are, to Perdita by Florizel (the prince, the almost-god, in disguise, descending to a lower sphere); picking up, as they do, the words which come at the beginning of the same scene—

> *This your sheepe-shearing,*
> *Is as a meeting of the petty Gods,*
> *And you the Queene on't*

—they tell us that Florizel and Perdita are more than just a nice young couple in love with each other, and the sheep-shearing feast is more than just a rustic revel. Their love, with what it will bring about, has something akin to the divine, and the union of divine with human and lower than human; for this love will redeem the suffering which Leontes' jealousy caused and bring together the opposing worlds of country and

70

court. The material of classical myth here serves a function deeper than decoration, more varied and dynamic than lyrical beauty; the difference can be seen in the language itself, in the farmyard evocations of "bellow'd" and "bleated". Donne's mind, more uncompromising, less all-embracing, than Shakespeare's, could only reject the decorative and superficial; Shakespeare, as always, retains but remakes.

Such, then, was the process in outline: the abandonment, by those writers who experienced the shift to the complex and dramatic, of an assortment of poetic dictions which had been evolved by, and were suited to, writers whose mentalities were static, simple, classical, and (in the old way) courtly. The dictions were not, of course, abandoned by all. They remained in use; but they do have an air, through the early decades of the seventeenth century (the Shakespearean moment, in fact) of becoming increasingly forlorn and forgotten, of drifting more and more surely into a stagnant backwater, of being the resort of those whose minds have ceased to grow. Drayton's enormous *Polyolbion* for instance, when at last it trails forth, slowly and piece-meal, into the world,[1] looks sadly old-fashioned and out of touch: this mausoleum of applied patriotism belongs in conception, as in diction, to the early Renaissance. *The Faerie Queene*, not Donne's *Anniversaries* and Webster's plays, is its true contemporary. It is fashionable to sneer at "fashions" in poetry; but the truth seems to be that to be "fashionable" (that is, to feel what style is possible here and now) is more important than critics and reviewers—when they happen not to like the contemporary fashion, or their own verse is not in it— are inclined to allow. It does seem true that at any given moment there are not more than one or two poetic manners in which success is possible—and a great many in which it is not. It would not be easy to discover good poetry in the Spenserian or Sidneyan manner after 1600; in the metaphysical style after the Restoration; in the Augustan after 1780; in the Romantic after—1920? Not much good poetry, but plenty of bad verse; for the progress of poetry is always attended by ghosts (many of them are prosperous, best-selling, and Laureate spectres)— those who went on writing in a fashion no longer alive. As did, for examples, Fulke Greville, with his Senecan "closet-dramas";

[1] First eighteen books published in 1612; the remainder in 1622.

71

Cowley, loyally metaphysical in language but not in mind; Samuel Rogers, vaguely and belatedly eighteenth century; Sir William Watson, a sad twentieth century Tennysonian echo. To be "fashionable" is of course no guarantee that the verse will be good, and there may well be ages—the 1780's, for instance, and (who knows?) the 1950's—in which good poetry is impossible in any fashion; but to be unfashionable does seem a sign that the verse will be bad. For poetry is the most sensitive of all kinds of writing; the insensitiveness which does not see when a style has lost its vitality is itself a guarantee that what is still written in such a style cannot wholly succeed. One can see the thing, and put it, from either side. *Because* A's style is in touch with the age, and B's is not, A is a true poet and B is not; or, *because* A is a true poet and B is not, A's style is . . . and B's is not. Or one can swing the emphasis from the age to the individual, and argue (as Wordsworth did) that in fact the great poet *makes* himself "fashionable", does not keep in contact with his age, but forces the age to come into contact with him. But whichever way, or with whatever emphasis, the thing is looked at, the relationship is always there.

Chapter 3

THE POETRY OF
THE SHAKESPEAREAN MOMENT

(Donne's "Anniversaries" and Shakespeare's last plays)

THE mature Shakespearean or metaphysical style—which, it must be repeated, is the same style used for different purposes and in different *milieux*—emerged in the last years of the sixteenth century and remained the most fruitful style for the first few decades of the next. The chapter which follows this will discuss what factors—social, intellectual, and spiritual—gave it birth and nourished it; this will show it, fully developed, in some of its greatest achievements: in Donne's *Anniversarie* poems, especially the second, and in the plays of Shakespeare's last years—*The Winter's Tale, Cymbeline,* and *The Tempest.*

These writings are nearly contemporary; the poems were written in 1611-12 and the plays from *c.* 1609 to 1612. There was doubtless no "connection" between them; by this time Donne had long left the world in which "Jack Donne" had flourished and enjoyed himself and was moving towards the world of the Dean of St. Paul's, and Shakespeare had left, or was leaving, the life of the Bankside for that of Stratford. These facts may account for what does seem to be a genuine, though tenuous and hard-to-analyse, affinity between the poems and the plays, taken as a group; they both seem to come from a certain "removal" from the world, they both have an effect as of bringing together all the strands of a crowded and passionate experience and weaving them into a new pattern. They both combine a fiercer realism, and a symbolism more remote, than their authors had made use of before. They both have an air, not so much of a valediction as of a renunciation and a re-ordering, which prepare for a new vision: which Donne was given the time to achieve, since he lived for twenty years more, but which eluded him, perhaps, to the end; which Shakespeare did achieve —on the showing of the plays themselves—in the shorter time he was given.

In 1611, when the first of the two *Anniversarie* poems was written, John Donne's worldly career was somewhat in the doldrums; as it had been, indeed, ever since his marriage, ten years earlier, and was to remain until his ordination, four years later. The years between made up, on the whole, a miserable existence of genteel parasitism, dependent on patrons, continually working to keep their favours by thick-spread flattery. Two personal factors must have made the strain more acute: Donne had a large, annually-increasing family of young children to maintain, and the way of escape from poverty and insecurity was all the time available, in the form of ordination as an Anglican priest—if only his conscience, still partly Roman, would allow him to take it.

This strand of his life—the flattery of patrons—makes a main strand in the material of the poems. For they are, in fact, an act of homage to a patron. Sir Robert Drury, for whose dead daughter the poems were written, was one of Donne's most valuable benefactors, taking him with him to the Continent and employing him as a sort of secretary. Donne certainly threw himself with overwhelming zeal into the job of flattering Miss Elizabeth Drury; she was in reality a 14-year-old girl whom Donne had never known, but in the poems she emerges as something very like the Virgin Mary. That comparison occurred to Ben Jonson, who told Drummond at Hawthornden that he had reproved Donne for saying things of Elizabeth Drury which were grossly blasphemous if applied to any other woman than the Virgin. But Donne had his answer ready: an answer which shows that he was perfectly well aware of the absurdity of his poems if judged by standards of realism. "He painted the Idea of a woman, and not a woman as she was."[1] "Idea" has of course the Platonic meaning: the abstraction, the quintessence, of womankind. The "she" of the *Anniversaries*—it is not with-

---

[1] The letter which Donne wrote from Paris to George Garrard (14th April, 1612) makes it clear that Jonson was not the only contemporary who misunderstood the poems and disapproved of them by the standards of commonsense. After apologizing in conventional fashion for having printed them, Donne goes on:

But for the other part of the imputation of having said too much, my defence is, that my purpose was to say as well as I could: for since I never saw the Gentlewoman, I cannot be understood to have bound myself to have spoken just truths . . .

out artistic point that Donne throughout calls her simply by the pronoun, never by her personal name, for he does not want the reader to think of any actual individual woman—the "she", then, derives from that Platonic worship of the Lady which one sees in such poems as *Twicknam Garden* and the *Nocturnall upon St. Lucies Day*: Donne's own personal version, modernized, intellectualized, infused with tinctures of bitterness and irony, of the old Spenserian Platonism from which he had revolted at the start of his career, and to which he now returns with all the weight of a complex and sometimes agonizing experience of life behind him.

That experience had not been agreeable in the years after Donne's marriage. His complex character included a sizeable streak of worldly ambition; it is not likely that these long years of frustration, dependence, and stagnation would have failed to make their mark upon him. There is, in fact, a wealth of evidence (in his letters, for instance) that they did. They sharpened in him, to a point of acute personal bitterness, that slowly increasing desire to renounce the world, the flesh (especially the flesh), and the devil, which is the major theme of the devotional poetry. Disgust with life, intense perception of its horror and ugliness, forms another main strand of the *Anniversarie* poems; but Donne does not exploit it for its own sake, as the satirists do and sometimes such dramatists as Webster: he does strive to give it a positive purpose, to place it in the setting of traditional Christian asceticism. Whether he entirely succeeds is another matter; perhaps the age, and his own sensibility, differed too widely from the ethos of the Middle Ages to be quite serenely sure of the value of such renunciation; perhaps the sensuous vigour with which he describes the world he aspires to renounce creates a poetry that effectively denies what its content affirms: but a real disgust is there, and a real craving to turn it to a better end.

Thus the raw materials of the *Anniversaries* seem very unpromising; they are made up of just those elements of seventeenth century life and taste most alien to modern experience. The flattery of patrons, together with what it involves—a deliberate indulgence in extravagances, both of language and thought; the wiredrawn, fantastic worship of a remote and impossible "she"; the feverish proclamation, and morbidly obsessed rendering, of the world's and the body's hideousness and hatefulness: when all three are combined in one poem, the obstacle, one would think, must be insurmountable; the bogey of "insincerity" will make its appearance, and the modern reader will retire defeated. But he need not, in spite of it all; for two reasons, the poems remain alive, however unpromising and limited to their age their contents may seem to be. In the first place, those contents meant more—far more—in their time than their modern equivalents (if such could be imagined) would mean to-day; and secondly, they were for Donne the deepest and most durable interests of his whole life. Court,[1] Church, and women: these are the materials of all his creation, and none of his poems unites them all so successfully.

It is presumably our vaguely democratic notions which are offended by the flattery of patrons: you may flatter a million readers, but you mustn't flatter one. The seventeenth century's cult of the Great Man did include, undeniably, a vast deal of quite insincere sycophancy; elegies and eulogies, epithalamia and birthday-odes, poured forth from an endless assembly-belt. But two things need to be remembered in order to put this activity in proper proportion. In the first place, since this was the accepted, the recognized way by which a writer could earn, not so much his income, as his "place", by which he could continue to write, it did not carry the slightest stigma; the writer was not put on the defensive, he did not feel guilty or ashamed. Secondly, all men—at least before the Commonwealth, and most of them during it—visualized society as thoroughly hierarchical. Virtually no one—certainly no one within the circles in which Donne moved—questioned for a moment the right of the great man, the grandee, to receive the homage and deference of those below him. The man who was a power in the State felt it his right—even his duty—to make his greatness visible to the world; he showed it in many ways, such as the immensity of his mansions, the number of persons in his household, the richness of his clothes, the number of his statues and paintings—and among these, in the quality and quantity of literary flattery expended upon him. That age would never have understood the modern way, whereby ministers of state and all-powerful

[1] Using this word to include the cultivation of great men (and women) as patrons and objects of reverence.

bureaucrats do their successful best to look as undistinguished and powerless as university lecturers; and hence, the flattering of patrons was at once more and less important than we are apt to think it. Less, because virtually all writers indulged in it: even the austere Milton does so, in *Comus* and *Arcades*. More, because it did form part of the age's total picture of society; for good and bad, it was in harmony with the age, with the deepest parts of the age's mind. It is not a contradiction, it is simply a more trivial expression, of that deep conviction of the necessity for a hierarchical order in the universe and society which Hooker and Shakespeare (among so many others) felt with such passion. And hence there is a real value in this element of the *Anniversaries*, which modern readers are apt to deprecate or forget, to regard as nothing more than the external "starting-point" of poems whose real meaning is very different. If the great man, the patron, were not there in the background, if the "she" of the poems did not have as original the great man's daughter, they would lose a quality hard to define but clearly present, a real element in the metaphysical manner: a quality of dutifulness, respect, reverence—the right word is hard to find, but it is something which made it easier than it would otherwise have been to build a bridge from the human girl to the divine symbol.[1] So in those poems of the *Songs and Sonets* which also deal in the symbolism of the partly dehumanized "she": if their addressees had not been, in all probability, great ladies— Magdalen Herbert or the Countess of Bedford—*The Funerall* and *The Relique* and *Twicknam Garden* would not be the poems they are, for Donne would not have felt as he did about their subjects.

Of the hyperbole which follows from the flattery of patrons, the same defence can be made: it was part of a greater whole, a trivial and superficial expression of something in itself essential and important. It attends, in varying fashion, virtually all poetry of the Shakespearean moment. All manners are tried by

[1] E.g., the lines in the prefatory poem (which was probably written by Hall) before the first *Anniversarie*:

> *And thou the subject of this welborne thought,*
> *Thrice noble maid . . .*

The transference of "welborne" from the "maid" to the "thought" indicates the quality.

that poetry, but rarest of all is plain simplicity. All subjects, to some degree, are elaborated and decorated, strained and twisted. Hyperbole is simply one form of this taste for elaboration; the subject in its natural proportions, as in its natural colouring, is felt to be dull: distorted and exaggerated, it takes on meaning.

> *My Love is of a birth as rare*
> *As 'tis for object strange and high*

—these opening lines of Marvell's *Definition of Love* define very fairly not only his "love" but also the style his poem is written in. "Strange and high"—seen from unexpected aspects, magnified more than nature—render it to perfection; the epithets may remind us—they should—of the saying of Bacon: "There is no Excellent *Beauty*, that hath not some Strangenesse in the Proportion."[1] The quality developed, no doubt, from the sort of hyperbole one sees in earlier writing such as Marlowe's. But that exaggeration was naïve; the later is thoroughly sophisticated, its makers are well aware of what they are doing. The later is complicated; the earlier straightforward. A piece of Marlovian hyperbole, such as the description of Tamburlaine, magnifies its object but does no more; it does not make it complex or strange. The baroque hyperboles of Donne and mature Shakespeare transform as well as enlarge; Elizabeth Drury is made into something not only greater than, but different from, a flesh-and-blood girl; and so, as we shall see, are the heroines of Shakespeare's last plays.

This leads us to the far-fetched, abstract "Platonism" of the *Anniversaries*' "she". This, as Donne uses it, develops into a remote symbolism in which "she" stands for life, goodness, joy, etc.—and, always, these qualities *lost*. Because "she" is dead, all things that are good and positive have died also; what remain are lifeless simulacra. Such was the "she" of the *Nocturnall upon St. Lucies Day*, whose death has reduced Donne's being to a state of total negation, has deprived it of "all that's good, life, soule, forme, spirit". It *is* a symbol ("the Idea of a woman, and not a woman as she was");[2] but its starting-point

[1] Many passages of Bacon's *Essays* are in what may be called a metaphysical prose.

[2] "She" is not only more perfect than a real woman could be, she is also different from what Elizabeth Drury could have been.

as a real woman is never quite forgotten—just as the fact that
Elizabeth Drury was the patron's daughter is never quite forgotten—and it always has a certain value. (To test how great
that value is, one has only to try, for a line or two, the sub-
stitution of "it" for "she".) The value is twofold: amorous and
devotional. The former because behind this symbol lie all the
complex and intense experiences which the love of women had
brought to Donne; of the total emotion resultant from these
experiences, this "she" (to use a metaphor Donne himself
would have used) is the quintessence. This fact enormously
enriches the poetry of the *Anniversaries*; for it means that the
poetry which is made out of Elizabeth Drury, the child whom
Donne never knew, and of her symbolized disembodied self,
can take over the emotions, and the language, of the sensual
and the secular; it can ascribe to her bodily beauty:

> *Shee, whose faire body no such prison was,*
> *But that a Soule might well be pleas'd to passe*
> *An age in her; she whose rich beauty lent*
> *Mintage to other beauties . . .*

—and it can celebrate her beauty with the same imagery as
Donne had used in earlier years for his "profane mistresses".
It uses the impassioned geography:

> *Shee, in whose body (if we dare preferre*
> *This low world, to so high a marke as shee,)*
> *The Westerne treasure, Eastern spicerie,*
> *Europe, and Afrique, and the unknowne rest*
> *Were easily found, or what in them was best*

—which differs in no way, but in an appropriate solemnity of
tone, from the lines in the cheerful and amorous *Sunne Rising*:

> *Whether both th' India's of spice and Myne*
> *Be where thou leftst them, or lie here with mee*

She is credited, for example, with the virtue of chastity:

> *And she made peace, for no peace is like this,*
> *That beauty, and chastity together kisse*

—a curious compliment to a 14-year-old.

79

—or from those in the nineteenth *Elegie*, the most unashamedly sensual of all Donne's poems:

> *O my America! my new-found-land,*
> *My kingdome, safeliest when with one man man'd,*
> *My Myne of precious stones, My Emperie . . .*

And the "she" of the *Anniversaries* can take over also that royal and courtly metaphor by which Donne transfers to his mistresses all the glamour and awe of Tudor and Stuart monarchy: the phrase of the *Second Anniversarie*:

> *Shee, who being to her selfe a State, injoy'd*
> *All royalties which any State employ'd*

—recalls that of the *Sunne Rising*:

> *Aske for those Kings whom thou saw'st yesterday,*
> *And thou shalt heare, All here in one bed lay.*
> *She is all States, and all Princes, I,*
> *Nothing else is.*

So much for the amorous value. As for the other, the devotional, there seems no doubt of what happened. For Donne, the Roman Catholic who abandoned his church with such slow reluctance, this was a means of retaining, by ways allowable in Protestant England, the emotions which he would otherwise have expressed through worship of the Virgin and feminine saints such as the Magdalen or St. Teresa. To theologians, Donne's transference from Roman to Anglo-catholicism is no doubt a matter of great importance, as it was to Donne himself, the ambitious individual with his way to make; to the literary critic, the effect seems imperceptible. In no sense of the word *except* the ecclesiastical, does it make the smallest difference. In so far as we are concerned with him, in so far as he was a poet, he never became a Protestant. And one suspects that for his particular temperament, in view of his particular experiences and needs, that part of Roman Catholicism which allows for the worship of the feminine was the part whose loss was most serious, for it deprived him of the readiest means, the easiest bridge, to connect the sensual with the spiritual. Hence, in many poems, probably earlier than the *Anniversaries*, one finds sly efforts to reintroduce it by back-doors, so to speak:

> *If this fall in a time, or Land,*
> *Where mis-devotion doth command,*
> *Then, he that digges us up, will bring*
> *Us, to the Bishop, and the King,*
> *To make us Reliques; then*
> *Thou shalt be a Mary Magdalen, and I*
> *A something else thereby.*
>   (*The Relique*)

> *What ere shee meant by'it, bury it with me,*
> *For since I am*
> *Loves martyr, it might breed idolatrie*
> *If into others hands these Reliques came.*
>   (*The Funerall*)

The Protestant disclaimings—"mis-devotion", "idolatrie"—cannot hide the fact that Donne is really getting what he wants: what is rejected theologically is kept poetically. In the *Second Anniversarie* itself, exactly the same trick is played, and here the distinction between theology and poetry is explicitly appealed to by Donne himself:

> *Here in a place,*[1] *where mis-devotion frames*
> *A thousand Prayers to Saints, whose very names*
> *The ancient Church knew not, Heaven knows not yet:*
> *And where, what Lawes of Poetry admit,*
> *Lawes of Religion have at least the same,*
> *Immortall Maide, I might invoke thy name.*

With a subtle disingenuousness entirely Donne's, the reader is being invited at the same time *not* to worship her as a saint (for that would be rank Popery) and to feel the emotions which he would feel if he did so. For Donne's poetry, this ingenious fence-sitting was pure gain; it meant that he avoided on the one hand the shrill monotony of Crashaw's ecstasies over St. Teresa—where the language of amorous sexuality strikes one as really distasteful because Crashaw is claiming that its object is a real saint and his emotion purely devotional—and on the other hand the thin, purely "literary" Lady-and-saint

---

[1] Presumably France, whither Donne had accompanied Sir Robert Drury.

worship of such thorough Protestants as Spenser. In the latter, one cannot credit the devotional aspect; in the former, it is the amorous that is unconvincing. But Donne gets both. One would not expect to find this theological tightrope-walking in the un-theological Shakespeare; but in fact its dramatic equivalent— astonishingly close—*is* to be found, both Catholic sentiment and Protestant apologizing for it, in Perdita's response to what she believes to be the statue (the "Image", as the Reformers would have called it) of her mother:

> *And give me leave,*
> *And doe not say 'tis Superstition, that*
> *I kneele, and then implore her blessing. Lady,*
> *Deare Queene, that ended when I but began,*
> *Give me that hand of yours, to kisse.*
>
> (V, 3)

Shakespeare, like Donne, like so many Elizabethans, may well have regretted what his conscious mind rejected as false; those lines of Perdita's may refer us back to the Sonnets' "bare ruin'd quiers, where late the sweet birds sang", which do seem to recall with nostalgic regret the ruined abbeys.

In all this, as in other things we have noted, Donne's *subject* is in no way new. It obviously descends from the medieval worship of the Lady, heavenly and human at once: but the split of the Reformation, and the particular tension which it caused round the figures of Virgin and saints, chief targets of reforming zeal, have filled the old figures, for one who was born a Roman Catholic like Donne but later changed, with a new tremor, as it were, of excitement; it has given them the attraction of the dangerous and the forbidden; it has taken them from the depressing atmosphere of a convention dutifully practised by all into the stimulating regions of the hotly-debated.[1] In this again, then, the *Anniversaries* play on a theme which had run through the whole of Donne's life: the theme which the third *Satire* had dealt with—which church will be his? Although by the time he

---

[1] Something similar—a stimulus or a distortion caused by aware-ness of hostile forces—may be seen elsewhere. The Continental art of the Counter-reformation (Bernini's sculpture, for instance) seems much more aggressively "Catholic" than does medieval art—which is simply Christian.

wrote the *Anniversaries* he was doubtless a good Anglican, their very subject involved the kind of emotions which kept alive his Roman Catholic past.

A closer examination of the *Second Anniversarie*—by far the better of the two—may show in more detail how much of Donne's mind this single poem contains. It begins with the statement that since "she" died, the real life of the world has also come to an end, though it still keeps up an appearance of living. The comparisons by which this point is made—the reflex actions of a man's body immediately after he has been beheaded, the sailing on of a ship after she has struck sail, the crackling of thawing ice, and the twanging of lute-strings breaking in the damp—are thoroughly Donne and thoroughly of the Shakespearean moment: rooted in reality yet entirely unexpected. Their function here is to emphasize the physical reality of the world—the world which is to be rejected. From this Donne goes to "a just disestimation of the world" (as the marginal heading puts it). The desire for renunciation: the central theme of all his devotional verse. But here, as always, the desire is expressed with a violence which makes one feel that Donne is forcing himself. The characteristic imagery is violent: thirst and disease. "Thirst for that time, O my insatiate Soule"—"drinke still till thou goe To th' only Health, to be Hydroptique so." Donne is not yet the famous preacher, not yet a divine, indeed; but the approach is already not far from that of a sermon, a hectoring, pleading exhortation of the self which shows how close to the dramatic tirade were the popular sermons of the seventeenth century and how little difference it made—as far as literature is concerned—when "Jack Donne" was converted into "Dr. Donne".

Next comes a "contemplation of our state in our death-bed". No passage of any writer expresses more intensely than this the age's cult, not so much of death as of dying, of all the ceremonial details and traditional behaviour which surrounded the act of death. What the ponderous and decorated tombs of the age, with their wealth of skulls and rows of kneeling children, expressed in one art, this poetry expresses in another. The passage is intensely dramatic; addressed to his soul ("thinke then, my soule . . ." it begins), written throughout in the second person, it makes one forget exactly who is being addressed:

Donne, or oneself, the reader, or all humanity. It visualizes the scene with extreme physical vividness: "thinke thy selfe labouring now with broken breath . . . thinke thee laid on thy deathbed, loose and slacke." It sees the performance surrounded by an audience—or rather, two audiences. One is spiritual: "thinke Satans Sergeants round about thee bee"—the deathbed of the medieval imagination, with good spirits and bad waiting to fight for the soul. The other audience is actual: "thinke thy friends weeping round . . ." The dramatic imagination passes without break or pause from the last moments of life to the first of death: "thinke that they close thine eyes . . . thinke that they shroud thee up . . . thinke that thy body rots." This tremendous passage anticipates, in spirit entirely, and even in many details, the actual "performance" (it merits the word) of Donne's own deathbed, which was played some twenty years later and which Walton's biography describes: the deliberate rehearsal:

> And now he was so happy as to have nothing to do but to die, to do which, he stood in need of no longer time; for he had studied it long . . .

—the crowding of friends:

> . . . and that week sent at several times for many of his most considerable friends, with whom he took a solemn and deliberate farewell

—the setting of his body in the pose of death:

> . . . he closed his own eyes, and then disposed his hands and body into such a posture, as required not the least alteration by those that came to shroud him.

The dramatic self-playing of the Renaissance mentality reaches in this its climax; the multiple vision—"this is myself; this is also my self as seen from outside; this is also *your* self"— which makes of Donne's mind a study of such fascination both to himself and to others, achieves its sharpest intensity at the moment when life is about to be lost. And that is just what happens when the heroes (or villains) of the contemporary theatre come to their ends; the Flamineos and Bosolas and Hamlets seem, at least—seem to themselves—to see things truly, and understand their lives, at the moment of death. "He had studied (death) long," says Walton of Donne; "he died," says Shakespeare's Malcolm of the Thane of Cawdor, "as one that had been studied in his death"; "he nothing common did or mean," says Marvell of Charles I on the scaffold, "upon that memorable scene." The vision in all is dramatic; for "studied" means the studying of his part by an actor, and Marvell's "scene" is *scaena*, the Roman stage. And Donne himself, in one of his sermons, foresees his deathbed and burial, explicitly, in terms of the scenes of a play:

> And when he (death) hath sported himselfe with my misery upon that stage, my death-bed, shall shift the Scene, and throw me from that bed, into the grave . . . (Sermon XV: *Eighty Sermons*, 1640).

Two sources fed this clear vision of the dying: the Stoical insistence that the end of philosophy was to die well, and the medieval Christian tradition of meditation upon the fact, the physical fact, of death, as training for the life beyond it. In the dramatists, the former counts for more; thus, Hamlet's last words are filled with concern not for his soul's fate in the next world but for his name's reputation in this, and Othello is interested in reminding his last audience that he had "done the State some service, and they know it". But for Donne the Christian and medieval tradition is the paramount impulse; this passage forms indeed its last triumphant expression in the language. Medieval in origin, but deeply changed; for just as it had happened to the worship of the feminine, so this tradition also was being questioned. The spirit of scientific concern for improving this life, and that of what one may call (for want of a better word) Protestant "progressiveness", deprecated what would very soon be thought of in almost a modern way—as "morbid". There is none of it in the strenuous Milton—"I cannot praise a fugitive and cloistered virtue . . ." expresses a spirit entirely opposed to it—there is none of it in the rational Dryden. Two things, then, give to Donne's "contemplation of our state in our death-bed" a flavour very different from that of its medieval ancestry, and a power far more vital and troubling to the modern reader: the ancient tradition, the medieval contemplation, is blended with the self-obsessed and self-dramatising genius of the Renaissance; and the tradition itself has the poignancy of an old thing which is nearing its end. That formula will account for much of what is most deeply moving in the poetry of Donne and his age.

From this, the poem takes us to consider "the incommodities of the soule in the body". The spirit of this—at least the doctrine of it—has more than ever the medieval bent.[1] With a violence of language greater even than before, the body is shown us as incurably sinful, as loathsome, filthy, corrupt, contemptible, the prison of the soul till death sets her free. No words are too bad for the body whose splendours Donne had enjoyed more than most men: "a small lumpe of flesh . . . this curded milke, this poor unlittered whelpe . . . a Province pack'd up in two yards of skinne." As before, he protests too much. As before, the power of the poetry comes from the fact that between this tradition of asceticism and the mind of Donne lies something of wider import and deeper effect than the pleasures of his own younger days: between them lies the Renaissance's cult and celebration of the human body, its proclamation through every medium that what Christian asceticism had pronounced to be loathsome and contemptible was in truth miraculous and lovely. Donne himself had proclaimed it; the doctrine of this passage opposes directly what *The Extasie* had argued—and does so, oddly enough, with the same metaphor. *The Extasie* had claimed that if the lovers do not "turn" to their bodies and use them in love, then "a great Prince in *prison* lies"; this passage answers by inviting us to consider the vileness of the body as a house for the soul—"thinke in how poore a *prison* thou didst lie." The "Prince" of *The Extasie* is the power of the body, if used and enjoyed, to release in love the otherwise frustrated soul; its "prison" is the denial of the body; the *Anniversarie's* "prison" is the body itself. Between these doctrines no reconcilement can be made. The relations between body and soul had formed another main strand of Donne's mind throughout his life; here, in the *Second Anniversarie*, the matter would seem to be decided—and decided in favour of the old asceticism: but what of the lines which describe the representative figure of that asceticism—the "stubborne sullen Anchorit", who

[1] In view of the existence of such sane lovers of life and humanity as Chaucer and Langland, it might be wiser to qualify this and say "the bent of medieval ecclesiastical asceticism".

> *. . . fixt to a pillar, or a grave, doth sit*
> *Bedded, and bath'd in all his ordures . . .*

—would he be described with such unpleasing and uncomplimentary vigour, if Donne's mind were wholly in favour of what he stands for? Donne is doing again, it seems, what he had done with the worship of feminine saints; but he does it here in reverse, and here, it is likely, unconsciously: the doctrine which he is advancing theologically, he is poetically rejecting.

This impression is confirmed by the next part of the poem ("Her liberty by death"), which describes the freed soul's transit through the spheres of the planets; the swift exhilaration of this passage and the light-hearted fantasy of its wit ("who findes in *Mars* his Campe no corps of Guard") seem designed to wipe out the ugly body-hating asceticism which preceded it; and when the poem reverts from the self-addressed soul to its main object, "she", then *her* body is described in terms that certainly cancel out what was said of the human body in terms of theological generalities. The image of a prison is picked up again, but now, for her sake, contradicted:

> *She, whose faire body no such prison was,*
> *But that a soule might well be pleas'd to passe*
> *An age in her . . .*

Sanctioned by which, the amorous hyperboles (already quoted) of geographical splendours are not out of place; *her* body is almost soul, and by another of those ingenious sleights of mind by which Donne gets the best of both worlds, a doctrine and spirit not far from those of such poems as *The Extasie* and *Aire and Angells* are imported into a poem, and a passage, ostensibly at the opposite pole. By *her* body, the soul was not hampered, but through it found its expression:

> *She, of whose Soule, if we may say, 'twas Gold,*
> *Her body was th' Electrum, and did hold*
> *Many degrees of that; wee understood*
> *Her by her sight; her pure, and eloquent blood*
> *Spoke in her cheekes, and so distinctly wrought,*
> *That one might almost say, her body thought . . .*

87

This physio-psychological theory, that in persons of exceptional purity and beauty the soul "shone through" its bodily covering, was easily adaptable to the purposes of directly amorous verse, and was much employed in it. The most notable example is perhaps the lines of the *Coy Mistress*, a poem whose spirit is entirely "Epicurean" and anti-ascetic:

> *And while thy willing Soul transpires*
> *At every pore with instant Fires . . .*

So in *The Extasie*—where the doctrine (as in Marvell's poem) leads to an explicit "moral" which the *Anniversarie* could hardly draw: but the doctrine itself is akin:

> *On man heavens influence workes not so,*
> *But that it first imprints the ayre,*
> *Soe soule into the soule may flow,*
> *Though it to body first repaire.*

Thus in these two sections of the poem ("Incommodities of the Soule in the Body" and "Her liberty by death"), two "theologies" apparently irreconcilable (and really so, in logic and plain prose) meet and blend in what Donne might have called the alchemy of poetry; and by their blending is created the poetry's richness. On the one hand, the medieval asceticism; on the other, that strange *ad hoc* amalgam of philosophies by which the Renaissance sought to give a philosophical basis to its conviction of the rightness of bodily beauty and pleasure—an amalgam compounded in part from Platonism, in part from Epicurean hedonism. Which of these sources and hence which tone you took, depended on your mood, solemn or flippant. Donne, in the *Second Anniversarie*, is of course solemn; he had used the other source in his time, in such poems as *Confined Love*;[1] but that tone was not for now.

[1] E.g.

> *Are Sunne, Moone, or Starres by law forbidden,*
> *To smile where they list, or lend away their light?*
> *Are birds divorc'd, or are they chidden*
> *If they leave their mate, or lie abroad a night?*
> > *Beasts doe no joyntures lose*
> > *Though they new lovers choose,*
> > *But we are made worse then those.*

In the section which follows, "Her [*sc. our* soul's, not Eliza-beth Drury's] ignorance in this life, and knowledge in the next," the tension is lowered; most of this is a flippantly sophisticated account of the age's scientific and philosophical problems and its attempts at solving them. Donne shows little real excitement; many of the "problems" he cites are quite frivolous ("why grasse is greene, or why our blood is red"); and the contrast is remarkable between the easy indifference of his conclusion on the matter of the four elements[1] and the bitter seriousness with which, in the third *Satire* some twenty years earlier, he had weighed the choice between the conflicting sects of the Church.[2] Then, and on *that* point, he was certain both that there *was* a final truth, and that that truth must at all costs (at the cost of the soul's welfare) be found; here, he is sure that we cannot know, and sure that it does not matter. Hence, what follows in the poem is not quite as absurd as it might seem; the declaration that she, Miss Drury, "all libraries had throughly read At home in her owne thoughts" makes some sense when Donne is seen to mean the only kind of knowledge, awareness (inborn in her) of spiritual things, which seems to him now of any importance or serious interest. Perhaps that had always been true of his mind; perhaps Donne had always been, in essence, a theologian, and all his other interests, all his busy, amused, "hydroptic" soaking-up of information about the sciences and so forth, were really eccentric to that. He was not, it may be, quite clear about it himself; the letter written in 1623 to the Marquis of Buckingham, with its wellknown remark about "the Mistresse of my youth, Poetry" and "the wyfe of mine age, Divinity", can be countered with the evidence which the first of his *Satires* gives us of the contents of his library some thirty years earlier, in which are listed in the place of honour "God's conduits, grave Divines". In any case, it is clear that this review of the age's intellectual problems has little serious

---

[1]   *And one Soule thinkes one, and another way*
        Another thinkes, and 'tis an even lay
—a fifty-fifty chance that the modernists are right: but it doesn't much matter.

[2] The 18th of the *Holy Sonnets* ("Show me deare Christ, thy Spouse . . .") proves that the problem was still agonizing him even later, in all probability, than the writing of the *Second Anniversarie*.

weight behind it; the spirit it betrays is not one of agonized doubt but of dry contempt: these matters are just not worth bothering about, not for a moment comparable, in emotional interest to Donne, with the death of the body and release of the soul, which had given the poem its climax of intensity.

The poem, indeed, is in some danger of running down; the parts which follow to the end give a certain effect of strain and dilution—a feeling betrayed, perhaps, in the line:

Then, Soule, to thy first pitch worke up againe.

The soul "works up" very hard, but not with complete success. "Of our company in this life, and in the next," "Of essentiall and accidentall joyes in both places": these, the topics of the concluding sections, seem outside the range of Donne's capacity. For what they attempt to render—the quality of blessedness, of uninterrupted contemplation of God—demands the mystical vision; and that Donne never had. His poetry is invariably both the product, and the expression, of a conflict; invariably, in other words, dramatic. Drama implies the clashing of opposing perceptions; the mystical vision requires the peeling away of all other perceptions, till only one is left. An almost abstract didacticism, most unusual in Donne, betrays a failure:

> *All will not serve; Only who have enjoy'd*
> *The sight of God, in fulnesse, can thinke it;*
> *For it is both the object, and the wit.*
> *This is essentiall joy, where neither hee*
> *Can suffer diminution, nor wee;*
> *'Tis such a full, and such a filling good;*
> *Had th' Angels once look'd on him, they had stood.*

Of these sections, the successful passages are those that deal with this life (and not the next): the scathing *Lycidas*-like lines on time-serving clergymen:

> *Shalt thou not finde a spungie slacke Divine*
> *Drinke and sucke in th' instructions of Great men,*
> *And for the word of God, vent them agen?*

—and those on the corruptions of the Court:

> *Are there not some Courts (and then, no things bee*
> *So like as Courts) which, in this let us see,*
> *That wits and tongues of Libellers are weake,*
> *Because they do more ill, then these can speake?*

Both themes are old ones for Donne, and favourite ones of his age; they, and their manner, go back to his early *Satires*. Their conclusion, too—"the poyson's gone through *all*"—reminds us of that universal railing which was a feature of the satirical spirit of the 1590's. The poem, before it ends, has another reminder that even the would-be mystical Donne is still the multiple man of the Renaissance, still intensely conscious of the flowing and changing nature of his ego. The soul which in this life loves beauty (women's beauty, as the context makes clear) may be loving the best that this life has to give—"and beauty worthy'st is to love"—but neither it, nor its object, is stable:

> *Poor cousened cousenor, that* she, *and that* thou,
> *Which did begin to love, are neither now;*
> *You are both fluid, chang'd since yesterday . . .*
> *So flowes her face, and thine eyes, neither now*
> *That Saint, nor Pilgrime, which your loving vow*
> *Concern'd, remaines; but whil'st you thinke you bee*
> *Constant, you'are hourely in inconstancie.*

The paradox of the last line is that of the nineteenth of the *Holy Sonnets*—"Inconstancy unnaturally hath begott A constant habit"—though there it is applied to the insufficiency of Donne's faith in God, and there it reverses the paradox seen here in the faith of the lover. The former is constant only in being inconstant, though its object, the Divinity, is worthy of constancy, being constant itself; the latter is constant in faith, but its object, forever changing, brings the shadow of inconstancy over the constant faith. This sense of a paradox, an essential discordance at the root of both relationships, that between God and man and that between man and woman, sends us back to the Shakespearean sonnets about the lady[1]—just as a later couplet in the *Second Anniversarie*, which describes the joy of the blessed in Paradise:

---

[1] *If thy unworthinesse raisd love in me,*
More worthy I to be belov'd of thee. (150)

91

This kinde of joy doth every day admit
Degrees of growth, but none of losing it

—returns us to its source in one of Donne's poems of secular
love (*Lovers Infinitenesse*):

And since my love doth every day admit
New growth, thou shouldst have new rewards in store.

This last echo—unlike the constancy-inconstancy paradox—
deals with a success, not a failure, in the relationships, with a
love and joy in both cases felt to be perfect; Donne can thus
merge his devotional and secular, can use the same sort of
language for both, from either aspect—can heighten the latter,
when it succeeds, by giving it the same expression as the
former, and can lower the former, when it fails, by using the
language of the latter. That he did this, in fact, is beyond
doubt; later—later than the *Second Anniversarie*, and after his
ordination—he seems to have done it in spite of himself, in
spite of his ecclesiastical self, so that one of the leading themes
of the *Holy Sonnets* is his bitter self-reproaching because he
cannot feel that he feels for God the intensity of emotion which
he had felt for what he now considers less worthy objects, his
"profane mistresses".[1] For which the real reason, presumably—
one cannot help finding the whole matter to be slightly, though
most humanly, comic—was the simple fact that the Donne of
the *Holy Sonnets* was not as young as he had been. All his
emotion—in so far as it emerged into poetry—was based on,
could only be based on, sensuous experience; that was the
governing condition of his art: and hence if the sensuous experience had become fainter, the emotion must become so too. To
put it crudely, Donne had left it too late. George Herbert
provides the contrast; he was still young when he made his
decision, and diverted the whole stream of his life from finery
and courtliness and worldly success, in which he had delighted

[1] E.g., the lines in the third sonnet:

O might those sighes and teares returne againe
Into my breast and eyes, which I have spent,
That I might in this holy discontent
Mourne with some fruit, as I have mourn'd in vaine;
In mine Idolatry what showres of raine
Mine eyes did waste? what griefs my heart did rent?

no less than Donne, to the life of devotion; the sensuous power of his mind—which also was no less than Donne's—was turned with no wastage to God.

But the *Second Anniversarie*, which is the "bridge-poem" of Donne's career, flung between secular and devotional, need not feel this carking sense of an emotion less powerful than it should be, which haunts the poems on the far side of the bridge. There is little of Donne that it does not contain and make good use of: use uninhibited and unashamed. It shows, more notably than any other of his poems, the immense capaciousness which is one of the secrets of its kind and age of poetry; it can take in everything, it is under no sort of compulsion—moral or æsthetic or psychological—to reject anything. It shows, too, another feature of its kind and age: a magisterial indifference to its subject-matter. The spirit that allows Donne to import into a poem ostensibly celebrating the saintly life and transit to heaven of a young girl, daughter of his patron, elements which derive from his own sensuality, his own sardonic experience of society, and his own sense of the ugliness and fascination of reality, is also the spirit which allows Shakespeare to be so completely indifferent to the nature of the stories, the mere "plots", from which he made his dramatic poems.[1] That indifference comes out most strongly, of all Shakespeare's work, in the plays of his last years, since in them the gap is widest between the nature of the plots, if they are looked at with the eye of commonsense—their absurd impossibilities and melodramatic situations[2]—and the nature of what is made from those plots.

We must go with care if we seek to bring out an affinity between different forms of poetry, as different in all externals as are Shakespeare's and Donne's; we must have made all allowances for incidental differences before we can isolate a central

[1] And also, the spirit which allows Montaigne's Essais to divagate from their set subjects in any direction that the natural movement of his mind wishes them to go. It is only the classicist type of Renaissance writing that "sticks to the point" with conscientious pedantry.

[2] Cf. Dr. Johnson's verdict on the story of *Cymbeline*:
   To remark the folly of the fiction, the absurdity of the conduct . . . were to waste criticism upon unresisting imbecility, upon faults too evident for detection, and too gross for aggravation.

likeness. For Donne, the writing of verse was not his career; for Shakespeare, it was. Donne was therefore free to change his verse, in subject or manner, or to give it up entirely, just as suited the requirements of his mind and emotions; he could make it express exactly what ideas, and in exactly what tones, he personally wished to express. He did not have to do what Shakespeare the dramatist always had to—unless his last plays were a partial exception—keep up a balance, partly stimulating, partly frustrating, always delicate, between his personal expression and his maintaining with his public a successful relationship. Because of that requirement, Shakespeare's poetry can never be analysed with the certainty that whatever is there represents what the whole of his mind would have wished to be there. The relationship between the self (as we know or conjecture it) on the one hand, and the poetry on the other, is simple in Donne, for nothing else intervenes, but difficult in Shakespeare, for a third party, the public, does intervene, and in just what ways, at what points, and with how much effectiveness, we have no means of knowing.

Hence the riskiness of deducing anything at all about "Shakespeare the Man" from Shakespeare's plays; it is trying to solve an equation which has too many unknown quantities. The plays of his last years, more than any other part of his work (except the Sonnets, which do offer some justification), seem to breed such false deductions; and if one asks why, perhaps the answer is comically elementary. Because in fact they *were* his last plays, we deduce that he knew they were. Because he did die soon after writing them, we decide that he wrote them as a last word, a valediction[1]; and since one of them happens to contain (as is completely appropriate to the plot) a magician's solemn abandonment of his art, we deduce—well, everyone knows that piece of false sentiment, which equates Prospero-abandoning-magic with Shakespeare-abandoning-poetry.[2] But if we look at

[1] The *only* basis for this belief is the fact that Shakespeare appears to have written nothing during the last three or four years of his life; but in the total absence of evidence on the reasons for this, it is quite unjustifiable to assume a deliberate cessation, announced in *The Tempest*. Poets, like politicians, very rarely retire; the great majority write on, ill or well, to the end.

[2] Mr. Ivor Brown provides perhaps the most notable piece of nonsense in this strain. He solemnly argues that Prospero's injunc-

these plays not from the viewpoint of afterwards, but as Shakespeare came to them himself, from what he had written before them and not knowing what was to come after, it will not be as an end, but as a new beginning, that we shall see them. They have many of the signs of an artist who is feeling his way towards a new use of his medium; they are experimental. There is never in them the kind of uncertainty found in the problem-plays, springing from a real confusion about life and values; the values here are as firm as in the great tragedies: but there *is* an exhilarating quality of surprise and searching and discovery. If Shakespeare had lived, if he had continued to write, these plays might be seen as "bridge-poems" in his career as the *Second Anniversarie* in Donne's; what they would have led to we must try to decide from themselves.

Lytton Strachey's verdict, that what they show is acute boredom, has been pretty thoroughly demolished; but in one respect it may stand. Bored Shakespeare does seem to have become with the commonplace stagecraft of the ordinary theatrical success. These plays are by no means less dramatic, but they do seem less "theatrical", than those which preceded them. They always were, and have remained, far less than the tragedies and some of the early comedies, the chosen vehicles of professional actors. Compared with his earlier plays, the stories are told with a slapdash indifference to plausibility even greater than before; the verse, amazingly subtle and rich, tends not to be of a kind which makes an immediate impact; set speeches, memorable tirades, are fewer than before, and so are "great scenes", enormously effective on their own, like the quarrel of Brutus and Cassius, Iago's persuading of Othello, or the murder of Duncan. It looks as if the loosening of the bonds (both geographical and financial) which had tied Shakespeare to his Bankside theatre had resulted in a comparative indifference to that theatre's requirements. By 1610 or so, the London theatre was in fact beginning to pass out of its greatest moment, beginning the swift decline of the following decades; one wonders if Shakespeare felt it.

tion to Ferdinand and Miranda not to anticipate their marriage expresses Shakespeare's remorse and regret for having done this himself, with Anne Hathaway, about thirty-five years earlier. He took his time about repenting.

Another form of drama, at its zenith in these years, seems to have attracted him with possibilities of new development. This was the masque. Shakespeare wrote no formal masque; but these last plays do show many of the masque's features and much of its atmosphere. Supernatural and ritualistic effects (such as the vision of the divinities in *Cymbeline* and the restoration of Hermione at the end of *The Winter's Tale*); the integral use of music, usually as part of these effects; the strong lyrical element: all these add up to a kind of drama much more symbolical, much nearer to allegory, than anything he had written before. It seems plausible to suppose that the contemporary vogue of the masque, coinciding with this impatience which Shakespeare had conceived for the kind of play and the kind of acceptance he had hitherto been contented with, induced him to try something in that direction. But only "in that direction": these plays remain absolutely *plays*, dramatic and alive in a way no real masques ever were or could be. The latter are terribly static and monumental; the dead hand of special occasions and courtly gentility lies heavy upon them. These Shakespearean plays, however fantastic and symbolical, never lose contact with life; they do not, as do the early fantasies, such as *Midsummer Night's Dream* or *As You Like It*, confine reality (broadly speaking) to the plane of low comedy and give to evil, when the plot requires it to appear, a certain sentimentalized softening. In the fantasy of the last plays, evil is an integral part, presented with the utmost intensity; the fantasy is never an escape. The evil of Leontes' jealousy, of Cloten and of Caliban, and the violence and ugliness of its expression, fill the part in these plays that the passages on the world's and the body's hatefulness fill in the poem of Donne.

What Shakespeare seems to have been moving towards was a kind of dramatic poetry quite unlike anything he had written before. It would have lived in the world of allegory and symbolism, but behind it, giving it backbone and force, would have been a lifetime of experience. It would have been less concerned with human beings as such, and more with human passions in their pure states: virtues and vices, good and evil, "the two contrary states of the human soul" (in Blake's phrase). This is the general point at which a parallel with Donne's *Anniversaries* might be legitimately made. Both Shakespeare and Donne had worked through a pre-occupation with real (i.e., particular, individual) experience towards a poetry which attempts to distil an essence out of the experience and also to transcend it. We have seen how the themes of Donne's earlier verse—that of the *Satires*, the *Elegies*, and the *Songs and Sonets*, which is *his* poetry of the concrete, particular experience—are summed up in the *Second Anniversarie*; so, in Shakespeare's last plays, the essence both of his tragic and comic experience of humanity receives its expression. Neither writer rejects the experience, they give it a positive purpose—though Donne, the smaller mind and the more theological, is impelled to attempt a rejection of part of it, which, luckily for his poetry, he can never entirely achieve. Shakespeare suffered from no such compulsion: what his "religion" was nobody knows or will ever know. His art, at least, rejected nothing.

This is the general resemblance; if we come to particulars, the clearest point of contact is in the treatment of the feminine—of the "she" of Donne's poem and the heroines of the plays. Any reader with sensibility feels at once that these heroines—Miranda, Perdita, Imogen—are in some way set apart from the heroines of their author's earlier work. The tone of their direct outspokenness may be given as a touchstone of this difference. Miranda's words to Ferdinand—"I am your wife, if you will marry me"—and Perdita's

> . . . *No more than were I painted, I would wish*
> *This youth should say, 'twere well: and onely therefore*
> *Desire to breed by me*

recall, but are not the same as, the outspokenness of the heroines of the early comedies: for their outspokenness had a tinge of the jest and the bawdy; this is of a kind that belongs (in Miranda's own phrase) to "plain and holy innocence". It is not exactly that these heroines are presented as perfectly good; it could be argued that all Shakespearean heroines are morally flawless—as stage convention, if nothing else, demanded—these women are seen as absolutes, they are felt as not merely exceptional, but as unique. "He himself [i.e., Prospero] calls her a nonpareil," says Caliban of Miranda, and "the nonpareil of this [time]" is Posthumus' phrase for Imogen. So, "peerless" is given to Miranda, to Hermione, and to Perdita: "so perfect and so peerless" for the first, "as she lived peerless" for the second, "the most peerless piece of earth, I thinke, that ere the Sun shone bright on" for the last. ("Peerless," but still, "a piece of earth": the transcendental, as always in this poetry, as we saw it in Donne, does not forget its roots.) They are absolutes, for whom such "flattery" is neither ridiculous nor disproportionate: "the Idea of a woman . . ." They are also essences of womanhood, and the love they evoke seems an essence of all earlier loves. Ferdinand describes his love for Miranda—

> *Admir'd* Miranda,
> *Indeede the top of Admiration, worth*
> *What's dearest to the world: full many a Lady*
> *I have ey'd with best regard, and many a time*
> *Th' harmony of their tongues, hath into bondage*
> *Brought my too diligent eare: for severall vertues*
> *Have I lik'd severall women, never any*
> *With so full soule, but some defect in her*
> *Did quarrel with the noblest grace she ow'd,*
> *And put it to the foile. But you, O you,*
> *So perfect, and so peerelesse, art created*
> *Of everie Creatures best*

(III,1)

—in terms which immediately recall Donne's phrase for his "she"—"she whose rich beauty lent Mintage to other beauties": they recall also the lines in his *Good Morrow*:

> *If ever any beauty I did see,*
> *Which I desir'd, and got, 'twas but a dreame of thee*

and those in Shakespeare's 31st sonnet:

> *Thou art the grave where buried love doth live,*
> *Hung with the trophies of my lovers gon,*
> *Who all their parts of me to thee did give,*
> *That due of many, now is thine alone.*

Both poets are doing, each in his own way and through his own form, the same thing: from the half-genuine, half-artificial hyperboles of lyrical love-poetry, whose absurd aspects both of them had very adequately exposed, they are making a poetry poised between human and divine. It looks as if both of them, after the crisis of the 1590's had passed, became more tolerant of the things which, during the crisis, they had violently rejected. The "Platonic" worship of the Lady, against which Donne had begun by reacting, returns, as we have seen, much modified but not unrecognizably altered; the last plays of Shakespeare show a similar return, with similar modifications, to a strain of romantic and lyrical beauty which the plays intervening had almost totally abandoned. Presumably this may often happen: a creative writer can afford to be more tolerant when his personal, immediate need to attack, discredit, and remove from out of his way has passed, when his own "revolution" has become accepted. Disconcerting, this is often, to critical but inelastic admirers, who are apt (the besetting sin of us critics) to stand still and label, while creators go on their illogical ways.

These heroines evoke, then, a poetry which bridges the human and the divine; and their own affinities with the latter are made explicit. Ferdinand and Miranda see each other as divinities at first sight. And this is more than the convention of amorous compliment (though it does derive from it—the process is still the same, the making of a new thing from the old resources), for Miranda has never before seen a man, other than her father, and Ferdinand is wandering bemused and magicked on a magical island. "What is't, a Spirit?" are her first words on seeing him; and her next: "I might call him a thing divine." And his on seeing her: "Most sure the Goddesse, on whom these ayres attend"—for he has been led to the meeting by the singing and playing of the invisible Ariel: music, as so often in these plays, both signalling and helping to create the suggestion of divinity. On Ferdinand's father, when he meets her first at the end of the play, she has the same effect: "Is she the goddesse," he asks, as his son had asked, "that hath sever'd us, and brought us thus together?" So in *The Winter's Tale*: on Leontes the first sight of his son's love produces an identical response. "And you faire Princesse," he begins, and corrects it at once to "Goddesse". For Perdita plays the same role as Miranda—she, too, first "severs", then "brings together", parents and children, country and court—and her divinity is as clearly established.

99

She is the "Queen" of the "meeting of the petty Gods" to which the sheep-shearing feast is likened; in Florizel's phrase, "no Shepherdesse, but *Flora*": in her own words, "most Goddesse-like prankt up". Shakespeare, of course, goes by the indirect ways of the dramatist; we must not expect that a point like this, the divinity of his heroines, will be argued and expounded, as it is by Donne for his poem's heroine; it will be simply created and presented. But it is none the less there for not being the subject of exposition.

A quality common to all these plays is one that might be called *extremeness*. Half-tones and qualifications are missing; this is a poetry, as it were, of primary colours. The strain of universal railing, with its key-word "all", continues here as it does in the *Second Anniversarie*. Posthumus, hearing of Imogen's supposed unfaithfulness, rails in this strain against all womankind:

> All *faults that may be nam'd, nay, that hell knows,*
> *Why, hers,*[1] *in part, or* all; *but rather,* all . . .
>
> (II, 5)

Imogen, hearing of Posthumus' unjustified suspicions, retorts with exactly the same response:

> All *good seeming,*
> *By thy revolt (oh Husband) shall be thought*
> *Put on for Villainy . . .*
> *so thou,* Posthumus
> *Wilt lay the Leaven on* all *proper men;*
> *Goodly, and gallant, shall be false and perjur'd*
> *From thy great faile.*
>
> (III, 4)

This is the dramatic equivalent of the lines in the *Second Anniversarie* which describe the total extinction of the world's goodness now that "she" is dead:

> *Yet a new Deluge, and of* Lethe *flood,*
> *Hath drown'd us* all, All *have forgot* all *good,*
> *Forgetting her, the maine reserve of* all.

[1] i.e., woman's in general, not Imogen's in particular: but *because* of Imogen.

And in these plays this irrational transference from the particular to the universal receives no dry criticism from the voice of commonsense, as the similar irrationality of Troilus had received from Ulysses; it does not get it here because here we are not in a world where commonsense has any validity. It would be as out of place in these plays as it would be in Donne's poem—as it was when his friends reproached him for overpraising the virtues of Miss Drury. For it is not only the heroines who are presented as absolutes: the extremeness extends to all the rest. Cloten and Posthumus, at the opening of *Cymbeline*, are described more as "ideas" of evil and of good than as anything remotely resembling real human beings:

> *He that hath miss'd the Princesse, is a thing*
> *Too bad, for bad report: and he that hath her,*
> *(I meane, that married her, alacke good man,*
> *And therefore banish'd) is a Creature, such,*
> *As to seeke through the Regions of the Earth*
> *For one, his like; there would be something failing*
> *In him, that should compare.*[1] *I do not thinke,*
> *So faire an Outward, and such stuffe Within*
> *Endows a man, but hee.*

$$(I, 1)$$

The hearer of this eulogy does demur (as Donne's friends demurred to his eulogies of Miss Drury): "you speake him farre," he complains, but the first speaker answers (as Donne's poem answers) by asserting that even such hyperboles fall short of the truth:

> *I do extend him (Sir) within himselfe,*
> *Crush him together, rather than unfold*
> *His measure duly.*

So with all the characters (that word, with its suggestion of "reality", is not the word for them): that these are absolutes and not real people, can be seen by the fact that their behaviour,

---

[1] Cf. Ferdinand's speech on other women compared with Miranda:

> *. . . but some defect in her*
> *Did quarrel with the noblest grace she ow'd,*
> *And put it to the foile.*

however inconsistent—and it is hopelessly inconsistent—
with their natures as described, is not regarded as in any way
demanding a change in one's verdict on their natures. Victorian
critics were wont to sigh heavily over the fate of poor Imogen,
united to such an unworthy husband as Posthumus; the truth is
that he is not meant to be in the least unworthy: on the contrary, he is presented as the one man in the world who *is*
worthy of her. He is perfect good, for a time corrupted and
almost ruined by the perfect, and monstrous, evil of Iachimo.
And when Leontes' jealousy has done its work, killing his son
and (as he thinks) killing also his wife, Paulina breaks off her
bitter reproaches with words which a modern reader is apt to
feel can only be taken as ironic—"he is toucht to th' Noble
heart." But ironic they are not: he *is* "noble", always has been,
and always will be. Noble, but corrupted: which makes the
corruption more dreadful. So, too, the death of his son is
explained as caused by the same, inherent nobleness:

> *To see his Noblenesse,*
> *Conceyving the dishonour of his Mother,*
> *He straight declin'd, droop'd, tooke it deeply,*
> *Fasten'd, and fix'd the shame on't in himselfe:*
> *Threw-off his Spirit, his Appetite, his Sleepe,*
> *And down-right languish'd.*

(II, 3)

To complain, as commonsense would, that a small boy does not
go into a decline and die because his parents quarrel, would
clearly be as irrelevant as to object that Elizabeth Drury had
hardly had time to practise the virtue of chastity. The death of
Mamillius is not the death of a small boy; it is the death of
innocence. The death of Elizabeth Drury is not (in the poem)
the death of a girl; it is the death of goodness.

In these plays, one feels that the meaning which Shakespeare
is striving to express lies almost beyond the capacity of a
drama filled only with human "characters": hence the monstrous, in Caliban and almost in Cloten—who is virtually a
monster, a "thing", not a man, as the first scene describes him.[1]
This quality of monstrousness enters even into others, not in
themselves hideous or evil. Evil invades them like a spirit—

---

[1] Iachimo also is thus described: "slight thing of Italy".

uninvited, it seems, by anything in their "characters"; as the age would have put it, they seem "possessed". No other plays of Shakespeare render evil with quite the same kind of unmotivated purity as these do; the evil of Claudius and Iago, in contrast, was seen as entirely human and explainable. The remorse of Claudius, Iago's explanations of his own motives (whether we credit them or not[1]), put their evil within the scope of human experience, comprehensible both by something outside and by something within themselves; but Leontes' jealousy, Iachimo's challenge and treachery, and Posthumus' crediting of his story, have motives so flimsy that they can, and in practice must, be disregarded. What is more dwelt on in these plays, and rendered with far greater force, than in any of the earlier work, is evil as a corrupter of the mind and imagination—of the soul, in fact. This aspect of it did, of course, exist, and exist very strongly, in earlier plays, as in the evil of Macbeth; but there the imaginative corruption is much more adequately, more realistically, balanced by actual events: what Macbeth *does* is good enough motive for what he *feels*. The jealousy of Leontes and Posthumus, so ill-based in fact, releases a flood of foul imaginings whose extraordinary physical violence seems completely disproportionate to what set it going, to the "nobility" of the men who pour it out, and to the loves which it defiles. They seem to throw themselves, at once and eagerly,

---

[1] I do not know if it has ever been pointed out that the first motive which Iago confesses to—that Othello had not promoted him as he thought he deserved—is exactly that which Clarendon attributes to John Felton, the assassin of the Duke of Buckingham:

John Felton, an obscure person, who had been bred a soldier, and lately a lieutenant of a foot company, whose captain had been killed upon the retreat at the Isle of Rhe, upon which he conceived that the company of right ought to have been conferred upon him, and it being refused to him by the duke of Buckingham, general of the army, he had given up his commission of lieutenant, and withdrawn himself from the army. (*History of the Rebellion*, Book I)

I cannot see why a motive which a seventeenth century historian thought adequate for a real person should not have been thought, by a seventeenth century dramatist, equally adequate for one of his *dramatis personae*.

as if this were what they really wanted, into a nightmare of obscenity:

> *And many a man there is (even at this present,*
> *Now, while I speake this) holds his Wife by th' Arme,*
> *That little thinkes she has been sluyc'd in's absence,*
> *And his Pond fish'd by his next Neighbor (by*
> *Sir Smile, his Neighbor) . . .*
>
> (*Winter's Tale*, I, 2)

> *This yellow Iachimo in an houre, was't not?*
> *Or lesse; at first? Perchance he spoke not, but*
> *Like a full Acorn'd Boare, a German one,*
> *Cry'de oh, and mounted . . .*
>
> (*Cymbeline*, II, 5)

Though it seems unjustified, for these plays as for any of Shakespeare's work, to use theological terms or to fancy that Shakespeare thought in such terms, one does feel that here is being presented a "state" rather than a human being: the state of damnation, as its victims present the state of blessedness. The pure evil of these imaginings is put beside the pure good of the women who are falsely accused, as the absolute corruption of the ordinary body, in Donne's poem, is put beside the absolute purity of hers. There is in fact, on this particular point, a particular link; the physio-theological theory which we have seen behind the lines of Donne on Elizabeth Drury:

> *Her pure, and eloquent blood*
> *Spoke in her cheekes, and so distinctly wrought,*
> *That one might almost say, her body thought*

—lies also behind Perdita's lines describing Florizel:

> *. . . but that your youth*
> *And the true blood which peepes fairely through't*

—and Camillo's describing Perdita:

> *. . . he tells her something*
> *That makes her blood look out.*

Both evil and good—in the poetry of both men—though presented as absolutes, are never made abstract; the concrete, particularized phrases by which the former is rendered—"Sir *Smile*, his neighbor", "this lumpe of flesh", "this yellow *Iachimo*", "two yards of skinne", "cry'de oh, and mounted"— keep the evil a physical reality, as the conceit (or rather the scientific belief, for it *was* believed in as science) of the pure blood showing through the skin the purity of the soul, keeps alive the physical presence of the persons who represent good.

From this putting beside each other—rather than formal comparison, which would not be appropriate—of Donne's theological and Shakespeare's dramatic poems, what conclusions can we come to on such qualities as are truly common to both? There is, first, inclusiveness: this has already been hinted at, the capacity for dealing with anything and everything. But that in itself has no great value; anyone can determine to shove in all he knows and all he has experienced, and the upshot may well be no more than a muddle. What preserved this poetry from that fate is its power of focussing. It has an extraordinary ability to concentrate on to a single point a wide range of different orders of experience: on the figures of the women in the poems we have been looking at, are focussed sexual desire and revulsion from it, love of bodily beauty and a sense of its inadequacy, youth as symbol of innocence and age as symbol of corruption, the world as desirable and the world as repellent. The least analytical reader, when he comes from the poetry of Spenser or Sidney or Marlowe to that of Donne and mature Shakespeare, is made aware of a difference which he might describe to himself as an increased thickness of texture: there seems much more to the square inch of it. The reason for this difference, which may not be as obvious as the difference itself, lies here: any given subject engages a far greater range of interests. The subject, indeed—as we saw—becomes in itself of minor importance: so does the form. If this poetry uses prescribed forms at all, it stretches them to the limit; as a rule it does not use them, it makes its own forms as it goes on, and the content determines what the form will be. The same holds good of the language. The tension and surprise which are major characteristics come partly from this: from the feeling that any- thing may happen and anything may be said, that the mould is, almost, cracking. This poetry is never complacent, never in that state of being smugly pleased with itself which so often vitiates the poetry of the classicist and genteel kind of Renaissance writing. It has the power of indefinite development—so that, with Shakespeare, even at what became the end of a long career of continuous writing, one feels that development is still active, experiment still alive. It is always working to be different from what it was; hence the aspiration, which we have found in both Shakespeare and Donne, to build a transcendental meaning out of particular experience, is not merely a desire imposed, as it were, from without, not merely a pious conviction of what ought to be done: it is integral with the nature of the poetry.

No English poetry, before or since, seems to have quite the quality of this. If that is so, it can hardly have been an accident: there must have been something in the climate of the first part of the seventeenth century peculiarly propitious to such an achievement. What that something was, the next chapter will try to discover.

Chapter 4

THE SOCIETY OF
THE SHAKESPEAREAN MOMENT

IF the essential features of this poetry be the abilities to include everything and to concentrate many orders of experience on to a single point, then it is clear that such poetry will be possible only in a society which both provides plenty to include and provides it in such a way that it *can* be brought together. The first requirement will be a view of life which does not specialize and does not exclude.

"Does not specialize" means, for our purposes, that sets of emotions and ideas which for us are non-transferable from one context to another, were in that age, for the kind of mentality that Donne and Shakespeare represent, fully transferable. It was always possible—and they were always attempting it—to build bridges from subject to subject, emotion to emotion; these bridges, increasingly fragile in the domains of pure ideas and practical politics, still held in that of poetry—and just because of their fragility in other domains, they were all the more tempting and precious. Between the spiritual and the political, for instance. A passage not yet looked at in the *Second Anniversarie* gives a perfect example. In the section "Of our company in this life and in the next," Donne evolves a series of elaborate conceits to establish a parallel between "her" and a sovereign State, all of whose functions she (in metaphor) performed: she made war and peace, she "did high justice", she gave pardons, she coined, she gave protections; and hence

> *As these prerogatives being met in one,*
> *Made her a soveraigne State; religion*
> *Made her a Church; and these two made her all.*

These lines touch one of the nerve-centres of the seventeenth century, and in particular of the kind of poetry we are analysing now. Without this intense feeling for a nexus, an absolute identity, between the spiritual, the political, and the personal— it could be, as here, the feminine, quasi-amorous personal—the

107

poetry of the Shakespearean moment would not be what it is. These three things—spiritual, political, personal—are united, in a way essentially the same, in Ulysses' words to Achilles in *Troilus and Cressida:*

> *The providence that's in a watchfull State,*
> *Knowes almost every graine of Plutoes gold;*
> *Findes bottome in th' uncomprehensive deepes;*
> *Keepes pace with thought; and almost like the gods,*
> *Does thoughts unvaile in their dumbe cradles:*
> *There is a mysterie (with whom relation*
> *Durst never meddle) in the soule of State;*
> *Which hath an operation more divine,*
> *Than breath or pen can give expressure to.*

(III, 3)

What Ulysses is talking about may seem to a modern mind somewhat inappropriate as basis for a passage of such mysterious, almost mystical, solemnity; he is assuring Achilles that the Greeks' Military Intelligence is well aware of his goings-on with the Trojan Polyxena. Spying, in fact; but this in no way debars Shakespeare from feeling and expressing the same union of spiritual and political that Donne felt: "providence", "like the gods", "mysterie", "divine"—the recurring key-words keep hammering at the spiritual note. Through poetry such as this—and through it alone—we can go some way towards restoring the flesh and blood of emotional reality to the dry bones of the clichés in the history textbooks. "Church and State", "divine right", "no King, no Bishop"—the twentieth century is apt to read them as if they were mere political slogans, on the level of "Votes for women" or "No taxation without representation": and so reading, fatally misunderstands them.

Divine right, it is true, was a Tudor, not a medieval invention; but it can be said that it was an invention in the medieval mode. It belongs to the same kind of thinking, represents the same sort of ambition, as that which made Dante see the fall of Troy as an event which led to Aeneas' founding of Rome, which led to the Roman Empire, which existed so that in due time—in God's time—a framework of political order might be ready for the reception of the spiritual order of Christianity: which double order should still (if things went right) be the pattern for

Emperor and Pope to follow. 'The society of Donne and Shakespeare, still medieval at least in this part of its mind, still pursued the medieval dream of synthesizing all things to a single system, with the spiritual at its head; it tried to realize, for the smaller field of England, and the Church of England, what had been a dream for Europe. It is by remembering the existence of this dream that we can understand what may seem to be—sometimes are—absurd excesses of sycophancy bordering on the blasphemous: such things as Donne's confident anticipating, for the benefit of his sovereign, the verdict of the Almighty (he is speaking of Queen Elizabeth and King James):

> Though then these two great princes (of whom the one con-regnat Christo, reigns now with Christ, the other reigns over us vice Christi, for Christ) were near in blood, yet thus were they nearest of kin, quod uterque optimus, that they were both better then any other, and equal to each other.
> (Sermon preached on 24 March, 1617)

Poets who thought and felt in this way would always be inclined, in their poetry, to unite rather than divide, amalgamate rather than distinguish; hence the conceit—most characteristic poetic weapon of the Shakespearean moment—is above all a device for uniting disparate things. And especially for uniting the concrete and the abstract, the sensuous and the spiritual; we have seen how this poetry is sensuous through and through, how it roots the transcendental in the earthy and renders in physical terms its mental and spiritual states. Of such a mentality the ecclesiastical concomitants are obvious: colour and music and ritual in the Anglo-catholic service. What goes with it in politics is equally clear: a reluctance to secularize, an instinct for seeing political processes as more than matters of merely rational "policy". Of all three the real meaning is the same: a preservation—precarious, soon to be lost, but alive for all that—of the medieval heritage. It is quite clear that to Donne, for example, it was the traditional theology of the Middle Ages, and not the new science, which "came home to his business and bosom"; it was the former, and not the latter, which was linked with his bodily and emotional life; the latter, not the former, which for him was the dry abstraction. "Medieval heritage" is a meaningless cliché in itself: what, in our context of a poetry which is permeated by the sensuous, did it actually mean? It meant, above all, a way of thinking about the human creature which united body and soul. This way of thinking was not in the least vague; it was thoroughly systematic and "scientific", however badly wrong. It could be, and was, systematized (the Middle Ages systematized everything), and a glance at it in the realm of physiology, at its view of the human body, will illuminate more than that realm alone.

Medieval physiology was also psychology. Its bases, of course (derived from Galen), were the four elements and the four humours. They in themselves need no elucidation. But for our purposes the point is that the humours were thought of as strictly and literally physiological realities. Their use as "metaphors" for human behaviour was secondary and very closely linked to the physiology which lay behind them. They were produced by the liver; they were liquids, spread through the body in the blood. The psychological conditions which resulted from an excess of one or the other were thought of as physical diseases, which drugs or dieting could deal with. Choler, for instance. When Hamlet tells Guildenstern (who has reported that the King "is in his retirement marvellous distempered . . . with choler") that he, Guildenstern, would do better "to signify this to his doctor", and when Petruchio remarks that he cannot eat mutton—"for it engenders choler, planteth anger"—neither is being fanciful: both are reproducing the medical commonplaces of their age. (Rhubarb was for choler a favourite prescription, as Webster's Ferdinand knew.) So with melancholy: this was seen as a "drosse and thicking" in the blood[1]—a physical condition, as Shakespeare sees it in *King John*:

[1] The phrase comes from Sir Thomas Vicary's *Profitable Treatise of the Anatomie of Mans Body*, published in 1548: the first textbook of anatomy and physiology printed in English. Vicary was a royal surgeon to four Tudor monarchs (from Henry VIII to Elizabeth); he was Master of the Barber Surgeons' Company and a governor of Bart's. His treatise (which I have drawn on extensively in this and following pages) is thoroughly representative of the orthodox medical ideas of the age. It goes back to a fourteenth-century MS. which in turn goes back still earlier. But the fact that the sixteenth century regarded it as authoritative is shown by its republication in 1577 (after Vicary's death) by the surgeons of Bart's; it seems to have been used as a textbook for at least a century more.

Or if that surly spirit melancholy
Had bak'd thy bloud, and made it heavy, thicke,
Which else runnes tickling up and downe the veines . . .
(III, 3)

This kind of physical-psychical parallelism runs all through the thought of the age, and is constantly appearing in its imaginative writing. A hot and moist humour led to (and was a symptom of) lechery: Othello brooding over Desdemona's hand ("give me your hand; this hand is moist, my Lady . . ."), and Cleopatra's maids joking with the soothsayer, are all referring to this:

—There's a Palme presages Chastity, if nothing els.
—E'ne as the o're-flowing Nilus presageth Famine . . .
Nay, if an oyly Palme bee not a fruitful Prognostication . . .
(I, 2)

The colour of the cheeks was symptomatic of the humour prevailing. If the cheeks are "full, ruddy, and meddled with temperate whiteness", the nature is "sanguin and temperat"; if they are "white coloured, without medling of rednes", it is "flematike"; if "browne in colour", choleric; if "as it were blowen in colour" (a livid yellowish pallor, presumably), then melancholy is the temperament.[1] So, when Agamemnon in *Troilus and Cressida* asks the assembled Greeks "Princes: what greefe hath set the Jaundice on your cheekes?" and when Viola talks of the "green and yellow" melancholy of her imaginary and lovesick sister, neither expression is merely figurative, as a modern reader is inclined to take them; both are literal, physiological as well as psychological. The "spirits", natural, animal, and vital, which in all this medical theory come second in importance only to the humours, are, like the humours, physical substances, conveyed in the blood. Liver, heart, and brain, regarded as the master-organs of the body,[2] produce the spirits: the animal spirit, produced by the brain, is that which makes Antony feel he is still young enough to fight:

[1] All from Vicary, op. cit.
[2] Cf. *The liver, heart, and braine of* Brittaine,
    By whom I grant she lives.
              (*Cymbeline*, V, 5.)

What Gyrle, though gray
Do somthing mingle with our younger brown, yet ha' we
A Braine that nourishes our Nerves, and can
Get gole for gole of youth.

(IV, 8)

If the humours of the brain be not properly balanced, then comes trouble:

Wherefore (sayth Aristotle) when it happeneth that the Brayne is eyther too drye or too moyst, then can it not worke his kinde; for then is the body made colde; then are the spirites of lyfe melted and resolued away; and then foloweth feebleness of the wittes, and of al other members of the body, and at the last death.

(Vicary, op. cit.)

On which physiology Falstaff bases his defence of sherris sack:

It ascends me into the Braine, dryes me there all the foolish, and dull, and cruddie Vapours, which environ it . . .

(2 *Henry IV*, IV, 3)

What all this amounts to is a link between body and character so close that it might almost be called behaviourist—would be behaviourist, indeed, but for belief in the soul. There seems a contradiction here: perhaps there is. On the one hand, this body-soul integration, based (as they thought) on real fact, exact science; on the other hand, the theology which (as seen in the *Second Anniversarie*) drew a very clear line between body and soul and in fact represented them as hostile. It was certainly a much-debated question of the age, just where the soul could be fitted into this framework so precisely marked out; Sir John Davies gives us some of the rival theories in the introduction to his poem *Of the Immortality of the Soul*:

In judgment of her substance thus they vary,
And thus they vary in judgment of her seat;
For some her chair up to the brain do carry,
Some thrust it down into the stomach's heat;
Some place it in the root of life, the heart;
Some in the river-fountain of the veins;
Some say, she's all in all, and all in every part,
Some say, she's not contained, but all contains.

112

The soul, then, was thought of both as something which fought against the body and aspired to escape from it, and as a part of the body; and it was this kind of thinking—there seems no doubt that Donne and Shakespeare and the rest thoroughly shared in it, took it for granted, indeed, as we take for granted (without, most of us, really comprehending) the existence of vitamins and their effects on our bodies—it was this that made it not only possible and easy, but inevitable, for the poets of the Shakespearean moment to fuse the physical with the spiritual. They still held the medieval integration. Their ideas on man's body, on his character and soul, on his religious and his political activities, still formed a whole—and formed it not merely in the sphere of metaphor but in that of science. In such a mental climate, it was not fancifulness to draw parallels between the order of the planets and that of human society (as it ought to be) and between the disorders of a troubled State and the diseases of a man's body. The poets who drew such parallels believed that all this was *true*. The forces which were to prove that in the sphere of science almost all of it was nonsense, and in the spheres of politics and religion all of it could be torn apart and defeated, were gathering and strengthening; the tension was steadily tightening, but the break was not yet.

Parallels between politics and literature should always be made with caution and received with scepticism; but perhaps it is not accidental that the age of the Shakespearean moment was one of comparative settlement between two great upheavals: the Reformation and its consequences before it, the Civil War after it. The settlement was highly precarious, what with Roman Catholic fanatics in the basement of the Houses of Parliament and Puritan or Arminian fanatics in half the pulpits of the land; the tension was held but only just held. And this is exactly the quality of the age's poetry. A poem like the *Second Anniversarie*, or a play like *King Lear*, maintains, but only just maintains, control over the clashing elements which compose it. Chaos is very near; its nearness, but its avoidance, gives the poetry its force. And the poetry delights in it; it takes the pure pleasure of the dramatist-as-artist in giving the maximum power and persuasiveness, the greatest possible chance of victory, to those forces which the dramatist-as-individual regarded as "enemies".

Such art—the art of true tragedy—is possible only to those whose view of life is tragic but not pessimistic; they must have no delusions, no wishful-thinking, about the actual behaviour, capacities, and fates of men on the human level, but must believe that there exists another level on which those fates are redeemed. If they have the delusions, they sentimentalize; if they do not have the faith, the tragedy turns to mere sadism—or masochism. For Christians, the terms by which the tragic sense can be kept are original sin (for the lack of delusions on the human level) and redemption (for the faith on another). By the former, one was disembarrassed from any hope that mankind, in this existence, would ever "progress"; by the latter, one felt no need for such a hope, since another, and better, was believed to be available. The dramatist could give the devil a good long rope—and thoroughly enjoy his capers at the end of it—because he knew that at last, the devil would hang.

Hence the poetry of the Shakespearean moment—which is shot through with the tragic sense—sprang from, and depended on, a view of politics essentially conservative, and a view of religion essentially orthodox: these two making up a view of humanity tragic but not hopeless. By such a view it was possible to give full value to all sides of human nature: which the progressive and optimistic mentality—represented, as the following chapters will argue, by the Puritan and the rationalist—could never do; for that mentality must always be tempted to minimize, or shut its eyes to, or try to suppress, some parts of the human variety.

Variety is one of the essentials of the poetry we are studying, and only a society which was various in itself could feed such poetry. But the variety must have some meaning: not chaotic, but ordered. And such was the variety of seventeenth century society: aristocratic but not snobbish; hierarchical without being petrified. The age of the first two Stuarts saw the English aristocracy reach a kind of distinction—not so easy to define but quite unmistakable—which, like the age's poetry, has a quality of its own. It seems—again, like the poetry—to get the best of all worlds, to be poised with a delicate force between extremes. The flamboyance, brutality, and whimsicality which so often give to the Elizabethan aristocracy an air of adolescence, are now toned down to a real refinement, but a refinement still far from the over-elaborate artificiality to which the aristocracy of the eighteenth century tended to bring it.

These aristocrats, the men of the early Stuarts, compared with their forebears or their descendants, seem much more often and more successfully in tune with the best of the spiritual and artistic worlds of their age. And hence the patron-writer relationship, notoriously one of the trickiest of all human associations, "comes off" then surprisingly well. Clarendon, for instance, testifies to Falkland's success with that most difficult member of the irritable genus, Ben Jonson:

> He seemed to have his estate in trust for all worthy persons who stood in want of supplies and encouragement, as Ben Jonson, and many others of that time, whose fortunes required, and whose spirits made them superior to, ordinary obligations; which yet they were contented to receive from him . . .

But the harmony went deeper than a tactful bestowal and a dignified acceptance of patronage; the relationship was often such that the very words "patron" and "patronage" seem hopelessly inappropriate. Imagine for a moment how utterly impossible it would be that a poet of the eighteenth century—or in fact after the Restoration—should feel for his patron anything like the depth and quality of emotion that Shakespeare felt for his Mr. W. H. Into such relationships—that of Shakespeare and Mr. W. H. was not the only one—there entered a warmth and sometimes a passion which did not destroy feelings of reverence and inequality—on the contrary, those feelings were intensified—but gave to the relationships a genuine value in themselves, not merely in the benefits they conferred. They could be, as they were for Shakespeare, not only the means by which the poet could live, but a valuable material for his poetic creation. So with Donne—though *his* patrons were apt to be women. For Magdalen Herbert (George Herbert's remarkable mother) Donne felt a complex of emotions which, allowing for the differences caused by the difference in sex and ages and by a strong devotional tone, are by no means incomparable with Shakespeare's feelings for Mr. W. H. The latter were a subtle and changing blend of love and tenderness for a beautiful and gifted young man, reverence and gratitude for a noble patron; Donne's feelings for Mrs. Herbert were a strange amalgam (strange to us, not to them) of a devotion almost religious, a respectfulness almost courtly, and a love which may or may not have had some tinge of the sexual. The sermon he preached at her funeral service gives the first of these aspects:

> For, as the rule of all her civil actions, was religion, so, the rule of her religion, was the Scripture; and, her rule, for her particular understanding of the Scripture, was the church.

The lines in his verse-letter to her, which say to the paper on which the letter is written

> *But when thou com'st to that perplexing eye*
> *Which equally claimes* love *and* reverence

(the emphasis is Donne's), give the courtliness and the love. And why "perplexing"?—because, presumably, Donne himself is not sure whether "love" or "reverence" is the right emotion. Jealousy too (as Shakespeare's Sonnets abundantly prove) could enter into such relations; the crowding of writers round a favourite patron could be thought of as if it were the attracting of lovers to a famous beauty. Donne again—still addressing his paper—sees it in Mrs. Herbert's cabinet, among its rivals, as if in a bundle of *billets doux*:

> *Who knowes thy destiny? when thou hast done,*
> *Perchance her Cabinet may harbour thee,*
> *Whither all noble ambitious wits doe runne,*
> *A nest almost as full of Good as shee.*

Even the cantankerous and commonsensical Jonson is not above such feelings; his epistle to the Countess of Rutland includes a few lines on Lucy, Countess of Bedford (also Donne's patroness):

> *. . . Lucy the bright,*
> *Than whom a nobler Heaven itselfe knowes not.*
> *Who, though she have a better verser got,*
> *(Or poet, in the court account) than I,*
> *And who doth me (though I not him) envy . . .*

Who the rival may be is not clear—it might be Donne, except

that one can hardly imagine Donne "envying" Jonson—but the feelings there, of a rivalry felt as something more personal than a mere competition for hard cash, are akin to Donne's for Mrs. Herbert, and akin to Shakespeare's for Mr. W. H. There is a vital difference between the literary-social world of the seventeenth century and that which we of the twentieth know and are conditioned to—a difference very obvious but rarely given its full value in criticism: the fact that in the seventeenth century a writer's public, those whom he wrote for and whose tastes counted in what he wrote, were actual individuals personally known to himself.[1] To this almost the only exceptions were the audiences for the popular drama and the public for pamphlets and broadsheets: once a writer left these worlds—as Shakespeare left the former in the Sonnets—he was committed to a kind of life in which personal relationships and personal emotions were inextricably involved with his literary career.

Such emotions, when blended with literary ambitions and a writer's career, the modern mind finds hard to comprehend: it asks with some bewilderment if Shakespeare was "in love" with Mr. W. H. and if Donne was "in love" with Mrs. Herbert? if she was his mistress? and if so, in what sense? Sir Herbert Grierson thought she was—in some sense or other; Professor Garrod, with indignation, declared she was not—in any sense at all.[2] Donne and Mrs. Herbert, one imagines, would have been much surprised, and somewhat amused, at such debatings. Of course (Donne himself would have answered) he loved Mrs. Herbert; but the word "love" had other and wider meanings than it has to-day, and its very narrowing indicates an impoverishment in a wider sphere than that of language alone.

[1] Poetry in the 1950's seems to be reverting to this condition. But since it is doing so not willingly but *faute de mieux* (*faute de* anyone willing to buy the stuff), the actual results may not be so happy.

[2] Walton's remark (in the *Life* of George Herbert) seems to show, by its protesting tone, that some contemporaries were a trifle dubious:

> This amity, begun at this time and place, was not an amity that polluted their souls; but an amity made up of a chain of suitable inclinations and virtues; an amity like that of St. Chrysostom's to his dear and virtuous Olympias; whom, in his letters, he calls his Saint . . .

The point is, for our purposes, that the word could be employed, without scruple and without insincerity, in a patron-poet relationship. When a poet of the early seventeenth century said that he loved his patron, male or female, more often than not he meant no less than he said.

And the patrons—the best of them—deserved it. Two of them we may take as specimens: Lucius Cary, Viscount Falkland, who was perhaps the best of all, and William Herbert, Earl of Pembroke—who may have had the most famous of "lovers".

For both of them the best source is Clarendon: best for our purpose, of imaginative reconstruction, as much as for factual information. For Clarendon himself came of this strain of Jacobean and Caroline gentry; his judgments and his emotions drew from the same sources as fed those men who read and rewarded Shakespeare and Jonson and Donne. His praises of Falkland, whom he loved more than he did any other man, make some of the greatest passages of English prose; that in the *History of the Rebellion* begins with two noble sentences which at once set the tone of the whole:

> But I must here take leave a little longer to discontinue this narration; and if the celebrating the memory of eminent and extraordinary persons, and transmitting their great virtues, for the imitation of posterity, be one of the principal ends and duties of history, it will not be thought impertinent, in this place, to remember a loss which no time will suffer to be forgotten, and no success or good fortune could repair. In this unhappy battle was slain the lord viscount Falkland; a person of such prodigious parts of learning and knowledge, of that inimitable sweetness and delight in conversation, of so flowing and obliging a humanity and goodness to mankind, and of that primitive simplicity and integrity of life, that if there were no other brand upon this odious and accursed civil war, than that single loss, it must be most infamous, and execrable to all posterity.

Turpe mori, post te, solo non posse dolore.

This is the monumental style, the weighty Ciceronian eloquence, the kind of prose which one feels should be carved on a tomb—and that, in words, is just what Clarendon has set himself to

make. The spirit it expresses was a vital ingredient in the
emotion which the age felt (or wished to feel) for those who
stood at the apex of its social order: the classical conception of
greatness, the classical and Renaissance conviction that poet and
historian must celebrate such greatness "for the imitation of
posterity". It takes us back to that sonnet of Petrarch which tells
how Alexander, coming to the tomb of Achilles, wept at the
thought that he, Alexander, had no trumpet as great as Homer
to keep his fame alive; and that in turn goes back to the lines of
Horace:

> *Vixere fortes ante Agamemnona*
> *multi; sed omnes illacrimabiles*
> *urgentur ignotique longa*
> *nocte, carent quia vate sacro.*

The spirit in which the Renaissance read and thought of its
ancient history Clarendon can transfer—not unselfconsciously
but not unnaturally—to the consideration of his own times and
the praise of his own most deeply-loved friend. It is not incomparable with what we have seen Shakespeare doing in the
Sonnets: transferring to the young man, and seeing in him
embodied, all the glamour of medieval chivalry.

But this alone—the monumental reverence—would not be
enough; more is needed, to account for the love that Falkland
evoked. What he possessed was the power of uniting worlds
which in our age seem irretrievably disparate, and of doing so
not because he thought it his duty (though no doubt he *did*
think so), but because he wanted to, because his deepest interests
embraced those worlds. Though he himself (it would have to be
"though" nowadays) was an aristocrat, a man of great wealth,
and a politician (Member of Parliament, and Secretary of
State), "his familiarity and friendship," says Clarendon, "for
the most part, was with men of the most eminent and sublime
parts, and of untouched reputation in point of integrity; and
such men had a title to his bosom." He was a patron and friend
to wits and poets—"he was a great cherisher of wit, and fancy,
and good parts in any man"—and also to scholars (these worlds
also were not then separate): "his house being within ten miles
of Oxford, he contracted familiarity and friendship with the
most polite and accurate men of that university."

119

His own intellectual life followed a pattern not unlike Donne's. It began in the tradition of the Renaissance courtier who was also an amateur writer—as Anthony Wood puts it:

> His first years of reason were spent in poetry and polite learning, into the first of which he made divers plausible sallies which caused him therefore to be admired by the poets of that time.

But—typical of his kind—theology was his deepest concern. The son of a Roman Catholic mother who made enormous efforts to convert her children (and succeeded with almost all save the best of them, Falkland himself), he regarded, as Donne did, the decision on the question—which church is the true Church?—as the most vital of all decisions. Medieval scholasticism was still alive for his mind: "he had read" (Clarendon again) "all the Greek and Latin fathers; all the most allowed and authentic ecclesiastical writers". But however deeply involved in theological controversy, in that age when such controversy was even more than normally un-Christian in spirit, he kept his tolerance and charity, his dislike of violence and rancour. In his own words: "Truth in likelyhood is where her author God was, in the *still voice*, and not the *loud wind*."[1] And although his opinions settled down as those of a moderate Anglican, he was very far from uncritical admiration of the Laudian party then dominant in the Church; Clarendon is rather worried by his dislike of Laud, and his speech in the Commons debate on the Root and Branch and the Ministers' Petitions contains as fierce an attack on the bishops' excesses and deficiencies as even a Milton could hope for—though Milton would not have approved its conclusion, that the men should be reformed, not the institution abolished. His friends among the clergy, the members of the *convivium philosophicum* which met at his house near Oxford, seem all to have had this moderation and decency: such men as John Hales, whose opinions Clarendon describes:

> Nothing troubled him more than the brawls which were grown from religion; and he therefore exceedingly detested the tyranny of the Church of Rome; more for their imposing

[1] From Falkland's one work of theology, *Of the Infallibility of the Church of Rome*.

uncharitably upon the consciences of other men than for the errors in their own opinions: and would often say that he would renounce the religion of the Church of England to-morrow if it obliged him to believe that any other Christians should be damned.

—and Chillingworth, whose own words show the same spirit:

> Take away this persecuting, burning, cursing, damning of men for not subscribing to the words of men as the words of God; require of Christians only to believe Christ, and to call no man master but him only; let those leave claiming infallibility that have no title to it, and let them that in their word disclaim it, disclaim it likewise in their actions. In a word, take away tyranny, which is the devil's instrument to support errors and superstitions and impieties in the several parts of the world, which could not otherwise long withstand the power of truth.
>
> (*Religion of Protestants a safe way of Salvation*)

That spirit was characteristic, if not of the age as a whole, at least of that part of it which not only seems, but in fact was, linked with metaphysical and Shakespearean verse. Such tolerant commonsense was also Donne's:

> You know I never fettered nor imprisoned the word Religion; not . . . immuring it in a Rome, or a Wittemberg, or a Geneva; they are all virtuall beams of one sun.

This is the equivalent, in theological thought, of the dramatists' art of seeing and valuing all sides.

And Falkland's politics were as decent and moderate as his theology; when the war began, he took—as his birth and background made certain he must take—the royalist side; but his intellectual sympathies were at least as much with the Parliament, and he told the King of his errors and deficiencies with a freedom which the latter did not always enjoy. His one desire was for peace. The war changed, as Clarendon most movingly describes, his very demeanour and appearance:

> From the entrance into this unnatural war, his natural cheerfulness and vivacity grew clouded, and a kind of sadness and dejection of spirit stole upon him, which he had never

been used to . . . and he, who had been so exactly unreserved and affable to all men, that his face and countenance was always present, and vacant to his company, and held any cloudiness, and less pleasantness of the visage, a kind of rudeness or incivility, became on a sudden less communicable; and thence, very sad, pale, and exceedingly affected with the spleen. In his clothes and habit, which he had intended before always with more neatness, and industry, and expense, than is usual to so great a mind, he was not now only incurious, but too negligent. . . . When there was any overture or hope of peace, he would be more erect and vigorous, and exceedingly solicitous to press any thing which he thought might promote it; and sitting among his friends, often, after a deep silence and frequent sighs, would, with a shrill and sad accent, ingeminate the word *Peace, Peace*; and would passionately profess, "that the very agony of the war, and the view of the calamities and desolation the kingdom did and must endure, took his sleep from him, and would shortly break his heart."

Trevelyan remarks that Falkland, with his negligence of clothing, unaccountable behaviour, and "spleen", behaved in this crisis with something of the manner of Hamlet in *his* crisis; he might have added that just as Hamlet was, before the fatal duel, so Falkland was plainly "fey" on the morning of his last day. He was killed at Newbury in September 1643; "in the morning of the fight he called for a clean shirt, and being asked the reason of it, answered, that if he were slain in the battle they should not find his body in foul linen."[1] His death, if not quite suicide (as many contemporaries thought it was), was certainly the action of someone who was less than normally anxious to live: he rode his horse at a gap in a hedge which was lined—as he knew—by musketeers. "He died," says Clarendon, "as much of the time as of the bullet; for, from the beginning of the war he contracted so deep a sadness and melancholy that his life was not pleasant to him; and sure he was too weary of it." Carlyle and Macaulay (as one might expect) both hold him in great contempt: no prophet certain of his own rightness, and no politician certain of his party's, could fail to do so.

The tragic sense: that is clear in all the men of Falkland's

[1] Bulstrode Whitelocke: *Memorials.*

kind.   That his behaviour should resemble Hamlet's is not
entirely fortuitous and insignificant; it signals his affinity to the
way of feeling which lay behind Elizabethan and Jacobean
tragedy; it proves him, a Caroline, to be still a true child of the
Shakespearean moment.   Men of his kind, confronted with the
brutal reality of civil war, responded as the tragic poets had
responded to the imaginary form of it they evoked in their plays.
The imagination of the Elizabethans had been haunted by a
presentiment of what reality brought to their children; their
plays of civil wars, medieval or Roman, were felt and presented
as ominously, potentially topical.   So the tragic sense, which is
in Falkland, is also in Clarendon who loved and praised him,
and in Andrew Marvell, on the other side in politics, but united
to them by this common quality which makes him also a poet of
the Shakespearean moment.   What Clarendon thought of his
country in civil war (he is writing of its happiness before the
war broke out):

. . . whilst the kingdoms we now lament were alone looked
upon as the garden of the world

echoes exactly the lines of Marvell in *Appleton House*:

Oh Thou, that dear and happy Isle
The Garden of the World ere while . . .

The tragic sense is seen again—and here the dramatic vision is
explicit—in the letter which Sir William Waller, the Parliamentary general, sent to his royalist friend Sir Ralph Hopton,
whose defeat and wounding he was fated to bring about at the
battle of Lansdown:

The great God who is the searcher of my heart knows with
what reluctance I go upon this service and with what perfect
hatred I look upon a war without an enemy.   The God of
Peace in his good time send us peace, and in the meantime
fit us to receive it.   We are both on the stage, and we must
act the parts that are assigned to us in this tragedy.

And the spirit of all of them had found its voice in Shakespeare's
histories, in which the tragedy of civil war in itself is a theme
felt far more deeply than attachment to one cause or the other;

the image of the violated garden, the wrecking of innocence and fruitfulness, is in Shakespeare too, in the talk of the gardeners in *Richard II.*

Falkland's was a character of exceptional beauty; as an individual, he would never, in any age, be typical. But the elements to which he gave a special beauty of his own can be found in others, whose characters were made out of earthier stuff—such as William Herbert, whom Clarendon thus describes:

> William earl of Pembroke was next, a man of another mould and making, and of another fame and reputation with all men,[1] being the most universally loved and esteemed of any man of that age; and, having a great office in the court, he made the court itself better esteemed, and more reverenced in the country. And as he had a great number of friends of the best men, so no man had ever the wickedness to avow himself to be his enemy. He was a man very well bred, and of excellent parts, and a graceful speaker upon any subject, having a good proportion of learning, and a ready wit to apply it, and enlarge upon it; of a pleasant and facetious humour, and a disposition affable, generous and magnificent. . . . He lived many years about the court, before in it; and never by it; being rather regarded and esteemed by king James, than loved and favoured. . . . As he spent and lived upon his own fortune, so he stood upon his own feet, without any other support than of his proper virtue and merit. . . . He was exceedingly beloved in the court, because he never desired to get that for himself, which others laboured for, but was still ready to promote the pretences of worthy men. . . . He was a great lover of his country, and of the religion and justice, which he believed could only support it; and his friendships were only with men of those principles. And as his conversation was most with men of the most pregnant parts and understanding, so towards any, who needed support or encouragement, though unknown, if fairly recommended to him, he was very liberal. And sure never man was planted in a court, that was fitter for that soil, or brought better qualities with him to purify that air.
>
> Yet his memory must not be so flattered, that his virtues and good inclinations may be believed without some allay of vice, and without being clouded with great infirmities, which he had in too exorbitant a proportion. He indulged to himself

[1] The contrast is with the Earl of Arundel.

the pleasures of all kinds, almost in all excesses. To women, whether out of his natural constitution, or for want of his domestic content, and delight (in which he was most unhappy, for he paid much too dear for his wife's fortune, by taking her person into the bargain) he was immoderately given up. But therein he likewise retained such a power and jurisdiction over his very appetite, that he was not so much transported with beauty and outward allurements, as with those advantages of the mind, as manifested an extraordinary wit, and spirit, and knowledge, and administered great pleasure in the conversation. To these he sacrificed himself, his precious time, and much of his fortune. And some, who were nearest his trust and friendship, were not without apprehension, that his natural vivacity and vigour of mind began to lessen and decline by those excessive indulgences.

Whether or not this *was* Mr. W. H., there is no doubt at all that it *could* be. Clarendon's portrait fits to perfection the character one deduces from the Sonnets: the charm, elegance, splendour, and wit, the independence and wilfulness, the generosity to men "of parts and understanding", the susceptibility to women and notorious proneness to amorous excesses,[1] and even the preference for women whose attractiveness (like that of the dark lady) came more from "character" and wits than from beauty of the chocolate-box order. This is clearly a man far removed from the almost-saintliness of Falkland; but the two have more in common than we could expect, or than most times could show, in characters on such different levels. The power of evoking not merely "esteem" but love; the unforced preference for the company of men of intellect; the insistence on a moral and political soundness (as he saw it), as well as intellectual distinction, in the men to be chosen for friends and beneficiaries:[2] these he had in common with Falkland. Herbert was

[1] Cf. the lines in the 95th Sonnet:
> That tongue that tells the story of thy daies,
> (Making lascivious comments on thy sport) . . .

[2] *If* Herbert was the young man of the Sonnets (we do know, of course, that he was Shakespeare's patron), and *if* Clarendon is correct in saying that he confined his favours to men whose opinions on Church and State coincided with his (that is, Anglican and royalist), one may have here a clue to Shakespeare's opinions. But two if's don't make one certainty.

born, one might say, with a patron's purse in his mouth. Son of that Countess of Pembroke for whom Sidney (her brother) wrote the *Arcadia* and whom Aubrey calls "the greatest patronesse of witt and learning of any lady in her time", tutored in his youth by Samuel Daniel, he was patron or friend or both to Donne and Chapman and Jonson (to whom he sent an annual £20 for the purchase of books)—as well as to Shakespeare: he was co-dedicatee with his younger brother of the First Folio, whose editors describe the two Herberts as having "prosequted both them [*sc.* Shakespeare's plays] and their Author living, with so much favour . . . for, so much were your Lordships' likings of the severall parts, when they were acted, as before they were published, the Volume ask'd to be yours." And there is no reason to doubt the evidence of Heminge and Condell: or to doubt the verdict of Aubrey upon the elder Herbert—"the greatest Maecenas to learned men of any peer of his time or since."

A quality of this aristocracy which counted for much in its value for the poets was that which the age called "magnificence": splendour and display, "conspicuous consumption" in the phrase of Veblen. To this the poets took up a doublefaced attitude, a characteristic blending of old and new, Christian-ascetic and Renaissance-æsthetic. They accepted—it is one of the commonplaces of their political thinking—the classical theory that "luxury" was the great destroyer of States; they accepted also the medieval Christian denunciation of it as a wrong to the poor and a distraction from thoughts of the life to come: but neither prevented them from not merely enjoying it but also giving it a value that can be called spiritual. Both Falkland and George Herbert—characters near to saintliness—show it, as Clarendon tells us of the former:

> In his clothes and habit, which he had intended before always with more neatness, and industry, and expense, than is usual to so great a mind . . .

and Walton of the latter:

> His clothes seemed to prove, that he put too great a value on his parts and parentage.

If one puts these with Sir Richard Baker's description of the youthful Donne—"not dissolute, but very neat"[1]—and with Ophelia's description of Hamlet before his troubles—"the glass of fashion and the mould of form"—one sees that magnificence, a taste for finery, was not alien, on the contrary it was natural, to minds of unusual refinement and power. It had even, it seems, an association with emotional intensity. Falkland's calling for a clean shirt on the morning of Newbury has a curiously close parallel in King Charles's conduct on the morning of his execution. "Herbert," he said to his attendant, "this is my second marriage-day. I would be as trim to-day as may be; for before night I hope to be espoused to my blessed Jesus." *The Spartans on the sea-wet rock sat down and combed their hair*: an anthropologist would no doubt see all these actions as deriving from the ceremonial washing and dressing of the sacrificial victim. Magnificence was allied to "nobleness", was its outward expression, as Clarendon sees it in William Herbert:

. . . but all [*sc.* his great wealth], served not his expense, which was only limited by his great mind, and occasions to use it nobly.

And "to use it nobly" did not mean to use it with senseless extravagance. Vulgar ostentation, avaricious "new men", and shameless profiteers, abounded then as much as at any time, and received their proper treatment at the writers' hands (Ben Jonson's plays are full of them, and Shakespeare's *Timon* is an essay on indiscriminating expenditure); but just as Falkland could denounce the misdeeds of the bishops without demanding the end of episcopacy, so in this matter of magnificence the writers of the age contrived to keep their moral judgments without losing their sensuous appreciation of the colour and variety which magnificence brought into life. They made it, as they strove to make all things, into a kind of symbol: magnificence was the symbol of the "great mind" and the "noble occasions". It gave them—or their imaginations so transformed it that it could give them—yet another field in which to make concrete and actual their spiritual perceptions—in this case, their perception that there must be a hierarchy in all things; and

---

[1] "Neat" had a wider and stronger meaning than it has to-day; its modern equivalent would be something like "finely dressed".

of the hierarchy in human society, magnificence was the outward show. Just so its equivalent in the Anglo-catholic service was the outward show of the spiritual hierarchy. The "philosophy" which linked the two may be seen in this passage from Donne's *Devotions upon Emergent Occasions*:

> In Heaven there are Orders of Angels, and Armies of Martyrs, and in that house, many Mansions; in Earth, Families, Cities, Churches, Colleges, all plurall things.

That was the theory; the practice is shown in the following account of the Laudian regime in the Church, where the "conspicuous consumption" for a spiritual end is perfectly clear, and the natural sympathy between a monarchy, a magnificent aristocracy, an Anglo-catholic church, and a sensuous poetry, appears in a concrete example:

> The churches or chapells of all the colleges are much beautifyed, extraordinary cost bestowed on them; most of them newe glazed, richer glasse for figures and painting I have not seen, which they had most from beyond the Seas . . . excellent pictures, large and great church worke of the best hands they could gett . . .[1]

"The Barge she sat in, like a burnisht Throne burnt on the water: the Poope was beaten Gold . . ."—the collocation is not inappropriate.

When such men as Falkland and William Herbert—and such women as Magdalen Herbert—were the flesh and blood embodiments of "nobleness", whom the poets of the age knew and wrote for and loved, then it becomes comprehensible that the word and the concept of "nobleness" should have gained, as it did, such richness and power in their writings. For Shakespeare in particular the epithet of "noble" is, above all others, that which renders both social and moral distinction—*the* word for the kind of conduct expected from those who are above the common herd, by station and no less (so, at least, it should be) by soul. Through *Antony and Cleopatra* the word rings like a refrain. It is Cleopatra's word for her own suicide, the act which

---

[1] From a letter by George Garrard, describing a royal visit to Oxford in 1636: cited by Mathew, *Social Structure in Caroline England*, p. 82.

is to prove her worthy of her queenliness and of Antony's
love:

> *What poore an Instrument*
> *May do a Noble deede . . .*
> *He words me Gyrles, he words me, that I should not*
> *Be Noble to my selfe.*

It is her praise for Antony:

> *Noblest of men, woo't dye?*

Antony's for her:

> *My Queene and* Eros
> *Have by their brave instruction got upon me*
> *A Noblenesse in Record.*

And Antony's for himself:

> *Bruised peeces go,*
> *You have bin Nobly borne.*

Two things were combined in this concept of nobleness: high
birth on the one hand, and on the other an inherent superiority
which was (or ought to be) the consequence of high birth, and
which, in those individuals worthy of their rank, became a
quality both physical and spiritual. We have seen that it was
this inherent "nobleness" which broke the boy Mamillius' heart
when he heard of his mother's disgrace; it shows also in
his sister, even when she is thought to be a shepherd's
daughter. "Nothing she do's, or seemes," says Polixenes,
"but smackes of something greater than her selfe, too Noble for
this place"; and when the old shepherd reveals that she is a
foundling, this same quality is cited as one of the proofs of her
royal blood—". . . the Affection of Noblenesse, which Nature
shewes above her Breeding".

Modern readers may be apt to find this not only incredible,
but a trifle sycophantic. And so, of course, in real life, it very
often was; when the rewards for pleasing a nobleman might be
as great as they frequently were, sycophantic adulation would
not be lacking. But at its best—and we are entitled to think of
it at its best, since we are concerned with it as refined into art—
it was not mere worldly wisdom or snobbery, because it was
never disjoined from moral judgment. Just as William Herbert,

in Clarendon's words, "lived many years about the court, before in it; and never by it", and held himself aloof from the King's favourites, so both Donne and Shakespeare—and indeed all the poets of their age and kind—could combine a deep reverence for the Court, thought of as ideal centre of the country's soul, with a bitterly accurate perception that the real Court, more often than not, was a centre of vice and intrigue; and Shakespeare's reverence for the true thing, the real "nobleness", did not exclude a thoroughly critical attitude towards its abuses. The King's speech in *All's Well* gives the Renaissance theory, which one finds also in Castiglione: that noble birth, if unaccompanied by noble conduct, loses its title to reverence:

> *That is honour's scorne,*
> *Which challenges it selfe as honours borne,*
> *And is not like the sire: Honours thrive,*
> *When rather from our acts we them derive*
> *Than our fore-goers: the meere word's a slave*
> *Debosh'd on everie tombe, on everie grave:*
> *A lying Trophee, and as oft is dumbe,*
> *Where dust, and damn'd oblivion is the Tombe*
> *Of honour'd bones indeed.*
>
> (II, 3)

The point is made, in another key, by the brilliantly farcical dialogue of *The Winter's Tale*, ending the scene in which Perdita's true identity has been discovered and her inherent nobleness accounted for. Enter then the Shepherd and Clown, who proceed to explain that they are now "gentlemen born . . . and have been so any time these four hours"; and the Clown announces that since he is a gentleman, he is perfectly entitled to tell lies and swear to them:

> —You may say it, but not sweare it.
> —Not sweare it, now I am a Gentleman? Let Boores and Franklins say it, Ile sweare it.
> —How if it be false (Sonne)?
> —If it be ne're so false, a true Gentleman may sweare it, in the behalf of his Friend.
>
> (V, 2)

The low, as so often in Shakespeare, criticize by parody and by comic misunderstanding—which is yet, in another sense, only too accurate understanding—the pretensions of the high.

When one looks at the men whom the great patrons favoured, one sees what seems to us a strange jumble of types: poets and wits, men of learning, scholars, divines. "Wit" and "learning" —by which the age meant, roughly, what we would mean by "imaginative writing" and "scholarship"—are equally the objects of patronage or friendship; the Sucklings and Carews— raffish and witty amateurs—jostle with the Shakespeares and Jonsons—professional and popular playwrights—with the Donnes and Earles—writers who lived and wrote in both secular and clerical worlds—and with the Chillingworths and Hales—scholars and theologians. Wherever one turns in this age, one comes across these blending groups. Donne is linked with Lord Herbert of Cherbury, poet and proto-Deist philosopher, and with his younger brother George, poet and divine; Jonson with Donne; Donne is a lifelong friend of Sir Henry Wotton, diplomat and Provost of Eton; Jonson is a protégé of William Herbert, who is also a patron of Shakespeare and of Chapman; Chapman is a member of Sir Walter Raleigh's circle, in which, earlier, was Marlowe; Jonson again is a protégé of Falkland, who is the friend of Earle, author of *Microcosmographie* and future bishop, and of Chillingworth, most notable of Caroline Anglican theologians. The materials of the pattern are always the same, though the variants are manifold: Church, aristocracy and gentry, the scholarship of the universities, poetry and drama.

An extraordinary cultural and spiritual unity: that is the irresistible impression, and the impression is true. This society, the dominant though not all-embracing society of the early seventeenth century, shows a short-lived and wonderful converging of elements which had been separate and were to be separate again. It shows, for example, the perfecting of a process the beginnings of which we saw in the 1590's. The popular drama of the London theatres finally grew out of the dis-esteem in which it had been held by the courtly and the scholarly; the Shakespeares and Jonsons were not despised by the heirs of the Sidneys (for the gentry) and the Halls (for the Church): they were admired, courted, and favoured. For Jonson, the evidence is overwhelming: he, more than any other man, perhaps, bridged this particular gap, for he alone of the dramatists had a weight of learning and a classical integrity that nobody could affect to despise. (And hence it is his name that is always recurring, more often than others, in the kind of groups described above.) But the bridging is equally clear for Shakespeare, in spite of his lack of "learning": for which we have the unimpeachable evidence of Dryden—later, of course, but not too late to have had it first-hand:

> . . . The consideration of this made Mr. Hales of Eaton say that there was no subject of which any poet ever wrote but he would produce it much better done in Shakespeare . . . and in the last King's court, when Ben's reputation was at its highest, Sir John Suckling, and with him the greater part of the courtiers, set our Shakespeare far above him.
>
> (*Essay of Dramatic Poesy*)

"Mr. Hales of Eaton" is that Rev. John Hales, friend of both Falkland and Clarendon, whose theological tolerance has been already cited; the "last King" is of course Charles I (Dryden is writing in the 1660's). Milton too, somewhat condescendingly, contributes his evidence to the same effect, in *Eikonoklastes*:

> I shall not instance an abstruse Author, wherein the King might be less conversant, but one whom we well know was the closet companion of these his Solitudes, *William Shakespeare* . . .

Church, courtliness, and popular drama have come together; scholarship also has joined them, for Hales was (in Clarendon's phrase) "the greatest scholar in Europe".

What this converging meant, in modern terms, was a bridging of the gulf between highbrow and lowbrow, Third Programme and Light. In the Elizabethan years, there had been such a gulf: one can see it in many things—in the utterances of Sidney and Hall on the drama, in the conscientiously "Senecan" closet-dramas of Fulke Greville and others,[1] and in the three "Par-

---

[1] Greville on his own plays is firm that they were not "intended for the stage": with a glance back at his adored Sir Philip, he writes:

And if in thus ordaining and ordering matter, and forme together for the use of life, I have made these Tragedies, no Plaies for the Stage, be it known, it was no part of my purpose to write

nassus" plays, which seem to set up, for a University audience, the correct and learned Jonson against the ignorant, amorous-mellifluous, popular Shakespeare. Why the gulf was bridged requires no elaborate explanation; it was bridged simply because the popular theatres began to turn out plays which deserved the admiration of the "judicious"—and the latter had sufficient sense and freedom from highbrow prejudice to admire as they should. The result of it is the extraordinary range of levels—it *is* extraordinary, when one thinks of it—which mature Shakespearean drama exhibits. It is incredible—to us—that poetry of the utmost difficulty and complexity, poetry such as this—

> *Affection? thy Intention stabs the Center.*
> *Thou do'st make possible things not so held,*
> *Communicat'st with Dreames (how can this be?)*
> *With what's unreall thou co-active art,*
> *And fellow'st nothing. Then 'tis very credent,*
> *Thou may'st co-joyne with something, and thou do'st,*
> *(And that beyond Commission) and I find it,*
> *(And that to the infection of my Braines,*
> *And hardning of my Browes).*
>
> (*Winter's Tale*, I, 2)

—should be not only in, but the very stuff of, dramas full of action and melodrama, full of horseplay, slapstick, and bawdy, dramas which—to reach the climax of incredibility—were produced with the greatest financial success in a London theatre. Because Shakespeare in his maturity wrote for, and was appreciated by, an audience—that is, a society—which ranged from the most vulgar to the most refined, his drama could be, and had to be, of corresponding range. It would be profitless to inquire which came first in this process—whether he deliberately deepened the tone and thickened the complexity of his verse in order to win the appreciation of the more educated tastes (the Sonnets seem to indicate a feeling that he *ought* to attempt this), or whether he won over his educated admirers because his work developed as it did. That we shall never know: presumably there was a constant and fluctuating inter-

for them, against whom so many good, and great spirits have already written.

(*Life of Sidney*)

action. It seems to have been round the turn of the century that highbrow and scholarly opinion began to show him favour. Gabriel Harvey's remark—

> The younger sort take much delight in Shakespeare's *Venus and Adonis*; but his *Lucrece*, and his tragedy of *Hamlet, Prince of Denmark*, have it in them to please the wiser sort

may be interpreted as a sign of this beginning, though one cannot much admire the critical judgment which links *Lucrece* with *Hamlet*; and in *Hamlet* itself—the Prince's talks with the players about the gagging of the clowns, the ranting of certain actors, and that "excellent play" which was "caviare to the general"—one sees a self-consciousness, an anxiety about the verdict of the "judicious", "those whose judgments in such matters cried in the top of (his)": put this together with the acute dissatisfaction voiced in *Henry V* (written about 1599, a year or two earlier than *Hamlet*) concerning the limitations and absurdities of the stage he had to work for; put both with the general uneasiness about his work that the Sonnets reveal, and the total picture is clear and coherent—of a writer who strove for, and obtained, the approval of those whom he regarded as both socially and intellectually the most gratifying of admirers. And it might be conjectured that his success in gaining this approval, the fulfilling of the ambition revealed in those of the Sonnets which deal with the subtler, more up-to-date rivals, was one of the causes which led to that re-establishing of settled values perceptible in the mature tragedies, when contrasted with the "problem-plays". The Sonnets show a Shakespeare uneasy about his status in society, as well as about many other things; for his later life we have no such "personal" document, but plays like *Macbeth* and *Antony and Cleopatra* show an easy certainty in portraying their courtly milieux as well as a firm foundation of moral values. Shakespeare shared in what he had greatly helped to bring about: the rise of the drama in all spheres, spiritual and intellectual as well as social. It is one of the surest signs of the fineness of Jacobean and Caroline society, that a rise in the first two spheres should have meant a rise in the third.

How it happened may be matter for doubt; what is clear is that it did happen; and this combination—of a thoroughgoing intellectualism prepared to go to any lengths of obscurity and subtlety, and a firm base of the popular and colloquial—is a vital component of all the poetry of the Shakespearean moment. The popular is of course more blatant in Shakespeare than it is in non-dramatic verse, since he had a directer incentive (the approval of his pit) to keep it prominent; but it is really no less in the sermons of Donne, with their purple passages of emotional rhetoric, and their jokes and puns, and in the poems of George Herbert, with their domestic imagery and colloquial language. When such blendings are no longer possible, the Shakespearean moment has come to an end. And they were possible only on the basis of a society with such spiritual unity as has been described.

Of this society and the attitudes to life which lay underneath it, what are the essential features from our point of view—the features which explain, as far as such things can explain it, the poetry which the society produced? First, it was a society which brought together, more successfully than most do, things which always tend to fly apart or to quarrel: spiritual and political, spiritual and physical, reverence and criticism, magnificence and simplicity; the hierarchical and the individualist, the popular and the esoteric. It was a society full of tension, ominousness, doubt of itself and its future; full, in consequence, of the tragic sense. But the traditional bases were still firm in men's minds; it had the medieval unity of thought without the medieval rigidity and fixed limitations. The feverishness and *naïveté* of the early Elizabethans were quietened and deepened; out of the turmoil of the 1590's—an incomparably fertile growing-time rather than one of full maturity—emerged this short-lived but perfect balance. It is not that the age was in any sense a Golden Age—in any case, the kind of society and mentality which this chapter describes was only part of the age's whole, as the following chapters will argue—it was just as imperfect as any other age, as full as any other of corruptions and brutalities. But this kind of society *was* dominant in the age, and it *was* peculiarly well-fitted—it is in this that its "perfection" lies—for the production of great poetry.

For poetry at its best is the least specialized of the arts; it employs a medium which everyone uses, its "technique" is of a sort which everyone has had a smattering of, inasmuch as everyone has learned his language. This fact, which should make it the least specialized of the arts, makes it also the most sensitive, since it uses a medium always liable to be corrupted by those wider corruptions in society which damage the society's language. Poetry is therefore peculiarly dependent on having a wide field of unspoiled stimuli available, on being in the midst of a society which excites the poet, excites him beneficially, and is excited by the poetry, which both esteems the art and can be esteemed by the artist. An age which largely rejects the poet and is largely rejected by him may produce a few good poems; it will never be a great age of poetry.

It seems also to be highly beneficial to poetry that it should be taken seriously but not solemnly, regarded as an art of the highest dignity, worthy of the full-time devotion of the finest spirits, but also as an occasional recreation for ordinary educated men. Hence one of the most reliable criteria for the state of poetry at any given time is the quality of its minor and "amateur" versifying, since that is an index of how near those who ought to be the best readers are, in spirit and comprehension, to the real and "full-time" poets. By that criterion, the early seventeenth century has no rival. Its Herricks, Sucklings, Wottons, and Lovelaces score the occasional bulls-eyes which are all that the part-time poet can hope to score, with a frequency and a satisfying confidence that their equivalents in other times can never achieve.

> *You meaner beauties of the night*
> *That poorly satisfy our eyes*
> *More by your number than your light:*
> *You common people of the skies . . .*

These lines, the work of a professional diplomat (written, it seems, while he was preparing in great haste and flurry to go on a highly important mission), written by a man for whom the writing of verse was a very occasional amusement, have an expertness of phrasing and rhythm which seems truly "professional". The English language, like so much else in the age, was not yet specialized.

Nor, in particular, was the language of poetry. For one thing, verse was still a natural and public medium: the medium for topical balladry and knockabout bawdy as much as for tragedy and devotional meditation. One of the reasons, no doubt, for the odd fact previously mentioned, that Shakespeare's intensely complex verse could be the medium for very popular theatrical successes, was simply that Jacobean audiences were far, far more sophisticated, in the matter of hearing verse, than the audiences of the twentieth century. The latter are completely at sea; either they listen with a strained awareness that this is something "special", or else—usually with the assistance of the actors' methods of delivery and often with that of the poet's rhythms—they do their best to forget that what they are hearing is verse at all. The Jacobean audiences must have been hearing verse all the time; the ballads and songs which they heard outside the theatre were part of their training for what they heard inside it. Inside the theatre, they expected verse; a play in prose would be for them the disconcerting exception. Looked at from the viewpoint of the audience, the whole extent of Elizabethan and Jacobean drama, from the jog-trot stuff of, say, *Ralph Roister Doister* through the rhythms of Kyd and Marlowe to those of mature Shakespeare, can be looked on as a long course of ever-increasing difficulty in the art of hearing verse. By the time of the Shakespearean moment their sophistication was complete.

The state of the language reflects it. In the early seventeenth century the language was poised between two extremes. It had outgrown the adolescence of early Elizabethan English, reflected in such whimsicalities as Euphuism, in shapeless outpourings like Nashe's prose, and in naïve pedantries like the experiments in classical metrics; it had not grown into the impoverishing "refinement" which overtook it after the Restoration. It stood between two "poetic dictions". Coleridge's brilliant remark about the metaphysical poets—they express "the most fantastic out-of-the-way thoughts, but in the most pure and genuine mother English"—(though one may doubt if the "thoughts" are really so "out-of-the-way") shows a true perception of the quality of their language.

Chapter 5

PURITANISM AND THE DRAMATIC ATTITUDE

"EVERY schoolboy knows" that the English Puritans of the sixteenth and seventeenth centuries were the English drama's most persistent and dangerous enemies. For this hostility the ostensible reasons, those which the attackers themselves brought forward, are not to seek. The dramas were full of bawdy and blasphemy; male actors were dressed up as women, and as women dressed up as men, in flat opposition to the Word of God (Deuteronomy 22. 5); the theatres attracted lewd women, and apprentices who should have been working; they increased the danger of plague, and lessened the chances of profit and salvation.

On such counts the campaign was waged which eventually triumphed, with the closing of the theatres in 1642. All this is more a matter of social history than of literature; it may even be doubted if its effects on literature were as great as one might imagine. The Puritan attack does not seem to have damaged the drama during the years of its greatness; and when the Puritans did succeed in closing the theatres, though they may have eclipsed the gaiety of the nation in the fifth decade of the seventeenth century, they inflicted no serious loss on posterity. They did no murder; they merely interred a corpse. But from a wider viewpoint, this campaign is of the greatest interest to literary criticism, for the Puritan objection to the actual theatres should be seen as a part and a symptom of a fundamental antipathy to that dramatic view of life and dramatic kind of art which were so vital parts of Shakespearean and metaphysical poetry. Before this is argued, however, it might be wise to attempt some definition of "Puritanism"—or at least (for exact definition will not be possible) to arrive at some idea of what it stood for in the age we are dealing with.

The word can be used to cover a very wide range of human beings, from the most fanatical of religious maniacs to men like Milton or Richard Baxter: men of the highest culture and refinement. It can mean either a fairly clear-cut religious-political movement in England during the late sixteenth and seventeenth centuries, or else a certain type of mind, constant and permanent in human nature, anti-sensuous, individualist, iconoclastic. Historically, the words "puritan" and "puritanism" (and so, presumably, the phenomena, as recognizable entities) appear to have originated in the 1560's. They began (like Whig and Tory) as contemptuous nicknames, bestowed on those who were notably insistent on "purity" of doctrine and ritual—which meant, in practice, purity from the corruptions of Canterbury and Rome. The first dated examples (both of 1572) which are given in the *O.E.D.*—an undated example from Stow is cited first—show the term as used by enemies, with the implications of hypocrisy and Pharisaical aloofness, which became commonplaces, already established. "Puritanes are they named, pure I wold they wer." "This name Puritane is very aptly giuen to these men, not bicause they be pure no more than were the Heretikes called *Cathari*, but bicause they think themselues to be *mundiores ceteris*, more pure than others, as *Cathari* did, and seperate themselues from all other Churches and congregations, as spotted and defyled."[1] On this level, there is not much difficulty, however many variants; the Puritan is one who objects to those features of the Anglican settlement which are obviously, or possibly, taken over from the Church before the Reformation. And this definition, though inadequate in itself, does form an element in all those who have any affinity to Puritanism: they all show a dislike for ritual, ecclesiastical hierarchy, and medieval theology.

It is when the meaning becomes wider that difficulties begin; for we shall find that many men who have, or seem to have, the pre-occupations and moral "tone" which one wants to call Puritanical, were not Puritans at all by any more accurate use of the word. Henry Vaughan, for instance. His preface to *Silex Scintillans* (his volume of devotional poetry) abounds in Puritanical denunciations of contemporary writings. He talks of "those ingenious persons, which in the late notion are termed Wits": persons who, he tells us, "dash Scriptures and the sacred Relatives of God with their impious conceits"; "stuff their books with oaths, horrid execrations, and a most gross and

---

[1] The quotations come, respectively, from J. Jones: *Bathes of Bath*; and Whitgift: *Answer to Admonition*.

studied filthiness"; are guilty, in sum, of "a constant, sensual volutation or wallowing in impure thoughts and scurrilous conceits, which both defile their authors, and as many more as they are communicated to". This is completely in the fevered style of Puritan invective, entirely (for example) in the manner of Milton:

> . . . And what a benefit this would be to our youth and gentry, may be soon guest by what we know of the corruption and bane which they suck in dayly from the writings and interludes of libidinous and ignorant Poetasters, who having scars ever heard of that which is the main consistence of a true poem . . . doe for the most part lap up vitious principles in sweet pils to be swallow'd down, and make the tast of vertuous documents harsh and sowr.
>
> (*The Reason of Church Government*)

But Vaughan was in fact an Anglo-catholic, member of a family of Royalist gentry, and his poetry is thoroughly in the metaphysical tradition: Herbert was (as he acknowledges) his master, and Herbert's master was Donne. Vaughan may have had Puritanical sentiments, but he was no Puritan.

This example will suffice to prove that the Puritans, properly so-called, had no monopoly of moral austerity. Revulsion from the life of the body, explicit rejection of sensuous beauty, intense conviction of sinfulness: all these will be found in many, who are outside the Puritan fold. But there *is* a difference: a difference in the manner, one might say the temperature, of such asceticism. When a poet like Donne or Herbert or Vaughan—and a dramatist like Shakespeare or Tourneur—expresses an ascetic revulsion from and rejection of the sensuous, their asceticism seems to express itself, paradoxically, in thoroughly sensuous terms, so that the physical world has returned, as it were, by a backdoor: we have seen that happening in the *Second Anniversarie*, but that is not the only work in which it happens. With the real Puritan, on the other hand, the rejection seems complete. There is with him no return of the sensuous, and the final result is an art permanently impoverished in that respect, rendered barer and more abstract. The difference can be seen more clearly in the visual arts. The baroque sculpture, painting, funeral monuments, etc., the equivalents of the poetry of Donne and Shakespeare and their followers, celebrate the mortality and unworthiness of the body with a great richness of sensuous detail; the Puritan equivalent is the bare chapel, from which all forms of art are excluded.

The Puritan, then, for our purposes, is a man whose rejection of the sensuous seems natural, a part of his very being, rather than simply a conviction. It *is* a conviction, of course, but it is also something more. He does not reject it with that intense blending of hate and love which springs from a real experience and a really passionate enjoyment of it (whether in the past, or continuing, in spite of himself, in the present); he rejects it, rather, with the sometimes puzzled disgust of a man who can't quite make out what all the fuss is about. Milton's *Comus*, for instance: there is something abstract, detached, almost academic, in that poem's rendering of the "sensual rout" of Comus and his followers. It is most intensely felt—Milton's hatred of the Bacchanalian is one of the deepest, and most enduring, of his emotions—but it is hated as an alien enemy, not as a part of himself. The Puritan in general tends to see sensuality as something *done by the other man*; and this is not as a rule hypocrisy, since as a rule he really did not do it himself. (The operative word is "do": we are not concerned with his dreams.) The violence of his denunciations of sensuality, and the fury of his iconoclasm against the sensuous in religion, may come in part from this incomprehension: he is honestly angered and bewildered at the value which others attach to those things which for him are mere baubles or delusions. Since he is by nature comparatively un-sensuous, ideas are in him farther away from sensations than they are in such men as Donne and Shakespeare and the society in which they wrote; his mind is in consequence simpler. It is easier for him—and therefore for us, when we read his writings—to know exactly what he means: no Puritan will produce a work as ambiguous as the *Second Anniversarie*. His passion tends to be for ideas and ideals in themselves, rather than for human beings; or for humanity as a whole, rather than for individuals.

This description—rather than definition—of the Puritan type of mind has already indicated some of the reasons that make it essentially un-dramatic and anti-dramatic. There are others. There is, in the first place, the Puritan tendency—strong to the point of the ridiculous in some, partially muffled by charity or commonsense in others—to see humanity as rigidly divided into black and white, the elect and the damned. Of which a comic—or tragic, if one likes—example may be seen in Richard Baxter's *Autobiography*:

> It is the most astonishing part of all God's providence to me, that he so far forsaketh almost all the world, and confineth his special favour to so few; that so small a part of the world hath the profession of Christianity in comparison of heathens, Mahometans, and other infidels; and that among professed Christians there are so few that are saved from gross delusions and have but any competent knowledge; and that among *those* there are so few that are seriously religious and truly set their hearts on heaven.

It must be remembered that Baxter was *not* a fanatic; he was a person of great intelligence and charity, who obviously, as this passage shows, believed with reluctance the nonsense which he *did* believe—this system of ever-narrowing circles which eliminates, first, non-Christians; second, Papist and Anglican Christians; and third, Christians of the right sect but insufficient enthusiasm. That such a man did believe such nonsense demonstrates its power in the Puritan mind. A mind like that is clearly disqualified at once for that willing suspension of damnation which constitutes dramatic faith—just as the opposite mind, with the tolerant commonsense which we saw in Falkland and Chillingworth and Hales, is allied to the dramatist's mind and will be able to appreciate his creations. One wonders how much the doctrine of predestination reinforced this difference. Perhaps there is no real connection; but certainly a doctrine which proclaimed[1] that the most important event in a human being's existence had been pre-determined by a power over which he had no control, and pre-determined in a way which made all his

---

[1] The account of it by Robert Burns can be recommended for brevity and accuracy:

> *O Thou, Wha in the Heavens does dwell,*
> *Wha, as it pleases best Thy sel,*
> *Sends ane to Heaven, and ten to Hell,*
> *A' for Thy glory;*
> *And no' for ony guid or ill*
> *They've done afore Thee . . .*

moral efforts irrelevant towards affecting that determination, does seem thoroughly destructive of the suspense and uncertainty, the feeling that enormous moral issues hang upon the characters' acts, without which there can be no true drama.

Whether crudely in the foreground—as in the passage cited from Baxter—or more discreetly in the background, this black-and-white dividing of humanity is always present in the Puritan mind. It was a mind which divided and excluded—in direct opposition to that society previously described, which aimed at uniting and including. It would be unjustifiably ecclesiastical, and absurdly narrowing, to describe the metaphysical and mature Shakespearean manner as an Anglo-catholic style *tout court*; but it is true that Anglo-catholicism agreed with it, while Puritanism did not and could not, and that the difference between an including and an excluding mentality is at the root of this difference. For the more you exclude, the farther you go from the rich variety and complexity of material which drama requires; and no amount of merely doctrinal varieties will compensate for an essential attitude which is plain black-and-white. The Puritan mind, for example, was not only not averse from the multiplication of sects; it welcomed it, as Milton does in *Areopagitica*, for evidence of spiritual liveliness, proof of the enlightenment to come. And this particular habit was but a symptom of the general Puritan bent for dividing: religious from secular, Church from State, Sundays from weekdays, levity from seriousness.

And religion from drama. One of the most notable differences between the popular drama of the Middle Ages and that of the Elizabethans and Jacobeans—probably the largest real difference, many of the others being matters of literary fashion alone —is of course that the subjects of the former are almost exclusively religious, those of the latter almost exclusively secular. And for this the Puritan-Protestant mind was mostly responsible, with its conviction that the Bible must be treated not merely seriously but solemnly, that its contents must never be joked about, as the medieval dramatists joked about Noah's reluctant wife, never embroidered with personal fancy, never made a storehouse of material for popular entertainment. (We may wonder if Shakespeare ever regretted it—if he ever looked with longing and irritation at the magnificent dramatic material which the Bible would have given him and which he could never use.) By this divorcing of religion from drama the Puritans could have done the latter great damage, since drama, which began from religion, always—at its best—strives to return to it. This is in fact what happened in the maturity of the Jacobean drama: it did return to religion, in its own way and without admitting it, so to speak. It may not be too fanciful to regard the steadily increasing depth and seriousness of the drama, from early Elizabethan to mature Jacobean, as an unconscious effort to bring back religion into a drama secularized against its will. Plays like *King Lear* and *Macbeth* are intensely religious, but religious in ways which the Puritan could not admit, perhaps could not "see" as religious at all. By his own act he cut off *his* religion from the possibility of being expressed in dramatic terms: hence the significant fact that virtually the only type of humanity in the whole Elizabethan and Jacobean scene which the Shakespearean *oeuvre* does not comprehend in its vast variety—is the Puritan. He is not there at all—unless one counts the slight and farcical caricature of him in Malvolio.

In spite of the gloominess of the dogmas which the extremer Puritans held, the Puritan was fundamentally an optimist. He was an optimist in so far as he was a revolutionary; he believed that changes in church and society ought to be made, could and would be made, and when made would bring about remarkable improvements in the human condition. The other side's conservatism, founded on pessimism about human nature (and also, of course, on the fact that they were in power), was not for him. He believed—in practice, whatever his dogmas told him—in human progress, if only (for examples) the episcopacy were abolished, or the King were eliminated, or a "free" Parliament were elected, or the Rule of the Saints were set up in the land. This optimism did not remain merely on the purely political and comparatively unemotional levels of the Puritan's mind, as it might remain in the mind of his equivalent to-day. For him, as for all men of the seventeenth century, there was no real break between politics and religion. His optimism, therefore, descended also into deeper levels: it became a genuinely apocalyptic vision, felt and expressed in religious, Biblical terms. Milton's prose—at least, that written in the early years of the revolution—abounds in such visions: the tremendous prayer in the *Animadversions upon the Remonstrant's Defence* is only the most extreme among many. Isaiah and the Song of Songs and the Book of Revelation lie behind this vision of what will happen when (it is bound to seem an anti-climax) the Bishops are at last got rid of:

> Come therefore O thou that hast the seven starres in thy right hand, appoint thy chosen *Preists* according to their Orders, and courses of old, to minister before thee, and duely to dresse and powre out the consecrated oyle into thy holy and ever-burning lamps; thou hast sent out the spirit of prayer upon thy servants over all the Land to this effect, and stirr'd up their vowes as the sound of many waters about thy Throne. Every one can say that now certainly thou hast visited this land . . . seeing the power of thy grace is not past away with the primitive times, as fond and faithlesse men imagine, but thy Kingdome is now at hand, and thou standing at the dore. Come forth out of thy Royall Chambers, O Prince of all the Kings of the earth, put on the visible roabes of thy imperiall Majesty, take up that unlimited Scepter which thy Almighty Father hath bequeath'd thee; for now the voice of thy Bride calls thee, and all creatures sigh to bee renew'd.

Of such ecstasies, disillusionment will be the certain obverse. "New Presbyter is but Old Preist writ large" is bound to come in a year or two. For our purposes, the point is that this apocalyptic optimism cannot exist with the tragic sense—the sense which we saw to be the common property of those who made up the society of the Shakespearean moment, and which depends on a clear-eyed, unshocked perception of the limitations of human possibilities in the moral sphere. Even the disillusionment which follows the apocalyptic vision will not yield the tragic sense: what it leads to is not tragedy, but disappointment. And that is a very different thing. True tragedy is not the result of disappointed expectations, of human beings behaving as one didn't expect them to behave, but of fulfilled expectations, of human beings behaving as a tragic philosophy of life, already formed, had always expected them to behave. Disappointment, the upsetting of one's expectations and disproving of one's philosophy, leads to a personal poetry—a poetry of self-adjustment, self-blame, or self-justification: for if, to put it

145

crudely, one has made a fool of oneself, one is far too occupied with understanding why one did, or proving that after all one really didn't, to achieve the impersonal detachment which tragic drama demands. Milton's ecstatic response to the first stages of the English Revolution in the seventeenth century resembles very closely Wordsworth's to the first stages of the French Revolution in the eighteenth: common to both of them was a sense of renewal and certainty:

> *Why should I not confess that Earth was then*
> *To me, what an inheritance, new-fallen,*
> *Seems, when the first time visited, to one*
> *Who thither comes to find in it his home?*
> (*Prelude*, XI)

From such a disappointment, both men made a poetry essentially autobiographical: the only kind of poetry that such an experience could lead to. Perhaps a dramatic and tragic poetry —unlike an autobiographical—can never emerge from one man alone; it must come from the interaction between the one man of genius and a society, of which he is part, deeply imbued with a tragic philosophy. And because such a combination is rarely achieved, the great ages of tragic drama are few and far between; great individuals are not so rare, therefore great poetry of the personal sort is a good deal commoner.

The Puritan, indeed, always tends to be an individualist, and if he is a poet, to write a personal and egoistic poetry. His theology—or rather, the whole spiritual cast of his religion— one can see either as springing from such egoism or as encouraging it. For men like Donne and Herbert, though the core of their religion, as must always be the case in any true religion, is a personal relationship between the individual soul and its God, that core was surrounded by a spiritual community, by a Church with strong and ancient roots—for they never saw *their* Church as beginning from the Reformation—by a priesthood itself hierarchical, and a hierarchy of spiritual beings in this world and the next: "all *plurall* things," as Donne expressed it. They saw their own personal drama of salvation or damnation as played on a crowded stage. For the Puritan, these "plurall things" were of vastly less importance. His tendency, his ambition, was always to deny to everything and everyone any

146

rights of interference in his private quarrel with God and the devil. He always worked to eliminate what he regarded as superfluous *personae*—such as the Virgin and the Saints—from his religious universe. Similar in origin was his dislike of ritual: that, too, he saw as a sort of crowding, a sensuous performance, a distraction from the one thing of real importance—as Milton sees it in *Of Reformation in England*, denouncing

> . . . the new-vomited Paganism of sensual Idolatry, attributing purity, or impurity, to things indifferent, that they might bring the inward acts of the *Spirit* to the outward, and customary eye-Service of the body, as if they could make *God* earthly, and fleshly, because they could not make themselves *heavenly*, and *Spiritual*.

Hence the Puritan's insistence on the "Spirit" as final arbiter: an elusive concept, but one which for him seems to reduce itself to nothing much more than the absolute right to private judgment in spiritual matters. Milton has it, with regard to interpretation of the Scriptures:

> . . . The Scriptures protesting their own plainnes, and perspicuity, calling to them to be instructed, not only the *wise*, and *learned*, but the *simple*, the *poor*, the *babes*, foretelling an extraordinary effusion of *Gods* Spirit upon every age, and sexe, attributing to all men, and requiring from them the ability of searching, trying, examining all things, and by the Spirit discerning that which is good.[1]

And so says the Westminster Confession of the Presbyterians in 1643:

> Our full persuasion and assurance of the infallible truth and divine authority thereof (*sc.* of the Bible) is from the inward work of the Holy Spirit, bearing witness, by and with the word, in our hearts.

The "Spirit", as here conceived, was a thing inward and private: to be found by introspection. Hence we would expect, what in fact we find, that when the Puritan turns to literature, his typical works are of those kinds that come from such introspectiveness: works of the single, not the multiple, vision. Baxter, in his *Autobiography*, describes the kind of thing which a Puritan

---

[1] *Of Reformation in England.*

reader looked for: "it is soul-experiments which those that urge me to this kind of writing do expect that I should especially communicate to them."[1] "Soul-experiments" is no bad description of Puritan writing: it is personal and propagandist, it does not make an objective pattern out of a variety of human events, leaving the "moral" which may be drawn from the pattern unexpressed and unemphasized; the moral is explicit, and the work, from beginning to end, directed towards it. Allegory; spiritual autobiography—either direct, or allegorized, partially or totally; argument and propaganda: these are the typical Puritan forms. *The Faerie Queene* and *Pilgrim's Progress*; *Grace Abounding*, Baxter's *Autobiography*, *Samson Agonistes*; *Comus* and *Paradise Lost*: these are Puritan creations. "To justify the ways of God to man" is a typically Puritan literary objective.

On mental and spiritual levels, then, the Puritan was deeply opposed to the dramatic attitude: as deeply as the Anglocatholic was in tune with it. There was also, reinforcing these levels, a social cleavage: the kind of society which the Puritan usually came from and the view of society which he always envisaged, ran directly counter to that which nourished the Shakespearean moment. One has to be careful at this point. Puritanism was not, of course, a class-doctrine, any more than Anglicanism; but, in practice, it did become more closely associated with the lower and middle classes than with the upper and courtly; it did increasingly slip into opposing the monarchy;[2] it did see its social ideal as nearer to egalitarianism than to hierarchy. Anti-puritan sentiment included a strong leaven of plain snobbery: witness, for example, the ragings of John Walker in his *Sufferings of the Clergy* (of the Anglican clergy, that is, dispossessed during the Commonwealth):

One . . . who was the Hogsherd's son of Little Houghton,

[1] Baxter—who was a "moderate"—indicates that he intends to disappoint this expectation: Bunyan's *Grace Abounding* fulfils it to perfection.

[2] E.g., to take an early witness, there is Donne's remark in *Paradoxes and Problems* (written in the 1590's) which purports to explain "why Puritans make long sermons":

And sometimes, that usurping in that place a liberty to speak freely of Kings, they would reigne as long as they could.

had been bred a knitter, became afterwards a horse-buyer, but then Mayor of Northampton, Colonel of the Town Regiment . . . If a cobbler or a tinker get into a pulpit and preach four or five hours for the Parliament, these are the men nowadays . . . They did put out good ministers and put in peddlers, tinkers, and cobblers.

In the same vein are the arguments of the magistrates who examined Bunyan for the offence of unlicensed preaching. They and their prisoner debated mightily on the text "As every man hath received the gift", which Bunyan interpreted as meaning that every man who felt it in him to "testify", might and ought to do so; one of the magistrates (parodying, it would seem, the Puritan jargon) expounded in reply:

> He said, Let me a little open that scripture to you: 'As every man hath received the gift'; that is, said he, as every one hath received a trade, so let him follow it. If any man have received a gift of tinkering, as thou hast done, let him follow his tinkering. And so other men their trades; and the Divine his calling, etc.

"Aiming it is like at me," comments Bunyan on another and similar occasion, "because I was a tinker." And to such snobbery the proletarian Puritan reacted with an inverted snobbery of his own, as one sees in Bunyan's unctuous glorification of his own lowness:

> For my descent, then, it was, as is well known to many, of a low and inconsiderable generation; my father's house being of that rank that is meanest, and most despised of all the families in the land. Wherefore I have not here, as others, to boast of noble blood, or of any high-born state, according to the flesh . . .
>
> (*Grace Abounding*)

Bunyan and the gentlemen who tried him represent the class-conflict in its simplest, most obvious form; but even in Puritans of a different social origin, and less intransigence, similar elements will always appear. What they all had was a distaste for courtliness and "magnificence". Such distaste is very clear in Milton, himself a highly cultured and unusually fastidious product of a middle-class home. The hatred of revelry and courtliness, which in his poetry runs clear from *Comus*, through the "sons of Belial, flown with insolence and wine" in *Paradise Lost*, to the feasting Philistines of *Samson Agonistes*, appears as explicit political argument in the last of his propagandist works in prose, the *Ready and Easy Way to Establish a Free Commonwealth*, which was written (ironically, when one thinks of the title) in the shadow of the imminent Restoration and the courtiers' return:

> And what Government comes nearer to this precept of Christ, than a free Commonwealth; wherein they who are greatest, are perpetual Servants and drudges to the public at thir own cost and charges, neglect thir own Affairs, yet are not elevated above thir Brethren; live soberly in thir Families, walk the Streets as other men, may be spoken to freely, familiarly, friendly, without Adoration? Wheras a King must be ador'd like a Demigod, with a dissolute and haughty Court about him, of vast expence and Luxury, Masks and Revels, to the debauching of our prime Gentry both Male and Female; not in thir pastimes only, but in earnest, by the loos imployments of Court-service, which will be then thought honorable.

The democratic spirit in politics is here linked—as the opening words of this passage indicate—to an anti-hierarchical sentiment which enters religion also; for Milton, the nearest approach to the Kingdom of Heaven which this world can reach to, is a levelled society (in his dream of the rulers of the State "walking the streets as other men", one imagines that the city-state of ancient Greece has also made its contribution)—just as clearly as for Donne and Shakespeare it was the ordered hierarchical pyramid. But not for Milton: "I cannot but yet admire," he says (in the same pamphlet), "how any man who hath the true principles of Justice and Religion in him, can presume to take upon him to be a King and Lord over his Brethren." In such passages—there are many more—one sees the natural anti-sensuousness of the Puritan reinforcing, probably causing, his political disapproval of courtliness. The Court he looks on (no doubt correctly) as the centre and breeding-ground of all sorts of excesses; he does not see, or if he sees does not value, what the poets of the Shakespearean moment both saw and valued—the compensatory quality by which the Court and aristocracy were also the breeding-grounds of elegance and splendour.[1] Thus the Puritan's distaste for a courtly society came from the same roots as his disapproval of ritualism in the Church—the natural form, as we saw, for the religion of a monarchical and aristocratic society—for both distastes had their origins in aversion from multiplicity, variety, and sensuous attractiveness; both show the same fanatical quality—an inability to criticize abuses without longing to eradicate *in toto*.

This social cleavage, which is one of ideals and ideas about society rather than of the individuals' social origins[2]—and for that reason goes far deeper and is far more important—makes itself felt with equal force and clarity in the particular field of the drama. But here again, caution is needed. It is quite clear that Elizabethan and Jacobean drama was not the product of, or designed for, or confined to, any one class; it was appreciated by all classes. But not by all types of *mind*: it sprang from, and for its appreciation demanded, a hierarchical view of society. Its tragedy is that of "noble" personalities, its comedy that of men who will not understand and remain within their social limits, like Malvolio and Sir Epicure Mammon. This is confirmed when we look at the actual social history of the theatres. The Marxist criticism which sees the Elizabethan and Jacobean drama as the expression of the *"rising bourgeoisie"*[3] shows a splendid indifference to the facts: the evidence is overwhelming

[1] It is therefore not unnatural that Charles I assembled the finest collection of paintings ever brought together by Royalty in England —and that Cromwell sold almost all of it.

[2] Most of the writers of the Shakespearean moment came from middle-class families; that class, then as always, was the great reservoir of talent. George Herbert is almost the only real aristocrat.

[3] E.g., "When these plays (*sc.* the medieval dramas) were taken over by the *bourgeoisie*, the rivals of the feudal nobility, and later patronized by the Tudors as leaders of the *bourgeoisie*, the drama was developed in conscious opposition to religious ritual, of which it rapidly became entirely independent." (George Thomson: *Aeschylus and Athens.*) It is true that *one* Tudor (Elizabeth) patronized the new drama (the others had died before it began)—but so did all the Stuarts, who spent most of their days in combating the *"bourgeoisie"*. And it is not at all true that in this patronage "the Tudors" (one ought, to be accurate, to say "the monarchy") were expressing their leadership of the *bourgeoisie*. On the contrary, on this point, they were going directly against it.

that the politically most "advanced" part of the middle-class, the commercial and largely Puritanized leaders of the City, were bitterly opposed to it, while the Court was its faithful and indispensable protector. Of many examples one may be cited: when the Lord Mayor of London, in 1580, petitioned the Council to suppress the theatres, the Council replied by ordering the Corporation to allow the players "to practise such plays in such sort and in the usual places as they had been accustomed", and gave as one reason that the players must be ready "with convenient matters for her Highness's solace this next Christmas". This is not to be explained away by Elizabeth's and James's addiction to playgoing, and the London merchants' dislike of seeing their prentices playing truant; both Elizabeth and James, however much they liked the play, regarded other things as of greater importance, were extremely sensitive to approval and criticism, and would never have patronized a drama which they did not recognize to be in tune with their own notions, their hierarchical and monarchist notions, about religion and society. The Court liked the drama—and by "the Court" one means not only the monarchy, but also the aristocracy, men like William Herbert— and the Puritan middle-class did not like it, for the perfectly simple reason that it expressed a viewpoint in harmony with the former's and out of harmony with the latter's.

The distaste which a Puritan who was very far from an uneducated ranter, and whose politics were revolutionary, could feel for the stage of his time, may be seen most remarkably in Milton. He, of course, was not only a Puritan, he was also a true son of the classical Renaissance; but in so far as he *was* a Puritan, he was a typical one: his mind and sensibility worked as the Puritans' worked. And in his reaction to the popular drama, one sees the classicist disapproval on grounds of literary dogma (the Sidneyan grounds), and the Puritan disapproval on moral grounds, coming together: but the latter more powerfully, and the latter, it seems, coming first. It looks as if he grew steadily less capable of appreciating the drama as he grew older. The complimentary references to Shakespeare, which one finds in *L'Allegro* and the verses prefixed to the Second Folio, both works of his youth, are quickly overbalanced by a series of sour and contemptuous snarls. There is that in the *Apology for Smectymnuus*, where Milton inveighs against the practice of

amateur theatricals by divinity students at Cambridge ("writh-
ing and unboning their Clergie limmes to all the antick and
dishonest gestures of Trinculo's, Buffons, and Bawds"), complains that in so disgracing themselves the students were
encouraged by the prelates,[1] and finally remarks:

> For if it be unlawfull to sit and behold a mercenary
> Comedian personating that which is least unseemly for a
> hireling to doe . . .

—how much more unlawful for such things to be done by
students of divinity. Such denunciations lead the way to the
contemptuous dismissal in the tract *On Education*—"what
despicable creatures our common Rimers and Play-writers be"
—and the final rejection of the living drama in the preface to
Samson Agonistes. They leave no room for doubt: the doctrines,
both Puritan and classicist, reinforce a natural fastidiousness—
"a certain niceness of nature" is Milton's own phrase for it[2]—to
produce a phenomenon not unknown in other ages, the friend of
progress and democracy who is very ill at ease with the arts and
amusements of the populace.

How this dislike of the drama fits in with the other convictions
of Milton's mind—which was a thoroughly integrated mind,
nothing occurring there that did not have the full weight of the
mind behind it—may be seen if one looks at some of his meta-
phorical uses of imagery taken from the stage. Ritualism in the
Church he sees as play-acting; in the *Apology for Smectymnuus*,
answering his opponent who had described that prayer previously cited (p. 145) as "theatrical" (and thereby, one imagines, touched Milton to the quick), he retorts:

> *It was theatrical*, he says. And yet it consisted most of
> Scripture language [Milton is right there]: it had no *Rubrick*

[1] That the Bishops allowed, even encouraged, the people to
amuse themselves, even on Sundays, is one of Milton's principal
complaints against them, as in *Of Reformation in England*:
> At such a time that men should be pluck't from their saddest
> and soberest thoughts, and by *Bishops* the pretended *Fathers of
> the Church* instigated by publique Edict, and with earnest indeavour
> push't forward to gaming, jigging, wassailing, and mixt dancing
> is a horror to think.

[2] In the *Apology for Smectymnuus*.

to be sung in an antick Coape upon the Stage of a High Altar.

"Antick" and "Stage" are of course precisely used: the image is of a theatre clown. So, in the same pamphlet, we get "the finicall goosery of your neat Sermon-actor"; and in *Eikonoklastes*, when Milton is concerned to ridicule the portrait of King Charles prefixed to *Eikon Basilike* and designed, he says, to present the King as a "Saint or Martyr", he does so by sneering at "the conceited portraiture before his Book, drawn out to the full measure of a Masking Scene" (i.e., the *décor* of a masque) and talking of "quaint Emblems and devices begg'd from the olde Pageantry of some Twelfe-nights entertainment at *Whitehall*". Such references to the stage are in remarkable contrast to those which, as we have seen, abound in the writings of men of the opposite temperament: when Donne or Marvell or Sir William Waller use the imagery of the theatre, it is in serious contexts and for the purpose of dignifying and intensifying the emotion. Donne, likening his own death-bed to a scene in a play; Waller, seeing himself and his friend-and-enemy as players in a tragedy; Marvell (this contrast is particularly pointed) seeing King Charles on the scaffold as a tragic actor: such usages would be possible only to men for whom the stage, the living drama, was associated with experiences of dignity and beauty—just as the tone of Milton's references could come only from a man in whom disgust, alienation, and a conviction of his own superiority were the feelings which the stage had provoked.

If the point is proved, then, that when the Puritan denounced the drama he was doing so not because a stern duty impelled him to reject what he liked but could not approve, but because a natural temperament made him eager to denounce as immoral what in any case he had no taste for, then the antipathy of the Puritan mind to the manner of the Shakespearean moment is seen as clear and inevitable: for that manner was dramatic through and through, dramatic beyond the confines of the theatre. It is, again, Milton who provides the most strik-ing example, just as it was he—the one great poet, almost the one poet of any quality, that the Puritan mind produced—who did more than anyone else to turn English verse away from the metaphysical and Shakespearean manner. (If, indeed, that *was* his work, or anyone's; one may doubt if anything could have held the Shakespearean moment.) The first of his many "manifestoes" (announcements, that is, of what he is going to do, what sort of poetry he is going to write) occurs in the *Vacation Exercise* written in 1627 (Donne had still four years to live) when Milton was 19: there he asks his "native language" to bring him

> Not those new fangled toys, and triming slight
> Which takes our late fantasticks with delight

—*not*, that is, the style of verse then dominant; and the first of these lines puts very well what a hostile critic would object to in the metaphysical manner. The young Milton, already astonishingly sure of himself, is already looking for other models; what he found is indicated in the remark he made to Dryden near the end of his life. "Milton has acknowledged to me," reports Dryden, "that Spenser was his original."

The lines of demarcation begin to emerge: the Puritan mind finds itself in poetry in a style which, turning from the drama and the non-theatrical poetry which is thoroughly dramatic, reverts to that earlier Elizabethan manner before the rise of the true drama—a poetry simpler in feeling, clearer in outline, explicit in moralizing, and remote from the popular in language. For the purposes of literary criticism, the last point is the most important. Nothing is more striking in Milton's writing than the difference—the obviously deliberate difference—between his language when he engages in prose controversy and that which he uses in his verse. (There is no such wide gulf between the language of Donne's sermons and that of his poetry.) Milton's prose abounds in intensely vivid, not infrequently coarse, colloquialisms; his verse has virtually none of them. For Milton, the poet was a mixture of Roman *vates*—the sacred seer—and psalmist; he sees him as a creature special and remote —"soaring in the high region of his fancies with his garland and singing robes about him"[1]—and the language he uses must have appropriate qualities. As with Milton's objections to the drama, the two chief sources of his mind contribute to this. On the one hand, the classical conception of the poet—as interpreted, at least, by the Renaissance—as one who employs a special lan-

[1] *Reason of Church Government.*

guage different from that of common speech; on the other hand, the Puritan aversion from contemporary popular entertainment. The two unite, as noted, in Fulke Greville's declaration that his dramas were not for the stage and Milton's similar disclaimer for *Samson Agonistes*. There *was* an affinity—a close one, even if sometimes unperceived at the time—between the classicist side of the Renaissance and the Puritan mind; the points of contact were two—contempt for popular art and contempt for medieval tradition.

All Puritans, before the 1640's (when they came into power), were in varying degrees revolutionaries—opposed to the *status quo* in so far as that consisted of an episcopal Anglican settlement supported by and supporting the monarchy. Being revolutionaries, they were hostile to tradition. And in particular to the tradition of the Middle Ages, of which the most living and controversial element in the realm of thought was scholastic theology. For that the Puritan mind had nothing but contempt. It is Milton's main complaint against the education he received at Cambridge that it still consisted of the old scholastic logic and divinity; men come to the universities, he complains,

> to store themselves with good and solid learning, and there unfortunately fed with nothing else, but the scragged and thorny lectures of monkish and miserable sophistry, were sent home again with such a scholastical burre in their throats, as hath stopt and hindered all true and generous philosophy from entring.
>
> (*Reason of Church Government*)

"Tradition" and "scholastic" are for him, invariably, words of abuse. "And must tradition then," he asks in the *Reason of Church Government*, "ever thus to the worlds end be the perpetuall canker-worme to eat out Gods Commandments?" "Full of nonsense and scholastick foppery"; "Scholastic grossness of barbarous ages"; "that asinine feast of sowthistles and brambles"[1]: some of his choicest phrases are reserved for this topic. Medieval thought he despises as radically as any pioneer of the new science, and much more violently, for to him it was linked more closely with his enemies: he saw it (correctly) as

---

[1] Respectively: *Apology for Smectymnuus; Of Education;* ibid.

still, in all essentials, the way of thinking of that society and form of religion which he set himself to destroy—the monarchical, hierarchic, and Anglo-catholic. Against it he sets up what was then, in comparison, a "modernist" blending: the classical humanism of the Renaissance and the Protestant theology of the sixteenth century. Such blending can be seen in his statement of the purposes of education and learning.[1] The task of education is to fit "a man to perform justly, skilfully and magnanimously all the offices both private and publick of Peace and War"; that is the classical spirit—"justly" and "magnanimously" have Plato and Aristotle behind them. And the end of learning is "to repair the ruines of our first Parents by regaining to know God aright"; that is the Christian objective. The Puritan and classicist affinity appears again: in both, one feels a simplicity and directness, a preference for plainness and loftiness, against the rich ambiguousness, the down-to-earth sometimes, up-in-the-air of involved conceits at other times, both possible at any times and in any blending, which characterize the minds and the poetry of Shakespeare and Donne. The Puritan, in fact, really preferred—would rather put up with, any day—the officially "heathen" thought and images of the classics (for they were safely dead) than the Christian thought and images of the Middle Ages (for they were still uncomfortably alive, still the objects of his enemies' worship). Of which preference a comic example is given in Stow: the Puritans of London pulled down an image of the Resurrection in Cheapside and replaced it by one of Diana, "with water . . . prilling at her naked breast". The heathen "idol" was less dangerous than the Christian.

By such activities and such thinking, the Puritans were engaged in a deliberate (and, in the long run, very successful) destruction of the immediate past, in a pulling-up of roots. They suffered, it seems, from none of that nostalgic regret for the Middle Ages which we have noted in Shakespeare and in other Elizabethans; Milton's contempt for medieval chivalry contrasts with the feeling for its glamour which Shakespeare's Sonnets reveal. The difference is just as clear if we look at literary forms. The popular Elizabethan drama carried within it a great deal of its medieval forerunner (the blending of comic

[1] In the tract *Of Education*.

and solemn, the colloquial speech, etc.); the dramas which derived from Renaissance classicism represented a total break. Such dramas, when they frowned on "tragi-comedy" (as Milton does in the preface to *Samson Agonistes*), were denouncing more than a fashion of the contemporary London theatre; they were repudiating a whole native tradition, which runs clear from the farce of the Towneley play's shepherds round the manger at Bethlehem to the gravediggers' scene in *Hamlet*. The Puritan spirit found the former blasphemous; the classicist thought the latter was "low". The profane was being divorced from the sacred, the popular from the highbrow; their precarious alliances, which we saw to be essentials of the Shakespearean moment, were fated to be dissolved.

In a different direction of Puritan activity, the same effect can be seen. Another thing which "every schoolboy knows" is that the Puritans pulled down the Maypoles. Not having the benefit of modern anthropology, they were no doubt unaware that they were pulling down a phallic symbol; but they did know (and say) that they were destroying something "heathen"[1]. They were putting an end to the relics of rustic paganism. The situation has something ironically paradoxical. The Puritans who could welcome, as Milton does, the pagan spirit when presented in the purely literary forms of Renaissance classicism, were also engaged in furious destruction of the only genuine and living paganism still in existence. Paradoxical, but easily understood: as with the images in Cheapside, the dead was safer than the living. So the Maypoles went, and with them what the Maypoles stood for: the folk-festivals of the countryside, still authentic and alive, not yet relegated to the "Ye Olde" and the researches of anthropologists. What this meant for poetry is not too easy to estimate. We had better be wary of entering that dubious and (at present) far too heavily exploited territory in which second-hand anthropology takes the place of first-hand criticism, and of subscribing to Chestertonian fables which present the Middle Ages as a kind of Christian Saturnalia, with a free and devout peasantry indulging in their merry junketings

---

[1] E.g., Phillip Stubbes, in his *Anatomie of Abuses* : . . . And then fall they to banquet and feast, to leap and dance about it (the Maypole), as heathen people did at the dedication of their idols, wherof this is a perfect pattern, or rather the thing itself.

under the benevolent gaze of broad-minded clerics; but it may be argued that the Puritan attacks on the Maypole and what it stood for, and on the popular drama and poetry and what *they* stood for, were connected on deeper levels, and with wider implications, than a general dislike of seeing people enjoy themselves. A play like *The Winter's Tale*, and poetry like Herrick's, clearly owe a very great deal to the existence around them of the folk-festivals, still alive and genuine, still imbued with a tinge of more solemn feeling, relic of the religion they had sprung from. When the "country matters"[1] are ended or driven underground, the poetry will no longer be the same. Another root will have been severed. And between this and the anti-medievalism on theological levels, a connection existed; under the old order and the old religion, the rustic paganism did flourish more successfully. For which there is the contemporary evidence of Bishop Corbet's poem:

> *Witness those rings and roundelayes*
>   *Of theirs, which yet remain,*
> *Were footed in Queen Mary's days*
>   *On many a grassy plain;*
> *But since of late, Elizabeth,*
>   *And later James came in,*
> *They never danced on any heath*
>   *As when the time hath been.*
>
> *By which we note the Fairies*
>   *Were of the old profession:*
> *Their songs were Ave Maries,*
>   *Their dances were procession:*
> *But now, alas! they all are dead*
>   *Or gone beyond the Seas,*
> *Or further for Religion fled,*
>   *Or else they take their ease.*

Not that the medieval Church was really more tolerant than the Puritans of rustic paganism; its attack was simply less effective —largely because it was not backed up, as the Puritans' was, by the forces of the classical Renaissance, with its tendency to

---

[1] Both senses of the phrase are applicable: they were in fact connected.

despise the arts of the folk as uncultured and "low",[1] and those of the new science, with its developing assault on the magical. All three, on this point, were working to the same end— Puritan, classicist, and propagandist for science—however unconnected or mutually hostile their individual representatives were or thought themselves: all tended to division and separation. The immense gains and achievements which Reformation and Renaissance brought about were bought at a very great price. Without those gains and achievements the Shakespearean moment would not have been possible; it could never have occurred in the cramped horizons of the Middle Ages: but neither would it have been possible unless there had been also, in Shakespeare and Donne and their like, an awareness of what had been lost as keen as of what had been gained. An awareness and a regret: the tension between gain and loss, exhilaration for the former and nostalgia for the latter, makes the Shakespearean quality.

To sum up, then: those qualities of the Puritan mind which made it not only alien, but opposed, to the mind of the Shakespearean moment, were its bent for dividing and excluding, its indifference or hostility to the sensuous, its dislike of the hierarchical and of the variety and magnificence which the hierarchical implied, its "progressiveness" and tendency to fanaticism, destructive both of the tragic sense and of the dramatist's balance, and its rejection of the medieval heritage. The opposites of all these qualities characterize, as has been argued, the mentality and society which Donne and Shakespeare represented and wrote for. Throughout the first forty years of the seventeenth century the Puritan ethos steadily gained ground: from being the philosophy of a sect, or variety of sects, almost universally despised by men of intellect, education, and imagination, it grew to be the dominant way of thinking in the country. The political effects of that progress need no emphasizing; the effects on culture and imagination are not so clear, but can

[1] E.g., the apologetic tone in which Sidney confesses his liking for the ballad of *Chevy Chace* and his suggestion that that ballad would be much improved if it were dressed up "in the gorgeous eloquence of Pindar". Sidney is here the lineal ancestor of a long line of classical improvers—of Pope improving Chaucer and Donne and Mr. Sturge Moore improving Hopkins.

hardly have been less. One effect, it seems probable, was the rapid decline of that form of art most particularly obnoxious to the Puritans, the drama. The Puritans had won their real war against it long before the actual theatres were closed; this, it seems likely, was the real reason—one important reason, at any rate—for the remarkably swift degeneration of the drama after about 1620: the Puritans had been so successful in discrediting it, even among those who were not themselves Puritans, that the best minds and finest spirits were no longer willing to write for it. By the 1620's and 30's, the drama is already living on its past, as far as the production of great works is concerned. Another consequence (essentially the same) which Puritan dominance brought in the sphere of poetry is the impoverishing of love-poetry. Puritans themselves, of course, don't write it at all—regard it, indeed, in Milton's phrase, as "the vapours of wine, like that which runs at wast from the pen of some vulgar Amorist"[1]—and their disapproval was in part responsible for that coarsening of fibre and narrowing of range which one sees in the love-poetry of Carew and Suckling as compared with that of Donne. What has come in is a tone of uneasy defiance, a determined heartiness and conscientious naughtiness—this does seem, very often, poetry written *pour épater le bourgeois*—instead of Donne's dramatic readiness to give full value to all notes in the gamut of love. The kind of tone which one calls "Restoration" can be felt already in the last years of Charles I's reign, those years of increasing ominousness and desperation, years in which the society represented by men like Falkland, Chillingworth, and Clarendon, increasingly uneasy, steadily losing its dominance, slowly but surely loses also its creative power, its power to attract the best and unite the disparate.

In this work the Puritan mind played the biggest part. But there was also another type of mind, in its own way just as alien to the mind of the Shakespearean moment, which begins to make itself felt as a real force in these early years of the seventeenth century, though it did not come into power and full self-awareness till after the Restoration: the sceptic, the rationalist, the man of Commonsense. To this mind, and in particular to one representative of it in the early years, the following chapter will be devoted.

[1] *Reason of Church Government.*

Chapter 6

THE BEGINNINGS OF RATIONALISM

(*Lord Herbert of Cherbury*)

THE sceptic or rationalist—the type of mind, that is, allergic to the mystical and miraculous, derisive or critical of ecclesiastical authority—is, like the Puritan, always with us: although, like the Puritan, he acquires a new status and a clearer definition from the seventeenth century onwards. Even in what are called "ages of Faith", the rationalist can be found, just as the mystic can be found even in what are called "ages of Reason". It is obvious that the Middle Ages had their rationalists; one may wonder how much real unbelief was expressed through the comparatively safe channels of railing at fraudulent friars and indolent monks or carving improprieties in the gloomier corners of churches—and what weight should one give, for example, to the sly defensive irony of Chaucer's lines in the prologue to the *Legend of Good Women*?

> *A thousand tymes have I herd men telle*
> *That ther is joy in heven, and peyne in helle;*
> *And I acorde wel that hit is so;*
> *But natheles, yit wot I wel also,*
> *That ther nis noon dwelling in this contree,*
> *That either hath in heven or helle y-be.*

Scepticism always exists; how much of it *appears* will depend mainly on the degree of safety with which it can be plainly expressed and on how much support it can win from the general intellectual climate of the age. In the Elizabethan age, it was very far from safe to express in public an outright rationalist criticism. Any sceptic was liable to be denounced, and proceeded against, as an "atheist" and a "blasphemer": words which seem to have been used, by the Elizabethan authorities, much as "Communist" is used in contemporary America, as a conveniently damning label for any one in any degree a nonconformer, a critic of official beliefs and venerated institutions.

162

Moreover, the Elizabethan age was, on the whole, solidly religious: its ethos lent no support to rationalist scepticism. Neither condition, then, was present for any large-scale and public rationalism.

There appears, in consequence, among the Elizabethans, not much of it. There existed, in all probability, a good deal more than appeared. It shows itself now and then in stray hints and isolated phenomena: most clearly in the person of Marlowe and in the circle—he seems to have been in it—which surrounded Sir Walter Raleigh. Marlowe is a difficult problem: sometimes, as in *Dr. Faustus*, he gives the impression of being thoroughly orthodox; at other times, as in *Tamburlaine*, he seems completely critical, attacking all organized religion under the guise of attacking Islam and standing for a sort of deist God, above the "gods" of official religions. "Daring God out of heaven with that atheist Tamburlaine" was how a contemporary saw it, and that was doubtless the popular verdict: the Elizabethans were not equipped to weigh the difference between deism and atheism. What Marlowe's mind was really like may perhaps be gauged by putting the scepticism of *Tamburlaine* together with his remark (reported by Baines, who witnessed against him when he was charged with atheism and blasphemy) to the effect that the only tolerable sort of religion, if you must have one at all, was the Roman Catholic, whereas "all Protestants are Hypocriticall Asses". Marlowe was by nature "agin the Government", a mind of extremes: the sort of mind which nowadays begins by being a Communist and ends by being a convert to Roman Catholicism. There is a quality of *wildness* about his mind (as also, according to contemporaries, about his character): and something of that quality, one imagines, adhered to all Elizabethan rationalism. Sir Walter Raleigh was also a wild man, feared and hated as much as admired, regarded by all as—unaccountable, not to be relied on.[1] Rationalism in that age, being against the stream, had an air of eccentricity.

At the same time, the forces which were to make it something a good deal more than an eccentricity were present and powerful, seeping downwards steadily if unperceived. Renaissance

---

[1] Raleigh, according to Aubrey, was "a-christ, not an atheist": which, if correct, would put his position near to Marlowe's.

and Reformation, working together, led to a general loosening, which in the end made for a change in mental climate that enabled scepticism and rationalism to come into the open as never before. What those forces were is well known: there is no need here for more than a brief indication of them. Most obvious was the breakdown of the Church's unity and the end of her virtual monopoly in the realm of thought and education. Next—and the main force which ended that monopoly—was the Renaissance's immense, almost uncritical admiration for pagan philosophy. This could, at first, and in many men, go more or less comfortably with Christianity, as it does in the English humanists such as More. Montaigne is a subtler case. He was perhaps, in some senses, a "good Catholic"; he was certainly firmly convinced, if not for entirely religious reasons, of the necessity for a dogmatic and accepted spiritual authority: but the *Essais* make it abundantly clear that his mind was nourished, almost exclusively, on pagan culture and thought. Compared with Plutarch, Cicero, Seneca, and the rest, Christian theology and Christian history meant nothing to him; and the complete scepticism which the *Apology* for Raimond Sebond reveals, with regard to the possibility of really knowing anything—though Montaigne, officially, uses it to argue the necessity for unquestioning faith—is the sort of double-edged weapon that could easily be turned the other way. And how did Montaigne intend it? Such an alliance, in any case, must be precarious; such a discrepancy, between real intellectual interests and official belief, cannot be hidden for long. Especially, perhaps, among the English, who always find it less easy than Continentals to be *croyants* without being *pratiquants,* or to be *croyants* with part of their minds and *incroyants* with the rest. The English freethinker becomes a freethinker *in toto*; we hardly know the type so common in the Continental intelligentsia—the anti-clerical who to us seems a thorough freethinker but contrives nevertheless to call himself a believer.

These intellectual developments were reinforced by some weighty facts: in particular, by the discoveries of the New World, with their revelations of non-Christian societies hitherto unimagined. More's *Utopia* and Montaigne's essay on "cannibals" show how these societies could be used as critical sticks wherewith to beat the Christian society of Europe. They furnished material for the first beginnings of anthropology and comparative religion. More, it is likely, meant merely to point out that if non-Christians could do as well as these Utopians, how much better should Christians do (instead of, as in reality, so much worse); Montaigne—ambiguous as always—may or may not mean a little more, and mean it a little less innocently: but as with the pagan philosophy, the dangerous material was there, only waiting for someone to draw the fatal conclusion—and for a society to be corrupted by it—that if non-Christian men can be at least as virtuous as Christians, then perhaps the beliefs which inspire them may not be entirely untrue.

Of all this—and one has to add, of course, the effects of the new science—the essential result was the displacement of theology, the Church's scheme of knowledge and wisdom, from being the one science dominant over all the rest (*una scientia dominatrix aliarum*) which the Middle Ages had made it. The way of thinking which lies behind the medieval pyramid of knowledge, with grammar as the base and theology as the apex, a way of thinking which the Middle Ages accepted even while theologians squabbled among themselves, was going, and going for good. That way we have found to be still vital, however much questioned, threatened, and tortured, in men like Donne and Falkland; its secular offshoots, so to speak, are still dominant in Shakespeare. Ulysses' speech on Order, that of the Duke (disguised as friar) urging the worthlessness of life on Claudio, and that of Burgundy (in *Henry V*) on the effects of war, are all, fundamentally, *sermons*: their thought is in essence theological. It is not a question of what Shakespeare "believed"—that question should be put aside at once as permanently insoluble—but of the terms of reference to which his mind turned when his drama demanded the expression of ideas. That is true of virtually the whole of Elizabethan and Jacobean drama. The rationalist mind is almost as absent from it as the Puritan; when it does put in an appearance, as in Edmund, Iago, and the villain of Tourneur's *Atheist's Tragedy*, it is subjected at once to an uncompromising moral condemnation. The dramatists themselves—with the possible and partial exception of Marlowe—do not share in it; for the rationalist's mind is perhaps as incapable as the Puritan's of true poetic drama, or of any art imbued with the dramatic spirit—and for not dissimilar reasons. Both rationalist and Puritan preferred to simplify, and both would rather argue than simply present.

These generalities may be tested by considering one remarkable example of the rationalist—incompletely, but unmistakably, rationalist—who lived in the first part of the seventeenth century, when to be rationalist was still to be eccentric. This is Edward Herbert, Lord Herbert of Cherbury. He is, from many viewpoints, a fascinating and unexpected person. Fascinating less for the qualities that he himself imagined to be his than for those which he did not realize; unexpected because he came from a background, and lived in a *milieu*, very unlikely to give rise to the rationalist mind. Of all those families which set the tone for the society of the Shakespearean moment, the Herberts were by far the most gifted and attractive: aristocratic, Anglo-catholic, magnificent, they were the very stuff from which meta-physical poetry grew and to which the Shakespearean drama aspired. Lord Herbert himself is a particularly interesting and profitable study because of the variety of his manifestations. He was a poet, who wrote in the time and (to the best of his ability) in the manner of Donne: we can therefore see what effects the rationalist mind will have on such poetry. He was a philosopher: we can examine the nature of his rationalism, and see where it comes into conflict with the attitudes of the Shakespearean moment. He was an autobiographer: the self he reveals, and the manner of his self-revelation, may show the effects of a way of thinking then unusual on a personality of the early seventeenth century. We may look at him first as a poet.

Lord Herbert, the elder brother of George, and the eldest son of that Magdalen Herbert whom we have met with as a patroness of Donne, has never, as the cliché goes, quite "found his niche" in English poetry. One or two of his poems may be found in anthologies; his poetical works have been printed in an Every-man volume;[1] but he has scarcely taken an assured place in the ranks of seventeenth century poets, he has remained not merely a "minor" (that could be said also of Herrick and Lovelace) but one of those "minors" who are read more for duty and incidental interest than for simple pleasure. Posterity's decision, in this case, seems perfectly just.[2] But what was the nature, and what

[1] *Minor Poets of the Seventeenth Century.*
[2] The exaggerations of some of his devotees betray an awareness

the causes, of this failure? Lord Herbert appears to have had all the talents—if one looks at them one by one—to make a true poet, and the age he lived in should have given him the maximum help; for, born as he was in 1583 (eleven years later than Donne), dying in 1648, he lived through the greatest moment of English poetry, and a moment which, as such men as Wotton prove, was unusually propitious to the fruitful development of minor talent. But something, in him, went wrong; some failure in fusion there must have been, some inability to weld his various gifts into a successful achievement in art. He was philosopher, courtier, soldier, diplomat, learned in many languages, the friend and disciple of Grotius and Casaubon on the Continent and of Jonson and Donne at home; he had a career of varied accomplishment which nevertheless rings hollow at the centre. It reminds one of Sir Walter Raleigh's, in whom one sees a similar array of real and most impressive talents and a similar comparative failure (in spite of a few poems which are astonishingly successful) to bring these talents to an assured artistic fruition. Perhaps, in both men, the failure came from the same causes. Both were sceptics in intellect; both had personal characters which strike one—and struck contemporaries—as somehow or other unsound: uncontrollable in pride, unpredictable in behaviour.

Of Lord Herbert's poetical output, almost the whole is thoroughly in the metaphysical manner; it is very clearly the work of a man who had read his Donne and taken him as master. He is in fact always "placed", in the literary histories, as a "minor metaphysical", and that placing is perfectly sound, as far as intention and surface technique are concerned. But one cannot go far in the reading before misgivings arise, before a gulf becomes apparent between master and disciple. Between Donne and others of those poets who learned from him, the other non-theatrical poets of the Shakespearean moment, such as George Herbert and Marvell, no such gulf appears; there, the differences are differences in scope and individual personalities; here, there is a crucial difference in quality, a real failure on the disciple's part to absorb the lesson of the master. And the

of this: thus, Mr. Moore Smith, the editor of the Oxford edition of his poems, commits himself to the unbelievable judgment that "in poetic feeling and art he outsoars his brother George".

reason, we may find, is that this particular disciple was not by nature intended to follow the example of that particular master.

The first symptom is seen in the rhythm. Lord Herbert's rhythm is, in general, depressingly nerveless; it trails on and on, following the stanza-form with a hopeless plodding fidelity:

> *I must depart, but like to his last breath*
> *That leaves the sea of life, for liberty*
> *I go, but dying, and in this our death,*
> *Where soul and soul is parted, it is I*
> *The deader part that fly away,*
> *While she alas, in whom before*
> *I liv'd, dyes her own death and more,*
> *I feeling mine too much, and her own stay.*

> *But since I must depart, and that our love*
> *Springing at first but in an earthly mould,*
> *Transplanted to our souls, now doth remove*
> *Earthly effects, what time and distance would,*
> *Nothing can now our loves allay,*
> *Though as the better Spirits will*
> *That both love us and know our ill,*
> *We do not either all the good we may.*

It is clear at once that Lord Herbert has quite failed to catch that organic and dramatic rhythm which is Donne's most essential quality. His rhythm does not mould and dominate the form; the reverse is what happens. This rhythm has not the faintest affinity to the verse of the theatres; it is not in the least —as Donne's is always—rhetorical. And allied to this—the same thing, perhaps, from another aspect—is a tendency to a desperately entangled and meandering syntax: of which the following stanza, with its string of "which's", is a not unfair example:

> *Nor here yet did your favours end,*
> *For whil'st I down did bend,*
> *As one who now did miss*
> *A soul, which grown much happier then before,*
> *Would turn no more,*

> *You did bestow on me a Kiss,*
> *And in that Kiss a soul infuse,*
> *Which was so fashion'd by your mind,*
> *And which was so much more refin'd,*
> *Then that I formerly did use,*
> *That if one soul found joys in thee,*
> *The other fram'd them new in me.*

Or this, where confusion of pronouns is the source of entanglement:

> *Of whom this might be said, should God ordain*
> *One to destroy all sinners, whom that one*
> *Redeem'd not there, that so he might atone*
> *His chosen flock, and take from each that staine,*
> *That spots it still, he worthy were alone*
> *To finish it, and have, when they were gone,*
> *This World for him made Paradise again.*

Even in his own time, Lord Herbert was reputed obscure; we know, on the evidence of Ben Jonson (talking to Drummond), that Donne wrote one of his own poems "to match Sir Ed: Herbert in obscurenesse". This, as Herford and Simpson remark in their edition of Jonson, was rather a cruel jest, since Herbert was so faithful a disciple; but the jest was deserved. For when Herbert is obscure, it seems to come always from sheer bad writing; neither subtlety of thought nor remoteness of imagery causes it, but plain incompetence in the shaping of his sentences and the fitting them to his form. The syntax of Donne and of George Herbert (and of mature Shakespeare), though often complex, is never confusing; the mastery of form and the drive of the rhythm always carry it through.

From the quotations already given, it will be apparent that Lord Herbert thinks very hard. One could certainly quote him in support of Dr. Johnson's dictum that to write in the metaphysical manner "it was at least necessary to read and to think". His poetry is never empty; there is always a brain behind it. Always; but, far too often, only a brain. Except in rare flashes, his thinking is terribly non-incandescent; it does not become concrete, passionate, and physical; it remains abstract and dry—what the eighteenth century was to call "frigid". Consider these

169   M

stanzas, remembering what Donne made of similar material in *Aire and Angells*:

> And as a Soul, thus being quite abstract,
> Complies not properly with any act,
> Which from its better Being may detract:
>   So through the virtuous habits you infuse,
>   It is enough that we may like and chuse,
>   Without presuming yet to take or use.

> Thus Angels in their starry Orbs proceed
> Unto affection, without other need
> Then that they still on contemplation feed:
>   Though as they may unto this Orb descend,
>   You can, when you would so much lower bend,
>   Give joys beyond what man can comprehend.

"Thus being quite abstract" is just what these verses are. They betray their lack of concreteness in another way—in the poverty of imagery (seen also in the previous quotations). For a man writing in the early seventeenth century, and in the metaphysical tradition, Lord Herbert, in this respect, is more than remarkable: he is almost unique. He has many whole poems with scarcely one live image; thus, the poem from which the above lines are drawn ("Madam, your beauty and your lovely parts") has only one, and that the well-worn trope of "Loves most sharp and piercing darts". The effect is extraordinary; it is as if one were presented with the complex and grotesque design of a baroque painting, without the rich life and colour that should fill it. That impression is given most sharply, perhaps, in Lord Herbert's satires, since metaphysical satire, with its convention of "roughness", was the most grotesque form of all. Lord Herbert's take Donne's as their models; but the difference is vast and revealing. For instance:

>   But that your view
> May comprehend at once them gone for Bloys,
> Or Orleans; learn'd French, now no more Boys,
> But perfect Men at Paris, putting on
> Some forc'd disguise, or labour'd fashion,

> *To appear strange at home, besides their stay,*
> *Laugh and look on with me, to see what they*
> *Are now become; but that the poorer sort,*
> *A subject not fit for my Muse nor sport,*
> *May pass untouch'd . . .*

Lord Herbert's "roughness" is quite disjoined from his meaning; it is imposed from above, as much as any "smooth" metre could be. But the roughness of Donne's satires reflects the rhythm's faithful, dramatic following of sense and emotion—the kind of roughness whose secret Coleridge recognized when he observed—somewhat pedagogically, but the remark goes wider than pedagogy: "If you wish to teach a scholar in the highest form how to *read*, take Donne—and of Donne this Satire" (the third, that on religion).

Donne's name must often recur in a discussion of Lord Herbert's verse, and not unfairly: a writer who follows a master so closely can be judged, at least in part, by the degree to which he comprehends what he follows. Every time, in this case, the disciple's effort betrays the failure of his comprehension. Take what is usually considered—with dubious justice—Lord Herbert's finest poem: the *Ode upon a Question Moved*. Behind that poem—not in its doctrine so much as its shape and *décor*—is undoubtedly *The Extasie*. Both poems begin with a pastoral setting. Herbert's is "innocent", in every sense: flat in its epithets, single in meaning:

> *The well accorded Birds did sing*
> *Their hymns unto the pleasant time,*
> *And in a sweet consorted chime*
> *Did welcom in the chearful Spring.*

Donne's setting conspires with the content: the sexual conceits establish at once an ironic, anticipating duplicity:

> *Where, like a pillow on a bed,*
> *A Pregnant banke swel'd up, to rest*
> *The violets reclining head,*
> *Sat we two, one anothers best.*

171

The difference is similar in the stanzas which render the lovers'
union. Herbert turns into vague naiveté—

> *While over eithers compass'd waste*
> *Their folded arms were so compos'd,*
> *As if in straitest bonds inclos'd,*
> *They suffer'd for joys they did taste*

—Donne's lightning interplay of solemn intensity and witty
suggestiveness:

> *Our hands were firmely cimented*
> *With a fast balme, which thence did spring,*
> *Our eye-beames twisted, and did thred*
> *Our eyes, upon one double string;*
> *So to'entergraft our hands, as yet*
> *Was all the meanes to make us one,*
> *And pictures in our eyes to get*
> *Was all our propagation.*

Along these lines each poem proceeds to its end. Herbert's,
below the surface, beneath the metaphysical modishness, is a
straightforward piece of Platonic pastoral idealism, in essentials
quite at home in the world of Spenser, poles apart from the
troubling ambiguity of Donne.

Lord Herbert, then, would seem to fail when he writes in
the metaphysical manner; but in other manners (and he has
them) he is much more successful. This sonnet, for instance:

> *Thus ends my Love, but this doth grieve me most,*
> *That so it ends, but that ends too, this yet,*
> *Besides the Wishes, hopes and time I lost*
> *Troubles my mind awhile, that I am set*
> *Free, worse then deny'd: I can neither boast*
> *Choice nor success, as my Case is, nor get*
> *Pardon from my self, that I loved not*
> *A better Mistress, or her worse; this Debt*
> *Only's her due, still, that she be forgot*
> *Ere chang'd, lest I love none; this done, the taint*
> *Of foul Inconstancy is clear'd at least*
> *In me, there only rests but to unpaint*
> *Her form in my mind, that so dispossest*
> *It be a Temple, but without a Saint.*

That poem surely "comes off"; the jerkiness of rhythm is still present, but here it has taken on a taut compactness, well matching the suppressed passion and anger of the theme. What has set it free? The fact that this sonnet is hardly at all in the metaphysical style. It has no "learning", no variety of mood, little complexity of thought. It is much more in the early Elizabethan manner, the manner of the sonnetteers; with the addition of a good deal of smoothness, and the subtraction of a little subtlety, it might remind one of Drayton's "Since there's no help . . ."

If this sonnet looks back to the Elizabethans, Lord Herbert has several passages which seem to look forward—to the Restoration. And this is no paradox. When the men of the Restoration rejected the metaphysical way of writing (which meant also, though they may not have known it, the Shakespearean way), and passed on it that verdict of "quaintness" and "harshness" which was scarcely to be questioned for two hundred years, they were also reinstating the earlier Elizabethan manner, which the metaphysical style, and mature Shakespeare, had turned against: the directness and singleness, the smoothness and polish, of Spenser and Drayton and Daniel. For reasons not altogether the same, but not entirely dissimilar, they went the way which Milton had pointed to. Behind Milton lies Spenser; behind Waller, Fairfax: Dryden is the heir of both Milton and Waller. So if it is the case that Lord Herbert was a metaphysical only on the surface, only (to put it crudely) because his friends were, it is not surprising that we find in him some passages remarkably Drydenesque. For instance:

> Our life is but a dark and stormy night,
> To which sense yields a weak and glimmering light;
> While wandring Man thinks he discerneth all,
> By that which makes him but mistake and fall:
> He sees enough, who doth his darkness see;
> These are great lights, by which less dark'ned be.
> Shine then Sun brighter through my senses vail,
> A day-star of the light doth never fail;
> Show me that Goodness which compounds the strife
> 'Twixt a long sickness and a weary life.

It is hard to believe that Dryden did not have that in mind when he wrote the famous simile which opens *Religio Laici* ("Dim as the borrowed beams of moon and stars . . ."). That passage is solemn in tone; the following, conversational and discursive, shows the same Dryden-like manner, tuned to a lower key:

> *Praises should then like definitions be*
> *Round, neat, convertible, such as agree*
> *To persons so, that, were their names conceal'd,*
> *Must make them known as well as if reveal'd:*
> *Such as contain the kind and difference,*
> *And all the properties arising thence.*
> *All praises else, as more or less then due,*
> *Will prove, or strongly false, or weakly true.*

"Round, neat, convertible" seems as appropriate a phrase for that verse as "thus being quite abstract" was for Lord Herbert's metaphysical manner. A simple and undramatic rhythm, a paucity and conventionality in the images, a lecturing manner, abstract and expository, an antithetical turn of phrase approaching the epigrammatic ("or strongly false or weakly true"): all the elements of "correctness" and "harmony", as the Restoration understood them, are here already. And surely Lord Herbert is incomparably more successful here, when he is anticipating Dryden, than he was when following Donne. This is good verse: not great but not despicable. Its "criticism of life"—and this too is a Restoration characteristic, reminding one of Dryden again—has no profundity, but it does have a clear, limited honesty. " 'Twixt a long sickness and a weary life" has something of that weight and tautness which Augustans like Pope and Johnson could give to a commonplace.

The conclusion seems to be, then, that Lord Herbert's bent was not, by nature, that of a metaphysical poet. He wrote the greater part of his verse in the metaphysical manner because that was the prevailing mode in his time and circle. But he lacked the essential qualities: the dramatic rhythm, the power to flood thought with passion which derives from the nearness of thinking to feeling, and the faculty of expressing abstractions in concrete and physical terms. His positive qualities were those of the Restoration, the embryonic Augustan. This conclusion, arrived at through an analysis of his poetry, is confirmed if we look at his other manifestations: his philosophy and his character.

As a philosopher, Lord Herbert has been long recognized as one of the founders—perhaps the principal source in England—of Deism and Natural Theology. What started him on philosophy, according to his own account, was his perception of the sad fact that Richard Baxter took note of: that the knowledge which theologians told us was essential to salvation was given to so few. But Herbert sees it in another spirit, he is more inclined to deny its reality, to blame it on the intransigent silliness of the orthodox, than to accept it in Baxter's way as the inscrutable will of God; and he draws from it a very different conclusion:

> Nothing ever troubled mee more then that a doctrine soe necessary as the knowledg of God and the true way to serve and worship him and the meanes to attaine everlasting Salvation should be soe variously delivered and taught in divers ages and Countreys and together urged in such perplext and difficult Termes . . . and after all this yet to finde it presented to me under such terrible menaces and threats, as if among the many Churches extant in the world I did not adhere to ye Right (which each said was theires), I could not justly hope for Salvation.[1]

From this impasse Herbert determined to attempt an escape; he set himself to investigate the religions and philosophies of mankind (Comparative Religion is beginning) and to see if from them he could deduce any "fundamentall Articles agreed upon by all". He found them, so he thought, and this theory of the Common Notions, as he calls them, is the core of his thinking, at least of that part of it still alive and interesting. These "Notions", he maintains, being held by all peoples and in all ages, make up the only religion that can be truly styled Catholic. There are five of them, and he lists them as follows:

1. There is a supreme God;
2. He ought to be worshipped;

[1] From a manuscript entitled *Religio Laici*, which may have been the first sketch for the Latin work of the same title published in 1645. The MS. was first printed by Mr. Herbert G. Wright in the *Modern Languages Review* for July 1933.

3. Virtue and piety are the principal parts of His worship;
4. We must repent of our sins and abjure them;
5. There are rewards and punishments for good and evil, in this life and a life to come.

Beyond these notions, it seems, Herbert is not prepared to be dogmatic.   In spirit if not in method—his method is often scholastic—he seems much more of the eighteenth century than the seventeenth: in the words of the modern editor and translator of Herbert's principal philosophical treatise, *De Veritate*:

> In spite of its traditional modes of thought *De Veritate* breathes the modern air. Herbert's approach to his investigation of truth is modern in spirit. He rejects all authority and tradition and applies himself to an independent examination of the facts as he finds them. . . . *De Veritate* is the prologue to two momentous courses of speculation.   It initiates in England the development of Natural Theology, and it anticipates the great sequence of rationalism in continental philosophy inaugurated by Descartes.   More definitely it forestalls by one hundred and forty years the doctrines put forward by the founder of the Scottish philosophy of common sense.[1]

Herbert has the theological optimism of eighteenth century deism; the doctrine of Original Sin can have meant nothing to him, he is convinced of man's innate capacity to find his own salvation: ". . . it having pleased God soe to implant the Love of Goodnes and Truth in the Soule that hee hath made them a part of Common Reason and Conspicuous by their owne Light."[2] "By their owne Light" brings one near to the "Spirit" of the Puritans; but the affinity, on this point, is limited, for Herbert has little real feeling for the Church and even less, perhaps, for the Bible. For both he admits to a certain "feeling"; he had been, as he says, brought up and instructed by them "even from [his] Infancy". He had been brought up, in fact (his father having died when he was a child), by the mother to whose orthodox piety Donne testifies and whose care of her eldest son went to the possibly ill-judged lengths that Walton describes:

[1] Meyrick H. Carré: introduction to his edition and translation of *De Veritate* (University of Bristol, 1937).
[2] *Religio Laici* MS.: op. cit.

. . . and having entered Edward into Queen's College, and
provided him a fit tutor, she commended him to his care;
yet she continued there with him, and still kept him in a
moderate awe of herself, and so much under her own eye,
as to see and converse with him daily: but she managed this
power over him without any such rigid sourness, as might
make her company a torment to her child; but with such a
sweetness and compliance with the recreations and pleasures
of youth, as did incline him willingly to spend much of his
time in the company of his dear and careful mother . . .

But whatever relics of emotional appeal his mother's care may
have preserved in him for the faith she taught him, Lord
Herbert's mind, when it turns to religion, is thoroughly enfran-
chised. For Church tradition his respect is lukewarm, and
colder still for theological controversy. The latter he despises in
the Augustan manner, as a waste of time, a war of meaningless
words; he resolved, he tells us in the MS. previously cited,
"for the disputes and Controversies of learned men to lay them
aside untill they were agreed among themselves": and the tone
makes it pretty clear that in his opinion that time will never
come. The contrast is striking with the Falklands and Donnes,
for whom theology was so much more than a subject one could
drop if it bored one. On the Bible Lord Herbert is thoroughly
critical, though his own temerity alarms him a trifle: "the
Bible," he suggests in *De Veritate*, "may indeed be the work of a
number of writers whose order has been settled in a remarkable
way by a later age." And on miracles especially his rationalism
takes on an aggressive and anti-clerical tone. Men are always
inclined, he argues, "to entertaine such beleifes as turne to their
Benefitte." All so-called miracles may not have been miraculous: "besides, things may bee done by naturall meanes which
some men may thinke miraculous." And the priests, as everyone knows, are always liable to "deceive and abuse the people".[1]
He is even—most remarkably for the age he lived in—tolerant
and sensible on the subject of atheists. Such men exist, he says,
in *De Veritate*, because they have been shocked by false notions
of God: "because they have noticed that some people apply

[1] The three comments on miracles are all from the *Religio Laici*
MS.

false and shocking attributes to God, they have preferred not to believe in God than to believe in a God of such a character."

There are English poets to whom these opinions—or some of them—would have been congenial: not Donne or George Herbert or Vaughan, but Marlowe and Milton and Dryden. Marlowe on miracles (as reported by Kyd) brings forward exactly Lord Herbert's second argument: "things esteemed to be donn by devine power might have as well been don by observation of men." Marlowe, like Herbert, has read the Bible with a critical eye (Baines is here the reporter): ". . . he saith likewise that he hath quoted a number of Contrarieties oute of the Scripture which he hath given to some great men who in Convenient time shalbe named." Milton, of course, is not to be found in this galley of sceptics; but Lord Herbert is with him in a withering rejection of medieval scholasticism. What Milton thought of that we have seen: Lord Herbert will supply an equally impressive collection of denunciations. "My Time was better imployd soe then in the inexplicable subtilityes of the schooles." "The influence of the ancient sects throughout the world will be destroyed as effectively as the power of the Schools in our own day." "There is hardly any type of argument in which the Schools cannot throw dust in the eyes of their disciples by their clever tricks."[1] And as for Dryden, there is not only the poetic derivation, suggested above, in *Religio Laici*; the title itself, there seems little doubt, derives from Herbert, and the account it gives of the deist's position (lines 42-61) is an accurate statement of the Common Notions. Dryden, of course, rejects them—his *Religio Laici* is an Anglican apology—but the spirit of Dryden's theology, with its calmness, tepidity, and fundamental alienation from tradition, even while affirming the necessity for it, is far nearer to Herbert's deism than it is, say, to the Anglicanism of Donne: far nearer, too, in the kind of poetry it nourished.

Thus, in philosophy, there is no doubt of Lord Herbert's position. He belongs not to that part of the seventeenth century which was still deeply medieval, the part which nourished the Shakespearean moment, and which virtually died without issue of any sort till Coleridge and the Oxford Movement revived at

[1] *Religio Laici* MS.; *De Veritate*; ibid.

least its theological aspect, but to that other part of the age, which "carried over" to the following century. It is here that a certain link with the Puritans can be seen, anathema though most of Herbert's opinions would have been to them,[1] and most of theirs to him. They meet in their common insistence, however divergent the motives and conclusions, on the right of private judgment; they meet also in their rejection of the medieval past.

Finally, there is Lord Herbert's personal character. For this, of course, his autobiography is the source. That book, in spite of many passages which are undeniably, if unintentionally, amusing, seems at last a tedious and unpleasing work. It is tedious because Lord Herbert has curious ideas of what will interest others in himself. He believed, for his own part, that his autobiography revealed his essential self: "I have thought fit," he declares, "to relate to my posterity those passages of my life which I conceive may best declare me." Yet what it "declares" is not, quite clearly, what its author can possibly have intended. What emerges is a naïve and ineffectual braggart. The poet and philosopher, the friend of Selden and Jonson and Donne, he leaves untouched, to expatiate at length on his duels (the great majority of which got no further than windy challenging), his diplomatic negotiations, and his triumphs as an amateur doctor. And the book is unpleasant not only because the revealed personality is itself unpleasant, but because one never feels confident that the personality is being wholly and honestly presented. Effect and intention are too far apart. This reaction, by the way, is not only that of a modern reader; Horace Walpole, the autobiography's first publisher, describes how he read the MS. to Gray and Lady Waldegrave and how the company "could not get on for laughing and screaming". "Laughing and screaming" were most certainly not the effects that the author would have desired. The book never yields that sense of a self-knowing being, sure of the terms on which he will present himself, which informs such nearly contemporary documents as the *Religio Medici* or *Grace Abounding* or Baxter's autobiography. The raw materials, so to speak, of a real human being—pride and vanity, courage and bellicosity and so forth—

[1] They are in fact denounced by Baxter, in *More Reasons for the Christian Religion*.

are there; but they never come together to form a whole. And it is not just a lack of literary ability that gives this impression; the fact is that Lord Herbert was *not* a "whole", not an integrated personality. He was deeply self-divided; the claims of the mind and of worldly ambition fought within him: neither triumphed, nor did they harmonize. "I ever loved my book," he claims for himself, "and a private life, more than any busy preferments"; but in fact the "busy preferments" never lost their power to attract him. His real political career ended when, in 1624 (he was then 41), James I summarily dismissed him from the post of Ambassador to France; but for all that the chance was not taken of devoting himself entirely to the "book" and the "private life". He became, instead, for the rest of his life, that common and disagreeable figure of the seventeenth century scene: the disgruntled courtier, the Disappointed Man, for ever petitioning and for ever rebuffed. It led him at last to his strange behaviour in the Civil War, when (less out of real conviction, it would seem, than simply from pique and weariness) he abandoned the solid royalism of all his family and all his friends, surrendered Montgomery Castle (the family seat—that "most romancy seate", as Aubrey calls it) to the forces of the Parliament, and died with the title round his neck of "the treacherous Lord Herbert". "Treacherous" we may discount; equivocal he certainly was. One can see the elements that must have made his royalism less certain than that of his family (the rest of whom suffered severely for their adherence to the King); the rationalist mind, deprived of any deep feeling for the Church-State nexus, could never draw its loyalty from the deepest sources. And once those sources were cut off, once Charles's cause appeared merely as one political case against another, it could not but seem very dubious. As it *did* seem to Falkland: but Falkland's religion held his allegiance steady—that, and his possession of an instinctive *pietas* which a rationalist can hardly feel. Intellectually, Lord Herbert's decision needs no defending. But being what he was and had been—member of a family at the very centre of the monarchist and hierarchical world, courtier and servant of the King—the decision was one of those that can be taken only by the sacrifice of all the deeper elements of a man's being; it was like the decision, in modern terms, to "collaborate". He was forced into a false position—a position of desperate loneliness, swimming against the stream of his kindred and *milieu*: the sort of position that only a character of quite exceptional strength and integrity could sustain without being twisted. His political eccentricity—for such it was, given that he was a Herbert—can be seen as the logical end of his difference from the mind and character which nourished the Shakespearean moment. His rationalism; his poetry, fundamentally if not superficially against the metaphysical manner; the equivocal unreliability of his character: all fall into place.

His own family will give us the contrast, in the person of his younger brother. George Herbert had many qualities in common with his elder. He had, as Walton tells us, the intense family pride and personal vanity:

> If during this time he expressed any error, it was, that he kept himself too much retired, and at too great a distance with all his inferiors; and his clothes seemed to prove, that he put too great a value on his parts and parentage.

He had also, as witnessed again by Walton and of course his own poems, the ambition for courtly success:

> . . . Hoping that as his predecessors, so he might in time attain the place of a secretary of State. . . . This, and the love of a court-conversation, mixed with a laudable ambition to be something more than he then was, drew him often from Cambridge, to attend the King.

He had—this time Lord Herbert is the witness—a proneness to anger:

> He was not exempt from passion and choler, being infirmities to which all our race is subject, but that excepted, without reproach in his actions

—a failing which Lord Herbert confesses to have been one of his own ("in mine own nature I was ever choleric and hasty"). And to these qualities we may add, on the strength of the magnificent stanza in *The Pearl*, the quality of sensuality.[1]

---

[1] *I know the wayes of Pleasure, the sweet strains,*
The lullings and the relishes of it;
The propositions of hot bloud and brains;
What mirth and musick mean; what love and wit
Have done these twentie hundred yeares, and more:

Between the two brothers there were thus close resemblances in particular qualities. But the difference in the sums—the difference between what the two men made of their qualities—is of course enormous. George Herbert, by some power which his brother lacked, was enabled to sublimate and canalize his qualities, including his failings, to a single and a noble end. And this is a power which he shared with the best spirits of the age. This is what gives to Shakespeare and Donne, as well as to George Herbert himself, the ability to concentrate in one poem, or one image, a host of disparate things. There *is* a connection —there must be, however hard to analyse or prove—between integrity of character and integrity of writing; the best men of the Jacobean and Caroline generations, in their lives no less than in their writings, possessed this power which could turn their pride into a devotion to the highest standards, their personal vanity into a fine fastidiousness of sensibility, their hot and hasty tempers into a lively alertness, and their sensuality into a powerful and delicate sensuousness. The original qualities are not lost; they were simply transformed: hence the art of a purely devotional poet, such as George Herbert, is as sensuous and lively ("my senses *live,*" in the words of *The Pearl*) as the love-poetry of Carew or Donne. Lord Herbert's poetry, as we have seen, is neither sensuous nor lively; *he* could not transform his personal qualities, he could only suppress them. The whole of his self is not there.

Lord Herbert, for his time and surroundings, was an oddity. The rationalist spirit which in part he represents did not become dominant till after the Restoration, just as the Puritan spirit, strong and growing in the early years of the century, did not become dominant till the Civil War and the Commonwealth. But Lord Herbert's poetic failure in the metaphysical mode anticipates what was to be the general course of English poetry; when a critical, anti-traditional, cool and level-headed mentality becomes the master and the ideal, then the metaphysical, the Shakespearean manner loses the climate in which it can grow.

I know the projects of unbridled store :
My stuffe is flesh, not brasse ; my senses live,
And grumble oft, that they have more in me
Than he that curbs them, being but one to five :
Yet I love thee.

And this mentality, after the Restoration—perhaps even earlier —spreads wider than the professedly anti-ecclesiastical unbelievers like Lord Herbert himself: they remained, then as always, a small minority. The qualities of mind, which are more important in determining poetry than mere "opinions"— qualities such as indifference to tradition, conviction of progress, dislike or suspicion of mysticism and "enthusiasm", common sense and critical irony—these spread from the professed unbelievers to believers like Cowley and Dryden. These two poets will confirm the link between failure in the metaphysical mode on the one hand and this sort of mind on the other—a link which might seem rather arbitrarily maintained if it depended on one case alone. What happens is that those poets of the time whose minds are of the commonsensical cool-headed sort either fail to achieve the authentic metaphysical manner or else abandon it when they find their true bents. Cowley is an example of the former, Dryden of the latter. For Cowley, as the *Ode to the Royal Society* proves, medieval scholasticism was what it was for Lord Herbert, a meaningless war of words. When one touches his mind at any point, one finds it to be the mind of an Augustan Whig, tepid, sensible, cheerful and progressive. He can stand at the head, for example, of a miniature anthology of utterances on that most Augustan of convictions, the necessity for Good Humour. If Cowley begins it—

> The truth is, for a man to write well it is necessary to be in good humor.

—Halifax and Shaftesbury continue it—

> *Religion* is a chearful thing, so far from being always at *Cuffs* with Good Humour, that it is inseparably united to it.
>
> Good Humour is not only the best Security against *Enthusiasm*, but the best Foundation of *Piety* and true *Religion*.

—and Addison, formulator of Augustan Whiggery as the others were its prophets, gives the doctrine its final seal:

> The man who lives under an habitual sense of the Divine Presence keeps up a perpetual cheerfulness of temper.[1]

[1] The quotations come from Cowley's Preface to his *Poems*, 1656;

With this in mind, it is not surprising that Cowley's verse shows what Lord Herbert's shows—in a very different way, for he was a far more expert and agreeable writer: but he too has the metaphysical manner without the metaphysical soul. His love-poetry, for example, is always tending to abandon the metaphysical intensity in favour of a graceful complimentary neatness, at once evocative of the Augustan manner:

> *How would those learned trees have followed you?*
> *You would have drawn* them, *and their* Poet *too* . . .

For Dryden's verse, the process is the same as for Milton's; it begins with metaphysical touches, it drops them with maturity and self-knowledge. The celebrated badness of his juvenile conceit on the pustules of Lord Hastings' smallpox—

> *Blisters with pride swell'd, which th'row 's flesh did sprout,*
> *Like Rose-buds, stuck i' the Lilly-skin about.*
> *Each little Pimple had a Tear in it,*
> *To wail the fault its rising did commit* . . .

is of course incomparably worse than the pleasantly comic clumsiness of Milton's conceit in the *Nativity Hymn*—

> *So when the Sun in bed,*
> *Curtain'd with cloudy red,*
> *Pillows his chin upon an Orient wave* . . .

but both show a radical disharmony between the style and its user. Thus the man of commonsense and the Puritan (when he turns to poetry) agree in one thing: the metaphysical style is rejected by both. And inasmuch as these two types were the parents of the future, that style was doomed.

Halifax's *Advice to a Daughter*; Shaftesbury's *Letter concerning Enthusiasm*; and the *Spectator*, No. 93.

Chapter 7

THE CIVIL WAR, AND THE SPLIT IN THE AGE

WHAT really destroyed the society of the Shakespearean moment, made it impossible that such a society should return, and therefore ensured that English poetry should not go the way of Shakespeare and Donne, was the great series of events, covering some twenty years, which split the seventeenth century into two, and which, for convenience, one may call the Civil War. The society was not "destroyed" physically, or even, on the surface, politically, since the Commonwealth came to an end. The destruction occurred at a deeper level and therefore one more important for poetry. What became impossible was to think and feel about human beings as Donne and Shakespeare did and to see that way of thinking and feeling as embodied, however imperfectly, in actual and contemporary society. One of the most moving passages in Clarendon's *History of the Great Rebellion* is that in the first book, in which he laments with bitter nostalgia the lost *douceur de vivre* which England had enjoyed before the war: a peace, prosperity, and happiness, so he claims, such as could scarcely be paralleled in history and which made the country the envy of all other lands. All that was wrong was that the enjoyers of this blessedness were not aware of it. That passage, if read purely on a political level, seems nothing much more than the sighings of a defeated reactionary, and there is something almost comic in the puzzled regret with which Clarendon has to admit the existence of a whole army of ungrateful serpents in this earthly paradise; but to read it on such a level alone is to misunderstand it, misunderstand Clarendon, and misunderstand the whole cast of mind which he stands for. On other levels, he was perfectly right. Whether or not the society he lamented involved more injustice than that which took its place, whether or not his cause was that of reaction and the Parliament's that of progress, something irreplaceable (as events proved) *was* destroyed, and the eventual "victory" of the royal cause did nothing at all to replace it.

What was destroyed was that nexus of Church and State, spiritual and political, which the earlier chapters of this book have described. The Restoration restored nothing but a simulacrum of it, as it did of all other things. Royalty returned, but never again would men feel for it as they had before the deluge: one was "loyal" to Charles II—aggressively, heartily, alcoholically loyal—but nobody felt for him the mystical reverence that had been felt for his father and grandfather.[1] The Court and courtiers returned, and so did poets to flatter them; but nobility and magnificence would never be what they had been to Shakespeare and Donne. The Bishops returned, and the Deans, and the country parsons—but no more Lancelot Andrewes, no more John Donnes, and no more George Herberts.

This is rather to anticipate; the point for us now is that the split of the Civil War went far wider and deeper than warfare and politics. Perhaps it was the first of ideological wars, certainly for England, unless one counts such Roman Catholic rebellions as the prayer-book rising of 1549 and the Pilgrimage of Grace thirteen years earlier. But in them the cause fought for was purely religious—politics did not enter their ideology, however mixed the actual motives—and in them propaganda of the modern sort, an organized warfare of spoken and printed ideas, had scarcely made its appearance. In the Civil War it did appear, to no small effect. And this contemporaries took note of; it was felt at the time that this was a war of the mind at least as much as of the sword, and therefore—for imaginative writers—as something which invaded their territory, queered their pitch, and ended their freedom from "engagement". Two contemporaries may be quoted who saw this, one from each side. The poem which Marvell, the Commonwealth-man, wrote for Lovelace's *Lucasta*, published in the year of the King's execution, laments what the wars have done to freedom and civilized taste:

[1] The typical tone of Restoration loyalty is a cheery back-slapping style, which would have been quite impossible before the Civil War. And the difference is not to be explained by the patent fact that Charles II was somewhat less austere than his father. James I was not, as an individual, inspiring or glamorous; but the awe which before the Civil War could be felt for the King had nothing to do with the particular monarch's personality.

> *Our times are much degenerate from those*
> *Which your sweet Muse, which your fair Fortune chose,*
> *And as complexions alter with the Climes*
> *Our wits have drawne th' infection of the times.*
> *That candid age no other way could tell*
> *To be ingenious, but by speaking well . . .*
> *These vertues now are banisht out of Towne,*
> *Our Civill Warres have lost the Civicke Crowne.*

And Cowley, the Royalist, in the preface to his volume of poems published seven years later (1656), complains of the infection of propaganda, the obligation imposed on writers to take sides:

> Now . . . in all *Civil Dissensions*, when they break into open hostilities, the *War* of the *Pen* is allowed to accompany that of the *Sword*, and every one is in a manner obliged with his *Tongue*, as well as *Hand*, to serve and assist the side which he engages in . . .

Of which situation, he argues, the result is a parlous state of affairs for poets and poetry:

> And if in quiet times they [*sc.* poets] meet with so small encouragement, what are they to expect in rough and troubled ones? if *Wit* be such a *Plant*, that it scarce receives heat enough to preserve it alive even in the Summer of our cold *Clymate*, how can it choose but wither in a long and a sharp *winter*? a warlike, various, and a tragical age is best to *write of*, but worst to *write in*.

The whole business wears quite a modern air—to be *"engagé"* or free, to collaborate or not to collaborate: for Cowley himself, in this preface, wrote the unfortunate passage in which he says, in effect, that since the Parliament has won its war, there is really no point any longer in keeping up a royalist intransigence—a passage which earned him many frowns and sneers, and possibly some more solid disadvantages, after the Restoration. He was, in fact, in exactly the position of those French intellectuals in 1945 who were suspected of having "collaborated"; his biographer, Bishop Sprat, has to shuffle with great uneasiness to defend him from that charge.

The Civil War, then, forced writers to "take sides". It did this more extensively and harmfully than simply by enlisting them as propagandists. It has already been suggested that the imaginations of the Elizabethans anticipated the reality of civil war which their grandchildren suffered; what is more, the ideological shape which the war took, and in particular its two central human figures, Cromwell and the King, made realities, and gave to those realities enormous emotional force, out of two of the most vital imaginative and dramatic *personæ* of the age. Cromwell embodied the military hero, the self-made conquering usurper; Charles the legitimate anointed monarch, the King by the Grace of God. These two figures are of enormous importance to Elizabethan and Jacobean drama; the struggle between them makes the backbone of Marlowe's *Tamburlaine*, of Shakespeare's English histories, and of *Macbeth*. The former stood for and satisfied the age's craving for individualist self-expression, for the great man who could revolt against the controls of orthodoxy, and defeat them; the latter was the central symbol of the other part of the age's mind, its deep reverence for order and tradition.

How completely Cromwell fulfilled the role of self-made hero, already worked out for him in the drama, will be seen in a moment; as for Charles, it is clear that his death became for the Royalists an event which concentrated all those feelings for Church-and-State-as-one which we have found to be dominant in the Shakespearean moment and its society. The "Martyr King" was not merely a figure of speech, as it is nowadays for all but a few determined eccentrics who confuse what they would like to feel with what they do feel; on the figure of Charles was focussed all that desire to *have* "martyrs" and "saints", and to celebrate them according to the Catholic pattern, which existed, in spite of Protestant qualms, in Shakespeare and Donne. The intensive cult of "relics" of the executed King is one proof of it; another is the drawing of parallels—sometimes hinted, sometimes explicit—between Charles's fate and that of Christ. Both friends and enemies made of him a religious symbol; against the Puritans' Man of Blood, the royalists made him a Man of Sorrows. This comparison, which to us may seem blasphemous, was quite clearly in Charles's own mind: when Bishop Juxon, on the morning of the execution, read the Lesson for the day, the 27th chapter of St. Matthew, "which relateth the Passion of our blessed Saviour", Charles inquired if he had picked out that chapter on purpose, as "being so applicable to his present condition". And in *Eikon Basilike* the parallel is often suggested—in the prayer in the 26th chapter:

> O let not my blood be upon them and their children, whom the fraud and faction of some, not the malice of all, have excited to *crucify* me

and in the verses printed at the end of the book:

> *With such a bloody method and behaviour,*
> *Their ancestors did crucify our Saviour.*[1]

Such an identification, between the deposed and martyred King-by-divine-Grace and the divine victim himself, was not in the least a new creation, invented for the special benefit of Charles; it was the natural outcome of a whole tradition, exactly anticipated in the words of Shakespeare's Richard II, speaking to the men who had deposed, and were to murder, him:

> *Nay, all of you, that stand and looke upon me,*
> *Whil'st that my wretchednesse doth bait my selfe,*
> *Though some of you, with* Pilate, *wash your hands,*
> *Showing an outward pittie: yet you* Pilates
> *Have here deliver'd me to my sowre Crosse,*
> *And Water cannot wash away your sinne.*
>
> (IV, 1)

By such a particular point as this can be justified the assertion that the dramatists anticipated in imagination what the later generation would experience, and by this anticipation helped to set the patterns of thought and emotion which determined how that generation would react to its experience. The same is true—exactly the same—if we look at the other great figure, both symbolic and real: Cromwell, the usurping hero.

For the type he came to fulfil, Marlowe's *Tamburlaine* is the starting-point in dramatic poetry: the perfect expression, in its clear outline and brilliant colouring, of the dream of the conqueror. But Tamburlaine the hero is a far more subtle, more

---

[1] *Eikon Basilike*, it seems conclusively established by now, was not Charles's own work: but the argument is not affected. It hit to a hair's-breadth—as its huge success demonstrated—what the royalists wanted to feel.

intelligent creation than his Technicolor trappings may suggest;
he is built on ideas, precise and intellectual. He is, above all,
the self-made man, the climber from obscurity to greatness.
"But tell me, Maddam," he asks of the captured Zenocrate,
"is your grace betroth'd?" "I am (my Lord)," she answers,
"for so you do import"; and he replies

> I am a Lord, for so my deeds shall proove,
> And yet a shepheard by my Parentage.

This self-made man is above Fate and Fortune; the powers that
control lesser men are controlled by him:

> I hold the Fates bound fast in yron chaines,
> And with my hand turne Fortunes wheele about.[1]

Nature too joins in to help him:

> Nature doth strive with Fortune and his stars
> To make him famous in accomplisht woorth.

And in Menaphon's description of the hero—a description
which seems to suggest a superhuman robot rather than a man
—the metaphor hints that the planets themselves, the whole
divine order, are moving at his command and for his advance-
ment:

> . . . Wherein by curious soveraintie of Art,
> Are fixt his piercing instruments of sight:

[1] Cf. *Jew of Malta*, at the end of which the Governor of Malta
(the legitimate ruler, who has defeated the self-made usurper of that
play, Barabas) explicitly rejects the forces that Tamburlaine relies
on, and appeals instead to God:

> So march away, and let due praise be given
> Neither to Fate nor Fortune, but to Heaven.

This view of the conqueror as especially "fortunate" descends from
the Romans. That Pompey was *felix* is one of the grounds advanced
by Cicero (*Pro Lege Manilia*) in support of his appointment to high
command. *Felix* meant "favoured by fortune", but it implied also
that such a condition was more than just a chance; it was a personal
quality, and it was one of the qualifications for being a hero. So
(in *Antony and Cleopatra*) Antony reluctantly endorses, as valid
evidence against himself, so to speak, the soothsayer's observation
that Octavius always defeats him at games of chance.

> *Whose fiery cyrcles beare encompassed*
> *A heaven of heavenly bodies in their Sphaeres:*
> *That guides his steps and actions to the throne,*
> *Where honor sits invested royally.*

The conqueror has, for his special function, that of the usurper, the destroyer of legitimacy, of those who rule by divine right and by the traditional sanctions and loyalties. In the comic cowardice of Mycetes, the King of Persia—

> *Away, I am the King: go, touch me not.*
> *Thou breakst the law of Armes unlesse thou kneele,*
> *And cry me mercie, noble King*

—it is the untouchability of divine right (what Claudius in *Hamlet* appeals to) that is ridiculed, and also the feudal obligation of loyalty ("the law of Armes"). So, too, when Cosroe, now king himself, learns that Tamburlaine has turned against him, he bases his defiance of the upstart on "love of honor and defence of right", and when he too has met with defeat, he simply cannot understand, this feeble representative of the old order, the new spirit of individualist rebellion: "the *strangest* men", he cries in puzzled despair—

> *The strangest men that ever nature made,*
> *I know not how to take their tyrannies.*

From enemy of legitimate ruler to enemy of orthodox religion was a short and inevitable step. And Tamburlaine is both. The Emperor Bajazeth, next victim on the hero's list, as he and his future conqueror are indulging in the flyting that precedes the battle, appeals to his State religion:

> By Mahomet, *my Kinsmans sepulcher,*
> *And by the holy* Alcaron *I sweare . . .*

but Tamburlaine answer with an appeal to his own native strength:

> *By this my sword that conquer'd* Persea . . .

When the battle has been fought, and Bajazeth is a prisoner, he is still appealing, and still in vain, to the priests of his orthodoxy, invoking their powers of magic:

Ye holy Priests of heavenly Mahomet,
That sacrificing slice and cut your flesh,
Staining his Altars with your purple blood:
Make heaven to frowne and every fixed starre
To sucke up poison from the moorish Fens,
And poure it in this glorious Tyrants throat.

And now Tamburlaine answers with a confident assertion (it is not a prayer, and it is not in vain) that a God who is higher than mere "religions", a sort of Stoic or deist First Cause, is his protector and favourer:

The chiefest God first moover of that Sphaere,
Enchac'd with thousands ever shining lamps,
Will sooner burne the glorious frame of Heaven,
Then it should so conspire my overthrow.

In the key of mockery, the same point is made through the jeers of Tamburlaine's followers:

—*Doost thou think that* Mahomet *will suffer this?*
—*Tis like he wil, when he cannot let it.*

The religion, in fact, is discredited because its anointed representative is defeated and humbled. "No king, no bishop": Marlowe is endorsing King James's dictum; but Marlowe is all for it.

Tamburlaine's "morality"—for he has one, he is not just a conqueror for the sake of conquering—is like his God, more Roman than modern. "Virtue" and "worth" are words he is always invoking; and the sense of his use of the former is far closer to the Latin *virtus* (manly accomplishment) than it is to moral "goodness". He defeats the legitimate Emperor, becoming Emperor himself, but still (though Zenocrate hopefully talks of his "*sacred* person" and begs him to give up his soldiering) he regards himself as dedicated to arms, he is still the champion of individualism and rejects the convention of primogeniture, saying to his youngest son

If thou exceed thy elder Brothers worth,
And shine in compleat vertue more than they,
Thou shalt be king before them, and thy seed
Shall issue crowned from their mothers wombe.

192

So, in the lines that end his most famous tirade—

> *. . . Shal give the world to note for all my byrth,*
> *That Vertue solely is the sum of glorie,*
> *And fashions men with true nobility*

—the context makes it painfully clear that "vertue" does not mean goodness; for the speech is sandwiched between the brutal killing of the virgins sent to beg peace for Damascus ("what, have your horsmen shewen the virgins Death?") and the mocking of Bajazeth in his cage.

Tamburlaine, in fact, is something of a Whiggish hero, and the Marlowe who created him[1] is almost a proto-Whig; sceptical of organized religion, contemptuous of traditional loyalties, advocate of *la carrière ouverte aux talents*. The line he began continues through the century; and when it encountered the person of Cromwell, it found at once that to praise the real hero the same terms were called for as had served for the fictional. Marlowe is to Tamburlaine as Milton is to Cromwell. Just as Tamburlaine had claimed to be in command of Fortune—

> *And with my hand turne Fortunes wheele about*

so Milton claims for Cromwell, that he

> *on the neck of crowned Fortune proud*

has "rear'd God's Trophies". Marvell has the same in the *Horatian Ode:* "the war's and Fortune's son." Cowley echoes Marvell: "this son of Fortune"; Dryden and Bishop Sprat, that dexterous pair of turncoats, complete the chorus. "For he was great," says Dryden, "ere Fortune made him so"; and the Bishop sings in tune:

> *Though Fortune did hang on thy Sword,*
> *And did obey thy mighty Word,*
> *Though Fortune, for thy side and thee,*
> *Forgot her lov'd Inconstancy . . .*[2]

---

[1] But not the Marlowe of *Faustus* and *Edward II*, who is far more critical, more traditional, and—possibly—more Christian.

[2] Milton: Sonnet on the Lord Protector; Cowley: Discourse by way of vision concerning the government of Oliver Cromwell;

They are, indeed, remarkably unanimous, the contemporary celebrators of the Lord Protector, whatever their judgments on his doings. They unite in putting, at the head of their accounts of him, his rise from obscurity to greatness ("who, from a Scythian Shephearde, by his rare and woonderfull Conquests, became a most puissant and mightye Monarque" is how the title-page of *Tamburlaine*—first edition of Part I—expresses it). Marvell's English verse in the *Horatian Ode*—

> *Who from his* private *gardens, where*
> *He liv'd* reserved *and austere*

—and Clarendon's English prose in the *History* (Book XV)—

> . . . who from a *private* and obscure birth, (though of a good family), without interest of estate, alliance, or friendships, could raise himself to such a height . . . yet as he grew into place and authority, his parts seemed to be renewed, as if he had had *concealed* faculties till he had occasion to use them

run parallel with Milton's Latin in the *Defensio Secunda*—

> Is matura iam atque firmata aetate, quam et *privatus* traduxit, nulla re magis quam religionis cultu purioris, et integritate vitae cognitus, domi *in occulto* creverat, et ad summa quaeque tempora fiduciam Deo fretam et ingentem animum *tacito* pectore aluerat.[1]

Dryden: Heroick Stanzas on the death of the Lord Protector; Sprat: To the happy memory of the late Lord Protector.

[1] To these could be added Waller (Panegyric to my Lord Protector):

> *Oft have we wonder'd, how you* hid *in peace*
> *A mind proportion'd to such things as these*

and Bishop Sprat (op. cit.):

> *So whilst but* private *Walls did know*
> *What we to such a mighty Mind should owe,*
>   *Then the same Vertues did appear,*
>   *Though in a less and more contracted Sphere,*
> *As full, though not as large, as since they were.*

The standpoints and conclusions of these three witnesses are entirely different. Clarendon, the royalist, condemns; Milton, the Puritan, approves; Marvell, the quasi-Puritan humanist, is balanced. Their agreement is all the more striking.

Tamburlaine, we have seen, was above all the destroyer of old-established things. And so was Cromwell, in the eyes of his contemporaries. Marvell's brief and pregnant phrases—

> *Could by industrious valour climb*
> *To ruin the great work of Time,*
> *And cast the Kingdoms old*
> *Into another mould*

—are echoed in Cowley's prose:

What can be more extraordinary than that a person of mean birth, no fortune, no eminent qualities of body . . . should have the courage to attempt, and the happiness to succeed in, so improbable a design, as the destruction of one of the most ancient and most solidly founded monarchies upon the earth?[1]

And just as Tamburlaine tells his Zenocrate that no success, no assumption of "sacred" legitimacy, will induce him to cease from his conquering career, so Clarendon reaches, with explicit condemnation, the conclusion that Marvell arrives at with judgment reserved:

They who enter upon unwarrantable enterprises, must pursue many unwarrantable ways to preserve themselves from the penalty of the first guilt.[2]

> *The same arts that did gain*
> *A power, must it maintain.*

The Wallers, Drydens, and Bishop Sprats need not greatly concern us; they were time-servers, from whom obsequious

---

[1] This is spoken not by Cowley *in propria persona*, but by the "devil" with whom he debates in the *Discourse by way of Vision*. But since it is a comment on the extraordinary nature of Cromwell's achievement, not a moral judgment on it, we may conclude that on this point Cowley and his devil are at one.

[2] *History*, Book X. The comment is made *à propos* of Cromwell.

panegyric could always be expected for whatever, and who-
ever, occupied the seats of the mighty. It is only in Marlowe
and Milton that uncompromising approval of the conquering
usurper is completely sincere; for both of them were, if not
fanatics, at least revolutionaries, men with very strongly-held
and clear-cut opinions, which made it difficult for Marlowe,
impossible for Milton, to do any sort of sympathetic justice to
the other side. But there was also another way of looking at the
usurping hero, a way different from both hired adulation and
revolutionary fervour: the balanced, half-critical and half-
admiring way, which is seen supremely in Shakespeare and in
Marvell's *Horatian Ode*, the characteristically "double-faced"
way of the mature Shakespearean and metaphysical manner. It
sees and judges the conqueror's destructiveness as well as his
greatness; it feels the case for traditional loyalties as strongly as
that for the upstart; it views the hero with irony as much as with
admiration; it is willing to agree that he is fortunate, but will
never claim (as Milton does for Cromwell) that his trophies are
also God's. Contrast, for example, Marvell with Dryden, each
describing the speed of Cromwell's victorious campaigns:

> *Then burning through the air he went*
> *And palaces and temples rent.*

> *Swift and resistless through the land he past,*
>   *Like that bold Greek who did the East subdue;*
> *And made to battle such heroick haste,*
>   *As if on wings of victory he flew.*

Marvell's image (Cromwell has just been compared with the
"three-fork'd lightning") is full of the sense of a destructiveness
terrible and indiscriminate—and almost devilish, for "temples"
are destroyed by it; Dryden has nothing of this. Dryden, again,
uncritically asserts that Cromwell was guiltless of ambition—
"and yet dominion was not his design"; Marvell, always
equivocal, implies the opposite:

> *So* restless *Cromwell* could not *cease*
> *In the inglorious arts of peace.*

Dryden swallows, without a hint of reservation, Cromwell's
claim to be fighting a "war to end war"—"he fought to end our

fighting"—Marvell, as noted above, obliquely warns his hero that they who won power by the sword must maintain it by the sword. Milton affirms the purity of Cromwell's religion; Marvell, on that, is most diplomatically silent.[1] If Milton is to Cromwell as Marlowe to Tamburlaine, then Marvell is to Cromwell as Shakespeare to Coriolanus. As Shakespeare, indeed, is to all his warlike heroes or self-made usurpers, to Bolingbroke and Hotspur, Coriolanus and Antony; the balance of admiration and criticism is always preserved. Bolingbroke is certainly meant to be admired; the weakness and foolishness of the king whom he deposes are relentlessly shown; yet the case for legitimacy, and the consequences of usurpation, are stated by the Bishop of Carlisle with a vigour as great as anything in the play ("The blood of English shall manure the ground, And future Ages groane for his foule Act"); and even the usurper's son, on the eve of his greatest triumph, is haunted by the guilt which his father incurred. Such balance, such freedom from engagement, is clearly the exact equivalent of Marvell's supremely generous tribute to Charles's conduct on the scaffold, and his plain assertion (in a poem ostensibly celebrating Charles's destroyer) that "Justice" is with the loser;[2] just as Marlowe's caricaturing of Tamburlaine's enemies is the parallel of Milton's harsh contempt for the King. Or consider—this may seem irrelevant but in fact is the same—the subtle Shakespearean use of his keyword "noble" in *Julius Cæsar*. "Noble" is, above all words, *the* word for the killers of Cæsar, the idealist slayers for liberty's sake, and especially the word for the most idealist, for Brutus himself. It is, says Cassius, the quality that Rome, under Cæsar, has lost—"Rome, thou hast lost the breed of Noble Bloods." It is the epithet that Antony, talking to Cæsar, awards to Cassius—"he is a Noble Roman,

[1] Richard Baxter—like Marvell, a Commonwealth-man but no fanatic—had similar doubts:

Hereupon Cromwell's general Religious Zeal, giveth away to the power of that Ambition, which still increaseth as his Successes do increase. . . . He meaneth well in all this at the beginning, and thinketh he doth all for the Safety of the Godly, and the Publick Good, but not without an Eye to himself. (*Reliquiae Baxterianae*, lib. I, part I.)

[2] *Though Justice against Fate complain,*
And plead the ancient rights in vain.

and well given." Cassius gives it to Brutus, prodding him up to the sticking-point—"well *Brutus*, thou art Noble: yet I see . . ." —but here already it has a tinge of irony, the practical man regarding the lofty hesitant idealist. The irony thickens, to explicit mockery, when Antony repeats it to the Roman mob:

> *The Noble* Brutus,
> *Hath told you* Cæsar *was Ambitious . . .*

—the equivocation is driven home when that same mob, turned inside out by Antony's rhetoric, transfers the word to Antony himself—"there's not a Nobler man in Rome than *Antony*"—so that when we reach the final use of it—

> *This was the Noblest Roman of them all*

—can we be sure (remembering that this is a "set speech" and that Antony's cynical cunning as a rhetorician has been well established) if true admiration or mocking irony is the dominant note?

This is the attitude, and therefore the kind of art, that the Civil War rendered impossible. By embodying in contemporary events both symbolic figures, conquering individualist usurper and divinely-sanctioned King, by forcing men to choose one or the other, the war brought to an end the conditions which made such a balance tenable. As long as these two figures were not in head-on and contemporary collision, it was possible for men to enjoy, in imagination, the tension between them and the tensions within their own minds of which the figures were embodiments, and to make from it all a tense but undistorted poetry; but as soon as they *were* in collision, there came, inevitably, the propagandist's lop-sided viewpoint. Imagine a *Macbeth* written after the execution of King Charles. It would then have been quite impossible to preserve, as Shakespeare does, both the mystical reverence for legitimate kingship, the sense that its destruction involves a violation of the divine and the natural orders, and the sympathetic dramatic presentation of the murderous usurper. One or the other would have had to go; what *is* a tragedy would be turned into a piece of propaganda. (This is not to argue that propaganda—that is, work intended to enforce a particular viewpoint—cannot be real art. It can be:

but it can *not* be true tragedy.) Of the balanced view Marvell's *Horatian Ode* is perhaps the last achievement; an astonishing achievement, considering its date—two years after the King's execution. But even Marvell could not hold it for long or with comfort: many of his other poems—*Appleton House*, for example, and those like it, which develop his special world of garden, country-house fantasy—have a strong tinge of escape; they seem the poetry of a man deeply disturbed by the chaos and horrors around him, who has managed, for a time, to construct a world of the imagination to keep out the conflict. But its fragility is evident even in the symbols which are used to create it; the garden-wall is no real defence against "ambition's heat" (Cromwell, after all, had begun in a garden, where he "tended the Bergamot"), and the "sweet militia" of the flowers is perfectly realized to be only a wishful fantasy. "Oh happy! *could* we but restore That sweet militia once more . . ."—but he knows quite well that we can't.

It is in Marvell and Milton that we can best study the effects of the Civil War on poetic sensibility, for it happens that they are the only poets of the first quality whose careers span this watershed of the century; the others are either entirely before it, like Donne and Herbert, or almost entirely after it, like Dryden. On Marvell the effect seems to have been a total destruction: the end of what had been one of the most delicate and exquisite sensibilities in the language. No poet's career provides a more striking, or more depressing, contrast than his does between his real poetry and the *Satires* which were apparently his only work in verse written after the Restoration. What impresses one in those satires, if one comes to them from *Appleton House* and *The Garden* and the *Coy Mistress*, is the coarseness and crudity of the wit and emotion; it is not merely that Marvell has become a propagandist and nothing but a propagandist, but that in so doing he has lost all the qualities which had made him a great poet. Dryden—with less to lose— loses a good deal less when *he* turns to propaganda; and the cause is this, that Dryden, a man of a later generation, with none but the most superficial traces of the earlier kind of sensibility, was not wronging the best part of his nature when he "to party gave up what was meant for mankind". Marvell *was* doing that wrong, for he had been a true son of the Shakespearean moment.

The sense of tragedy is lost, succeeded by a bitter one-eyed railing; the metaphysical wit, never divorced from feeling, is displaced by the kind of wit which aims at nothing more than creating contempt and dislike; above all, there is lost the ability to stand aside from contemporary events even while writing of them and judging them. That ability the *Horatian Ode* had shown supremely; its quality comes from the fact that—partly by the aid of the "Horatian" form, partly by the parallels with Roman history—Marvell was able to place the conflict between Charles and Cromwell in the perspective of history. But now, after the Restoration, he is totally involved: up to the neck in it, a Party man.

With Milton, the process is not the same, nor so clear; the effect of Civil War on him was a change, not a destruction. What the change was is perfectly clear: it is the change from the poetry of the minor poems to the special style created for *Paradise Lost*. That a change of some kind would have occurred when Milton at last came to write the great epic which had been his lifelong objective, is also clear; for to make a special diction for the special purpose of the Epic was for him a purely literary requirement, obeying one of the dogmas of Renaissance classicism, and to blame him for doing so is really to blame the whole concept of classical epic as model for modern tongues. (A concept which has, in fact, been responsible for more wasted talents and a greater number of unreadable lines than any other one can readily think of.) But what may be argued is that Milton's "epic dialect" took the form it did take largely through his long absorption in political propaganda. No other poet's career shows quite the pattern of Milton's: an early beginning, the conviction that poetry was his true vocation being there from the outset; some ten years of production; then about fifteen years—the central years of his life, from his thirties to the end of his forties—of virtually total abandonment of poetry; then another fifteen years or so of poetic creation. The break in the middle can hardly have failed to make some effect. It was filled, of course, by political activities and the writing of propagandist prose; and it is these prose writings which provide the real link —as far as style is concerned, the only link—between early Milton and late. What Milton shows, then, is not the natural kind of development, of which Shakespeare is the supreme

example—a flow of style always changing but never broken—
he shows instead a development interrupted and deeply affected
by an alien power. For prose he did feel as something alien,
not part of his true creation: something to which he reluctantly
descended—and condescended—giving it, in his own phrase,
only his "left hand". This alien power, the prose, has many of
the features which were to make the manner of *Paradise Lost*.
It is, first of all, supremely argumentative, it has always a stated
objective, as plainly as has *Paradise Lost*. Milton is always
arguing a case, always writing for the victory of a cause, and
never—by the nature of propaganda as well as in accordance
with his own personal nature—never capable of allowing the
smallest grain of reason or goodwill to the enemies of the cause.
Hence, in a purely literary sense (Milton's personal sincerity is
never in question), there seems a kind of utilitarian cynicism in
this prose; Milton is willing to adopt any manner, use any
weapon, if he thinks it will make for victory. The manners of
his prose run from a sort of cold-blooded scurrility, a conscientious slinging of Billingsgate strangely unreal on the part
of one who was by nature (as we have seen) unusually fastidious,[1] to a re-modelling for English of the style of the classical
orator. The latter is perhaps the dominant and the favoured
manner; behind much of this prose one can easily see its model,
its ideal figure: the toga'd spellbinder in that much-idealized
Roman-cum-Athenian Senate which so powerfully impressed the
Renaissance imagination.[2] From this model comes the heavily

---

[1] E.g. (from the *Ready and Easy Way*, etc.):

Let our zealous Backsliders forethink now with themselves,
how thir Necks yok'd with these Tigers of *Bacchus*, these new
Fanatics of not the preaching but the sweating-tub, inspir'd with
nothing holier than the Venereal Pox. . . .

[2] And was still impressing even the satirical mind of Swift:

I desired that the senate of Rome might appear before me in
one large chamber, and a modern representative in counter-
view, in another. The first seemed to be an assembly of heroes
and demi-gods; the other a knot of pedlars, pick-pockets, highway-
men, and bullies.

Contrast that extremely silly remark with the commonsense of
Dr. Johnson's comment on Shakespeare's character of Menenius:
". . . and wanting a buffoon, he went to the Senate of Rome for

Latinized form, which Milton must have made—perhaps deliberately, perhaps by instinct—to fit his imagined orator. To think of the Latinized form as beginning with *Paradise Lost* is entirely incorrect; it begins in the prose pamphleteering. The opening sentences of *Areopagitica* make as good an example as any—a perfect specimen both of the Latin mould and of the oratorical model behind it:

> They who to States and Governours of the Commonwealth direct their Speech, High Court of Parlament, or wanting such accesse in a private condition, write that which they foresee may advance the publick good; I suppose them as at the beginning of no meane endeavour, not a little alter'd and mov'd inwardly in their mindes: Some with doubt of what will be the successe, others with feare of what will be the censure; some with hope, others with confidence of what they have to speake. And me perhaps each of these dispositions, as the subject was whereon I enter'd, may have at other times variously affected; and likely might in these formost expressions now also disclose which of them sway'd most, but that the very attempt of this address thus made, and the thought of whom it hath recourse to, hath got the power within me to a passion, farre more welcome then incidentall to a Preface.

It is possible (*experto crede*) to have known that passage for years without having realized that "High Court of Parlament" is, as the grammars would say, "in the vocative case". And the general syntax, with its picked-up relatives ("they who . . . I suppose them": *illi qui . . . eos puto*) and its inverted word-order ("And me perhaps . . . these dispositions . . . affected": *et me fortasse . . . tales motus animi . . . commoverunt*), is in the purest and finest tradition of Latin Prose Composition, and exactly the syntax of *Paradise Lost*:

> The aggregated Soyle
> Death with his Mace petrific, cold and dry,
> As with a Trident smote . . .
>
> (P.L. X, 293)

that which the Senate of Rome would certainly have supplied him." Milton and Swift, the intolerant propagandists, are much more easily bamboozled than Shakespeare and Johnson, the charitable humorists.

Such style, and such self-presentation, are entirely in the manner of *Paradise Lost's* orations: Satan, preparing for the tempting of Eve, is imagined as Milton imagines himself, preparing to argue his case before Parliament:

> *As when of old som Orator renound*
> *In* Athens *or free* Rome, *where Eloquence*
> *Flourishd, since mute, to som great cause addrest,*
> *Stood in himself collected, while each part,*
> *Motion, each act won audience ere the tongue,*
> *Somtimes in highth began, as no delay*
> *Of Preface brooking through his Zeal of Right.*
> *So standing, moving, or to highth upgrown*
> *The Tempter all impassiond thus began.*
>
> (P.L. IX, 670)

Thus, the years of absorption in politics and political writing had on Milton's use of language the effect of enormously increasing the proportion of what one might call the forensic; they made it less of an instrument for seeing and recreating and more of one for enforcing and persuading: less of a natural growth and more of a manufactured tool. Style for him has become a thing which anticipates feeling; something to be learned, practised, applied to whatever point is to be enforced, not something which grows with the content and cannot be detached from it. (The proof of which is the ease with which the Milton of *Paradise Lost* can be—and has been—imitated, contrasted with the virtual impossibility of imitating Shakespeare.) The traces of the dramatic attitude which are in *Comus*, and of the metaphysical in the *Nativity Hymn*, disappear entirely and for good. The splitting of men's minds which the Civil War brought about did not utterly destroy, in Milton, the power to write great poetry, as it had done in Marvell; it diverted him to the writing of great poetry *of another kind*. And for this the reason may be the same (*mutatis mutandis*) as it was for Dryden: Milton had never been a writer of the balanced Shakespearean kind, he had always been, in a sense, a propagandist. His true nature was not being wronged; the experience of the Civil War only intensified what had always been part of it. But this intensifying was of vital importance both to his own verse and, through it and its immense influence, to the rest of English poetry. For Milton now becomes a poet whose essential way of using language is thoroughly acceptable to Restoration and Augustan ideas. The serious poetry of the Restoration and early eighteenth century tends, most of it, and especially the best of it, to the argumentative and expository: it tries to enforce, against opposition, a particular point of view. If it is not always (it very often is) the poetry of a political party, it almost always has something in its methods akin to those of party-propaganda.

In this way, the outburst of propagandist literature which the Civil War brought about had an effect on English literature much more durable than the events which began it. From it a great deal of eighteenth century literature received its bent. For from those events sprang English party-politics; with them political propagandist literature rose to a status of real import-ance in the literary scene. In the Elizabethan age, by com-parison, such literature had been low and furtive, a matter of ephemeral squibs like the Marprelate pamphlets. Now—from the Restoration onwards—to that sort of Grub-street activity is added a kind of writing more dignified and less anonymous. The "party spirit" begins to permeate the republic of letters—to the great disgust, it is true, of both Swift and Addison. "Whig and Tory," grumbles the former in a letter of 1706, "has spoiled all that was tolerable here, by mixing with private friendships and conversation, and ruining both": and Addison, more priggishly, makes the same complaint:

> If this party-spirit has so ill an effect on our morals, it has likewise a very great one on our judgments. We often hear a poor insipid paper or pamphlet cried up, and sometimes a noble piece depreciated, by those who are of a different prin-ciple from the author. . . . As men formerly became eminent in learned societies by their parts and acquisitions, they now distinguish themselves by the warmth and violence with which they espouse their respective parties. Books are valued upon the like considerations: an abusive scurrilous stile passes for satire, and a dull scheme of party notions is called fine writing. (*Spectator*, No. 125.)

That complaint is really the same as those earlier ones of Marvell and Cowley: politics are ruining literature. But Swift and Addison were complaining against an activity in which both of them had to some extent indulged, and their complaints were in any case of no avail: the party spirit had come to stay. It produced on imaginative literature an effect which might be seen as both a prolongation and a widening of the effects which it had on Milton; it made a completely all-round view of any subject much harder to achieve. Men, one might say, now had "ideas"—and ideas ultimately political—readymade before they began their creation; their ideas, moreover, belonged to one or the other way of thinking, and possession of one excluded complete sympathy with the other.

Of such a mentality one effect on poetry will be the use of a "diction"; an accepted, known-beforehand kind of language with which readers will at once feel at home, by which they are ready to be persuaded, as they would not if the language were an individual's creation. Hence in this too, Milton, a master of poetic diction, is at harmony with later opinion and practice. It is not merely that his particular diction became one of the standard models, so that there is scarcely a line of eighteenth century blank verse which is not to some degree Miltonic; Milton's power went wider than that, his whole practice of first making a diction and then applying it to whatever one wrote of, became the received practice of Augustan verse in every mode. His taste shows it as well as his practice. The *Apology for Smectymnuus* has a passage making fun of Hall's *Satires* (Hall had been, for purely ecclesiastical reasons, one of Milton's opponents, but anything was relevant by the canons of seventeenth century controversy):

> And turning by chance to the sixth Satyr of his Second book[1] I was confirmed; where having begun loftily *in heavens universall Alphabet* he fals downe to that wretched poorenesse and frigidity as to talke of *Bridge street in heav'n, and the Ostler of heav'n,* and there wanting other matter to catch him a heat, (for certaine he was in the frozen *Zone* miserably benumm'd) with thoughts lower then any Beadle betakes him to whip the signe posts of *Cambridge* Alehouses, the ordinary subject of freshmens tales, and in a straine as pittifull.

[1] Actually, the seventh Satire: Milton was following a misprint in the edition of 1598.

What is notable there is not so much Milton's disapproval in itself (the passage he mauls is in fact pretty bad) as the critical canons by which he does his demolishing. It is the blending of "high" and "low", solemn subject and familiar words, it is the forced, unnatural witticism, that he cannot abide; and there, both in the general viewpoint and the particular term he uses ("frigidity"), he is thoroughly Augustan, anticipating exactly the canons by which the eighteenth century rejected the metaphysical way of writing. He is, for example, showing precisely the critical viewpoint of that pioneer of Augustan criticism, John Dennis, commenting on a couplet of Waller:

> So Jove *from* Ida *did both Hosts survey,*
> *And when he pleas'd to thunder, part the fray.*

—Is not that a noble Similitude?
—Yes; but the word Fray is altogether unworthy of the Greatness of the Thought and the Dignity of Heroick Verse. Fray is fitter to express a Quarrel betwixt drunken Bullies than between the *Grecian* and *Trojan* Heroes.
                    (*The Impartial Critick*: Third Dialogue)

And it is by obeying the same canons that Dr. Johnson was unable to accept Lady Macbeth's use of such words as "dunnest", "blanket", and "knife", of which the domestic associations ruined for him the tragic solemnity. Dennis and Johnson, in these instances, are working purely as literary critics; but Milton's handling of the passage from Hall shows that there had been a connection between this type of literary criticism and the party or propagandist approach. A mind limited in sympathies, strongly inclined for one side and against its opposite, will show the equivalent in language: the rejection of the Shakespearean and metaphysical all-inclusiveness in language went together with the rejection of that Shakespearean society and way of thinking, which also aimed at including all.

The total effect of the Civil War on literature might be summed up as this: it gave to the whole of the literary scene an air recognizably nearer to that which we know to-day. Modern literature—if one wants to make an epigram of it—begins in 1660. The last links with the Middle Ages are broken. Patronage becomes increasingly cynical and deprived of emotional value, the writer works more and more for an unknown amorphous "public". And—in consequence—he is increasingly anxious to argue and convince, to mould or follow public opinion, and in so far as public opinion becomes increasingly party-opinion, the writer is more and more inclined to become the "representative" of this political grouping or that. Writers, in general, before the Civil War, had to bother very little about public opinion or the reading-public; for the former, in politics, was of much less account, if indeed it existed at all as we know it, and the latter was smaller and less economically important to most writers' welfare. A writer like Shakespeare, to be secure in his career and his place in society, had presumably to satisfy two demands: he had to convince his playhouse audience that he could entertain them, and his patrons and friends that he was worthy of their favour. A writer like Donne had only the second of these demands to cope with. Whether writers were really more or less "free" when they worked in this way, whether one pays more or less in spiritual wear-and-tear when one has to satisfy a patron rather than a public, can be inter-minably debated; what is clear is that the change was a vital one, and it does seem likely—the concrete results bear it out—that the change to the modern shape of the literary world was destructive of tragic and dramatic poetry. Such poetry seems to depend on a certain intimacy between the poet and his com-munity, such as cannot be attained if the latter is large and amorphous; on a stability of the emotional relationships and the assumptions shared between them, which is easier achieved if the poet knows whom he has to please and can sense their reactions at once; and on his ability to preserve a fundamental detachment in spite of these close relationships—a detachment not easy to maintain if he must always be reckoning with a fluctuating and intangible public opinion.

Chapter 8

THE CLASSICAL LINE

THE dramatic and metaphysical way of writing was not the only way of the early seventeenth century, though by far the most fruitful. Along with it was the tradition which can be called the classical: a kind of poetry, that is, clearly and more or less directly derived from classical models. Not that this way can be rigidly separated from the other—all divisions between kinds of writing, after all, like all divisions into "ages", are not much more than artificial conveniences. Often, indeed, the two overlapped, and the same man was capable of both. Ben Jonson especially: the only writer who was completely a native both of the living theatre and of the world of classical learning and doctrine. But even in him the two worlds seem not quite in harmony: when the latter is too dominant, as in *Catiline* and *Sejanus*, the virtues of the former are lost, and the verdict of contemporary audiences, as reported by Leonard Digges—

> . . . *they would not brooke a line*
> *Of tedious (though well-labour'd) Catiline*[1]

has become the judgment of posterity.[2]

Of this classical poetry, the origin was of course Renaissance classicism: the group of doctrines which can be summed up as maintaining that one should take the classics as models, and on those models make an English poetry by adapting their forms and catching their tones. When one says the "classics", what one should really mean, certainly for the sixteenth and seven-

---

[1] Verses prefixed to the Second Folio.

[2] Cf. Jonson's *Ode* "Come leave the loathed stage", in which, disgusted with the bad taste of the playhouse (which had hissed *The New Inn*), he turns for consolation to the classics and to verse written by their lights:

> *Leave things so prostitute,*
> *And take the* Alcaick *lute,*
> *Or thine own* Horace *or* Anacreons *lyre;*
> *Warme thee by* Pindares *fire . . .*

teenth centuries, is Latin. Greek, then as always, counted for very little: it was the possession of a small minority, never backed up by the enormous weight of educational monopoly which Latin enjoyed. One ought, indeed, to narrow it still farther: it was not so much Latin, as "classical" Latin. By way of demonstrating their superiority to the monkish barbarism of the Middle Ages, which had had the bad taste to keep Latin a living language, the scholars and humanists of the Renaissance performed that curious trick from which some of us have still suffered in twentieth-century schools: they extracted some hundred years of Latin literature, pronounced this to be "pure" and "classical", and condemned the rest to darkness. This tract of literature became the raw material for Renaissance education and a standard unquestioned by classicist taste. Thus the only kind of classical "influence" which, as critics of poetry, we are really concerned with—the direct action of one language on another—was limited to that particular age of Latin poetry which centres round the age of Augustus.

To be "Augustan" is not only an eighteenth century ambition; it can be seen operating as an ideal all through the classical tradition from the Renaissance onwards. Ben Jonson, commenting on Shakespeare's excessive fluency, finds it natural to enforce his reprimand with an Augustan example: *"sufflaminandus erat; as Augustus said of Haterius."* The same standard Waller finds appropriate for the praise of Cromwell—

> *As the vex'd World to find repose at last*
> *It self into Augustus arms did cast;*
> *So England now does with like toyle opprest,*
> *Her weary Head upon your Bosome rest* [1]

Dryden for the celebration of Charles II's restoration—

> *Oh Happy Age! Oh times like those alone,*
> *By Fate reserv'd for great Augustus throne!*
> *When the joint growth of Arms and Arts foreshew*
> *The World a Monarch, and that Monarch You* [2]

and Dr. Johnson for the praise of Dryden's achievement:

---

[1] *Panegyrick to my Lord Protector.*
[2] *Astraea Redux.*

What was said of Rome, adorned by Augustus, may be applied by an easy metaphor to English poetry embellished by Dryden, "lateritiam invenit, marmoream reliquit." He found it brick, and he left it marble.

(*Life* of Dryden)

Both for political and literary judgments, the Augustan standard would serve.

Why the Augustan age should have exerted such an attraction, is not hard to see. Whether or not justified by the reality, an ideal picture was formed of a court at once powerful and tasteful (*"joint* growth of Arms and Arts"), both favouring poets and favoured by them. It provided them with something worth singing *about*—in the shape of great men who were not arrant scoundrels and great deeds which extended civilization—and provided them also with something worth singing *for*. To fit this picture certain adjustments, no doubt unconscious, had to be made: the "rebels" and individualists of Roman poetry, such as Catullus and Lucretius, were comparatively depreciated; the equivocal aspects of Horace—his irony and cynicism—and of Virgil—his deep melancholy—were little dwelt on, if indeed they were felt at all. They did not fit. Horace had to be an urbane and contented celebrator of the golden mean and the Augustan achievement, Virgil a highly-polished, untormented praiser of rusticity and prophet of imperialism. These two, above all others, were the influences, and these views of them—not wrong, perhaps, but certainly inadequate—coloured a great deal of the English poetry written in the classical vein.

Especially, perhaps, those poems which celebrate great men and great occasions. Their tradition starts from the success of the Renaissance humanists in persuading their "princes" that literary fame was a desirable possession and themselves the right persons to supply it. Poetry, it was generally agreed, had a State function to perform: it should elevate, magnify, and preserve. Hence the unvarying tone of these State poems: they are always seeking for that "marmoreal" quality which Clarendon's prose on Falkland[1] achieves, perhaps, more finely than any of the age's verse. They are looking for something in English like Horace's Latin—

[1] Quoted above, p. 118.

. . . per quas Latinum nomen et Italae
crevere vires famaque et imperi
porrecta maiestas ad ortus
solis ab Hesperio cubili[1]

—and if they never quite find what they seek, the cause is perhaps a deficiency of the language—for the fluid ambiguities of
English are not meant for marmoreal effects, in which each word
must stay still, as it were, and Dr. Johnson was quite right to
think Latin the language for inscriptions—or perhaps it is a lack
of the kind of emotion which Horace could entertain for his
Rome. Whatever the cause may have been, it was certainly not
lack of trying. The poems just cited, of Waller and Dryden, will
do as well as any for specimens: in them are the characteristics
of all this poetry—a conscientious and exhausting inflation, a
desperate striving for elevated dignity:

> *If Romes great Senate could not wield that Sword,*
> *Which of the Conquer'd world had made them Lord,*
> *What hope had ours, while yet their power was new,*
> *To rule victorious Armies but by you?*
> *You that had taught them to subdue their Foes,*
> *Could Order teach, and their high Spirits compose,*
> *. To every Duty could their Minds engage,*
> *Provoke their Courage, and command their Rage.*
> (*A Panegyrick*, etc.)

> *And now times whiter Series is begun,*
> *Which in soft Centuries shall smoothly run;*
> *Those Clouds that overcast your Morn shall fly,*
> *Dispell'd to farthest corners of the Sky.*
> *Our nation, with united Int'rest blest,*
> *Not now content to poize, shall sway, the rest.*
> *Abroad your Empire shall no Limits know,*
> *But like the Sea in boundless Circles flow.*
> *Your much lov'd Fleet shall with a wide Command*
> *Besiege the petty Monarchs of the Land:*
> *And as Old Time his Off-spring swallow'd down,*
> *Our Ocean in its depths all Seas shall drown.*
> (*Astraea Redux*)

[1] *Odes* IV, 15.

One can easily see why it was to become a critical commonplace that Mr. Waller had "refin'd English numbers". His verse, no less than Dryden's, seems at once what one wants to call eighteenth century or Augustan (English Augustan), in its crudity of language and thought, its simplicity of feeling, with no double-meanings and no undertones, and the unvarying thump of its rhythm. Yet in fact these are poems of the mid-seventeenth century; what makes them not merely seem to belong in spirit to the later age is that they were written in that classical tradition which the eighteenth century, far more than the seventeenth, took for its guide. Only a touch of bombast—metaphysical hyperbole gone wrong—betrays their true date; and even that, in such panegyrics-to-order, continued through the eighteenth century: continued, but steadily degenerated, in the drier, more critical air. Poets abandoned it to the care of Poets Laureate. But the manner of self-conscious inflation did continue, easily diverted to other purposes: to the purposes of parody, for instance, serving the great Augustan cult of mock-heroic. Such lines as the opening of Dryden's *Macflecknoe*—

> *All humane things are subject to decay,*
> *And when Fate summons, Monarchs must obey:*
> *This* Fleckno *found, who, like* Augustus, *young*
> *Was call'd to Empire and had govern'd long:*
> *In Prose and Verse was own'd, without dispute,*
> *Through all the realms of Non-sense, absolute*

—are an absolute parody of the serious manner of *Astraea Redux* and of all such poems of State pomposity: the parody, no less than the originals, invokes the Augustan standard. Change a few words, and what results would sink with no trouble into a setting of solemn insincerity:

> *. . . This* Lewis *found, who, like* Augustus, *young*
> *Was call'd to Empire and had govern'd long:*
> *In Land and Sea was own'd, without dispute,*
> *Through all the realms of* Europe, *absolute.*

So, in Pope's epistle *To Augustus* (the imitation of the first epistle of Horace's second book), some inside knowledge is needed—one must know what Pope and his friends really thought of King George II—to perceive that this "heroic" is "mock":

> *To thee, the World its present Homage pays,*
> *The Harvest early, but mature the praise:*
> *Great Friend of Liberty! in Kings a Name*
> *Above all Greek, above all Roman Fame:*
> *Whose Word is Truth, as sacred and rever'd,*
> *As Heav'n's own Oracles from Altars heard.*
> *Wonder of Kings! like whom, to mortal eyes*
> *None e'er has risen, and none e'er shall rise.*

The ease with which this manner could be used for effects of parody, and the speed with which real poets found that use was the only one for them, may be taken as an index of its unreality. In English society, such inflated and humourless panegyric of the State has no true roots: it seems alien, and it is.

Together with panegyric, as a "public" kind of poetry, was elegy. This, of course, is one of the mass-produced forms of the seventeenth century: there is no better illustration both of the naturalness with which the age turned to poetry—its feeling that poetry was a proper and inevitable thing—and of the remoteness of much of its poetry from what we would call genuine "feeling", than the whole bookfuls of elegies called forth by the deaths of such persons as Prince Henry, Edward King, Lord Hastings, *et alii*. Here, at least, the age is as far as it can be from the romantic conviction (or heresy) that true poetry can be made only from "spontaneous expression" and "powerful emotion". Still, it can be said that such elegies-to-order achieve poetry only in two ways. If they follow the classical mode, they must have some true feeling of personal sorrow. If they follow the metaphysical, they make their poetry by that process, observed in Donne's *Anniversaries*, of using the ostensible subject as nothing more than a centre round which to move in an orbit as wide as the poet fancies. (And if they follow the Miltonic, as in *Lycidas*, they must be concerned with John Milton.)

The classical kind of elegy has to be distinguished from the metaphysical. The difference lies in its sticking to the point and also in a fundamental tepidness, in spite of—and often badly clashing with—the frequent lavishness of eulogy. Dryden's

Eleonora ("A Panegyrical Poem: dedicated to the Memory of the Countess of Abingdon") provides an admirable specimen of the contrast, since he wrote it, avowedly, in emulation of Donne's *Anniversaries*. Dryden, like Donne, had never known his subject. "One Disadvantage I have had," he remarks in the prefatory letter to the lady's widower, "which is, never to have known, or seen my Lady." But, as he observes, "Doctor *Donn* the greatest Wit, though not the best Poet, of our Nation, acknowledges that he had never seen Mrs. *Drury*, whom he has made immortal in his admirable *Anniversaries*": and as Dr. Donne did, so will Mr. Dryden—he will so praise the Lady Abingdon as "to raise an Emulation in the living, to Copy out the Example of the dead". That was, no doubt, Donne's "official" objective—what he would have declared to be his motive—but of course it is not the only or even the principal theme of his poems. But it is of Dryden's: *Eleonora* is really nothing but a recital of the lady's virtues, with appropriate morals extracted therefrom. Thus the classical elegy, by sticking to its point, impoverishes the result—if there is not, as there certainly is not here, any personal sorrow for the elegy's subject. What the difference really amounts to is that the thought of death in general, and of a woman's death in particular, cannot release in Dryden that flood of intense associated thoughts and emotions which they released in Donne—for the good reason that those thoughts and emotions are not in him. For since real poetry cannot be attained unless there has been true emotion somewhere, for something, then clearly, if you choose a subject which in itself has no emotional value for you, poetry can come only if that subject leads on to others, which do have such value. But this Dryden's subject cannot do for him, since he suffers both from classical "decorum"—which will not allow him to digress—and from those spiritual blockages which, since the Restoration, made impossible the free metaphysical-Shakespearean transfers from one sphere of the mind to another. And he suffers, too, from a real tepidness. *Eleonora* has a passage which shows it exactly: describing Lady Abingdon's piety, he tells us:

> *Such her Devotion was, as might give rules*
> *Of Speculation, to disputing Schools;*

214

And teach us equally the Scales to hold
Betwixt the two Extremes of hot and cold,
That pious heat may mod'rately prevail,
And we be warm'd, but not be scorch'd with zeal.

This, of course, is the Augustan ideal—this praise of the luke-warm is entirely Swiftian[1] or Addisonian—but however admirable it may be as opinion, it is poetically ruinous when it occurs in a context of fervent hyperbole.

Thus a certain paradox appears to be evolved. The classical elegy, which pretends, as it were, to be impersonal, marmoreal, dignified, and so forth, in reality depends far more than meta-physical elegy—apparently a much more "personal" poetry—on the existence of a personal grief. Dryden himself, in another poem, will prove it. *To the Memory of Mr. Oldham* is a real poem; when Dryden is lamenting a brother-poet, in a poem written neither for cash nor for favour, he reaches an eloquence and beauty far superior to anything his public elegies (and eulogies) can attain to. The feeling of equality and affinity saves it:

One common Note on either Lyre did strike,
And Knaves and Fools we both abhorr'd alike

—for the Restoration, unlike the Jacobean and Caroline ages, could never quite set free its tributes to the Great from the taint of obsequious insincerity. And in this elegy it is worth noting how much of the emotional power comes from the classical, Virgilian allusions—here also set free from the pompousness of State and allowed to be natural and direct:

Thus Nisus *fell upon the slippery place,*
Whilst his young Friend perform'd and won the Race . . .

[1] Cf. Swift on love, in *Cadenus and Vanessa*:

Love, why do we one passion call
When 'tis a compound of them all?
Where hot and cold, where sharp and sweet
In all their equipages meet . . .
But friendship in its greatest height,
A constant rational delight,
On virtue's basis fix'd to last
When love allurements long are past,
Which gently warms but cannot burn . . .

> *Once more, hail, and farewell! farewell, thou young,*
> *But ah! too short, Marcellus of our Tongue!*

Both in State panegyric and in elegy, the presence of Horace counts for much. On the whole, indeed, if we exclude epic and pastoral as special kinds, and therefore Virgil, the standard for both, it is Horace who seems to be the strongest power over all this classical poetry. (Ovid, his only rival, the true classicists regarded with some disdain: his luscious eroticism and verbal conceits appealed more to the world of the "sugared sonnets" and mythological sensualities.) The manner of the Horace who is not a lyricist—the Horace of the *Satires* and *Epistles*, familiar and talkative—is overwhelmingly the presiding tone of two other kinds of seventeenth century verse: the friendly, unbuttoned discourse and the literary causerie.

The tone which the former sets itself to render is that of the cultured but unpedantic gentleman, living in comfort but not in luxury, knowing the great world but not tied to it, amiably chatting with a friend of equal status and similar type. Horace on his Sabine farm—dearest and most durable literary daydream of those who enjoyed their classical educations—is always there in the background. Jonson's *Inviting a Friend to Supper*, for example, with its opening of modest confidence and decent, not lavish hospitality:

> *To-night, grave sir, both my poore house, and I*
> * Doe equally desire your companie:*
> *Not that we thinke us worthy such a guest,*
> * But that your worth will dignifie our feast,*
> *With those that come; whose grace may make that seeme*
> * Something, which, else, could hope for no esteeme.*
> *It is the faire acceptance, Sir, creates*
> * The entertaynment perfect: not the cates . . .*

When the "culture" comes along, it is (as it ought to be in this kind of context) exclusively Latin:

> *   How so e'er, my man*
> *Shall reade a piece of Virgil, Tacitus,*
> * Livie, or of some better booke to us,*
> *Of which wee'll speake our minds, amidst our meate.*

If one encountered nowadays that tone of serene classical superiority, one would probably find it thoroughly infuriating, for one would expect it, justifiably or not, to be allied to a taste essentially dead. At the safe distance of three hundred years (and when uttered by a man of Jonson's creative achievement) it rings true and evokes no protest. This tone of familiar talk is responsible for some of the most delightful verse of the seventeenth century; another such is Drayton's epistle to Henry Reynolds:

> My dearely loved friend how oft have we,
> In winter evenings (meaning to be free,)
> To some well-chosen place us'd to retire;
> And there with moderate meate, and wine, and fire,
> Have past the howres contentedly with chat,
> Now talk'd of this, and then discours'd of that,
> Spoke our owne verses 'twixt our selves, if not
> Other mens lines, which we by chance had got,
> Or some Stage pieces famous long before,
> Of which your happy memory had store . . .

The poem goes on to Drayton's endearing picture of his own schooldays:

> In my small selfe I greatly marveil'd then,
> Amongst all other, what strange kinde of men
> These Poets were; And pleased with the name,
> To my milde Tutor merrily I came,
> (For I was then a proper goodly page,
> Much like a Pigmy, scarse ten yeares of age)
> Clasping my slender armes about his thigh.
> O my deare master! cannot you (quoth I)
> Make me a Poet, doe it if you can,
> And you shall see, I'll quickly bee a man.
> Who me thus answered smiling, boy quoth he,
> If you'll not play the wag, but I may see
> You ply your learning, I will shortly read
> Some Poets to you; Phoebus be my speed . . .

This kind of verse has a very clear connection with that of the eighteenth century; the line runs straight—with the Horatian

influence always present and keeping it recognizably the same—
from such poems as these, through Dryden's epistle to his kins-
man John Driden, to Pope's *Imitations of Horace* and *Epistle to
Dr. Arbuthnot*. Pope gives it the final perfection, raises it from
the level of delightful verse to that of great poetry; he does it
by letting himself go a good deal more, widening the range so
that real passions—anger and venom and moral solemnity—can
be brought within it: but the essential tone, the familiar talking
voice, is never lost.

The literary causerie comes very close to it. Behind it, as a
rule, are the grand exemplars, Horace's *Ars Poetica* and the
first epistle of his second book, which takes one on a rapid
gallop through his Roman literary past. Drayton's epistle,
already cited, follows the latter model: it lays down what was
beginning to be the conventional view of the history of English
poetry—that Chaucer began it, doing remarkably well considering the limitations of the language in his benighted times—

> *That noble* Chaucer, *in those former times,*
> *The first inrich'd our* English *with his rimes,*
> *And was the first of ours, that ever brake,*
> *Into the* Muses *treasure, and first spake*
> *In weighty numbers, delving in the Mine*
> *Of perfect knowledge, which he could refine,*
> *And coyne for current, and as much as then*
> *The* English *language could expresse to men,*
> *He made it doe . . .*

—Gower came next; Surrey and Wyatt, Spenser and Sidney,
continued it. Drayton deals also with his contemporaries: with
Marlowe, among others, whom he sees as the type of "poetic
madness", and with Shakespeare, whom he seems to think of as
solely a writer of comedy—betraying in this, perhaps, a kind of
inadequacy not rarely found in this sort of verse. Still, in such
poems as this will be found a remarkably high proportion of
what is really alive and interesting in the literary criticism of the
early seventeenth century. The poems of Jonson, Leonard
Digges, and the unknown "I.M.S." on Shakespeare, of Carew
on Donne, of Cartwright on Fletcher, and of Sir John Beaumont
"concerning the true form of English Poetry"—these are some

of the best examples of a species which has many more. Beaumont's poem is particularly interesting as a remarkably early (1629) and close anticipation of the canons of eighteenth century criticism. It affirms the value of rhyme—

> *In ev'ry Language now in Europe spoke*
> *By Nations which the Roman Empire broke,*
> *The relish of the Muse consists in rime,*
> *One verse must meete another like a chime*

—recommends the rhymed couplet rather than stanzaic forms—

> *In many changes these* [sc. *rhymes*] *may be exprest:*
> *But those that joyne most simply, run the best:*
> *Their forme surpassing farre the fetter'd stave,*
> *Vaine care, and needlesse repetition save.*

—quotes the classics as standards ("whose heate the Greek and Roman works inspires"), emphasizes fitness and sobriety as poetical virtues—

> *Pure phrase, fit Epithets, a sober care*
> *Of Metaphors, descriptions cleare, yet rare,*
> *Similitudes contracted smooth and round*

—and deprecates "pedantry"—

> *A language not affecting ancient times,*
> *Nor Latine shreds, by which the Pedant climes.*

All this is thoroughly Augustan, as is the form of Beaumont's own verse. It is clear, in fact, that the rhymed couplet is already, in the early seventeenth century, the chosen form for these kinds of poetry which, in manner and content also, anticipate the later age.

Of all this seventeenth century verse in the classical line, the common feature is that it is always, in varying senses, a public kind of poetry. Even when it is not "occasional"—celebrating some great occasion or great person—it always assumes the existence of a listener, a sympathetic listener usually, on good terms of understanding with the writer. By that assumption this poetry is precluded from dealing with depths and extremes of emotion, of analysis or subtlety. For this is a poetry in which *communication* is the first consideration; it must limit itself to what the other man is sure both to understand and to appreciate. State poems, by their very nature, can hardly afford themselves the luxury of original ideas or unexpected sentiments—the commonplace is of their essence—and the poems of familiar discourse are also limited—limited by their Horatian convention of quiet good sense and easy good breeding. "We know, of course—talker and listener—we *both* know what sensible well-bred gentlemen don't talk about": that is the standard implied. This classical verse thus shows a self-consciousness very different from that of metaphysical or Shakespearean. The latter's self-consciousness is dramatic, that of the actor, who can let himself go—to all appearances—completely, because he knows that in reality the part he is playing need not be identified with his self: and because of that, his parts can always be changed, his range is infinite. But the self-consciousness of the classical verse is that of someone obliged to behave according to a certain code, who would feel himself disgraced or humiliated if he went outside it.

This is the real point at which such verse has an affinity to the poetic ideals and practice of the eighteenth century, and here too is the point at which it is radically different from the poetry of the Shakespearean moment. For the latter, as earlier chapters have argued, has as one of its vital characteristics the willingness to include everything, the refusal to leave out anything, whether on grounds of relevance or morality or taste. The classicist taste—reinforced by that "refining" on moral grounds in which the eighteenth century carried on the work of the Puritans—was more than anything else a system of pruning and selecting: it rejected some things in the hope of achieving a more manageable and comprehensible order out of what was left. This pruning and selecting, which, when the time came (after the Restoration), it was going to apply to English, it already applied, as we have noted, to the raw material on which its judgments were based: to the classics themselves. And between the two—between the principles behind the two selections, English and Latin—there is a real likeness: between the poetry of Catullus and Lucretius on the one hand, and that of the Roman Augustans, especially the two most influential, Virgil and Horace, on the other hand, there is a difference not at all unlike that which came over English poetry between the age of Shakespeare and Donne and that of Dryden and Pope. The language of the earlier poets in both is much richer, more flexible and uninhibited, more natural, nearer to the speaking voice, than that of their successors, which has been subjected to a process of refinement, to a pruning of vocabulary, a chastening of material, and a standardizing of rhythm.[1] Coleridge—or Coleridge's headmaster—perceived that difference where the Roman poets were concerned, as *Biographia Literaria* tells us:

> He habituated me to compare Lucretius (in such extracts as I then read), Terence, and above all the chaster poems of Catullus, not only with the Roman poets of the, so called, silver and brazen ages; but with even those of the Augustan aera; and on grounds of plain sense and universal logic to see and assert the superiority of the former in the truth and nativeness both of their thoughts and diction.

Whether Coleridge recognized that the taste which his headmaster protested against in Latin was the same as that which he himself scarified in English—the false kind of poetic diction, as exemplified by Gray—is not quite clear; he probably did, since he certainly recognized that the traditional kind of classical education, with as its finest flower that absurd bi-lingual acrostic known as "Latin Verses", was largely responsible for bad taste in English poetry; and *that* sort of education was the pedagogical infant of Roman and English Augustan taste.

Coleridge and his master put their fingers on the quality which the earlier poetry had, and the later lost, in the word "nativeness". This is the quality which keeps the language of poetry in an unselfconscious, probably unconscious, harmony and kinship with the current colloquial speech of the age; and this is what was partly lost when classicism became the dominant standard for English poetry, and would have been entirely lost if its victory had been total instead of partial. For classicist doctrine works by imposing a set of principles created for one language on to another: it is thus the negation of "nativeness".

---

[1] What Dr. Johnson remarks of Pope, that he was "a master of poetical prudence", in that he virtually confined himself to one metre, could be said equally of Virgil.

In this too there is a certain parallel between English and Latin: with, for the latter, Greek models performing the function that Latin performed for the English classicists. As Horace advises in the *Ars Poetica*:

> *vos exemplaria Graeca*
> *nocturna versate manu, versate diurna.*

"Nativeness" almost goes; and its loss is most intimately connected with the final, post-Restoration collapse of the quality of poetic drama; perhaps it was really the same thing, since the existence of a drama both popular and poetic had been by far the most effective bridge for the linking of poetic and popular language. Once this bridge ceased to be effective, the connection could be kept only by individual *tours de force*, such as Pope continually accomplishes in such works as the *Imitations of Horace*; but writers of lesser genius had to take refuge in the easier resource of a prefabricated diction. The last forty years of the seventeenth century—the years after the Restoration—show the confused beginnings of this process; they show English poetry still struggling to keep the drama as its centre and fount of its life, but more and more aware of the vast inferiority of its own achievements in that sphere to those of the drama before the Civil War, and more and more, in consequence, tending to find its real bent in other spheres. They show, too, an effort on the part of criticism to excuse this inferiority by claiming some compensatory gains. They are, for poetry, confused and unsatisfactory years, these last decades of the seventeenth century; the old way has been irretrievably lost, the new has not yet been conclusively found. But the classical tradition which this chapter has examined was one of the new way's parents. The other was Milton, whose true nature is much more justly seen if he is taken as the first of the Augustans than as a poet whose lifetime overlapped those of Shakespeare and Donne. And in the decades after the Restoration the new way is born.

Chapter 9

CRITICISM AND POETRY AFTER THE RESTORATION

CRITICS always suffer from a tendency to judge the total quality of an age or a civilization by the quality of its achievement in the particular activity they are concerned with: they suffer, in other words, from the usual tendency to overestimate the importance of their own interests. The age of the Restoration[1] was not a great age for poetry; but there is no need to go from that to denounce it as a whole. "Milton lived on, illuminating by his presence an age unworthy of him"— Victorian critics were partial to that kind of rhetoric; but in fact this "unworthy" age was a great age of music—the age of Purcell; of architecture—the age of Wren; of science above all—the age of Newton and Boyle. It was perfectly worthy of Milton or of anyone. What is undoubtedly true is that something did go wrong with its poetry, and it may be true that a failure in poetry—the most intense and refined use of the medium of communication which all society uses—both reflects and intensifies some wider failure. Perhaps failure is not the right word for what went wrong in Restoration poetry. Confusion would be better. Both the language itself, and the status and functions of poetry, were in a state of uncertainty. The language was in process of settling down from the rich complexity it had displayed before the Civil War into the plain, chastened, sensible "modern" manner which was to be its Augustan form; and the state of poetry was settling with it in the same directions. Both language and poetry, of course, went these ways because the society they existed in and for was taking them thither. If we take one example, if we look back to King Charles's execution and the symbolic value it had had, it soon becomes clear that that event was not only the climax of the strain of Church-and-State feeling, it was also its death-blow. Never again would it be part of the main stream of

[1] Used here as a convenient term for the last forty years of the seventeenth century.

English sensibility; it took on irresistibly an air of crankishness, sentimentality, and superstition. Never again would it be possible for men whose minds were *not* crankish, sentimental, and superstitious, to bring to bear on the head of the secular State that cluster of emotions which centre round saintliness, martyrdom, and, in the last resort, the supreme martyrdom of Christ. When a Restoration Royalist like Dryden expresses "horror" at the memory of Charles's execution, and talks about the country's bearing "the marks of penitence and sorrow" for that crime at Charles II's return from exile,[1] the texture of the poetry makes it perfectly clear that though he is "sincere" in a way (but only a year earlier he had published his quite uncritical panegyric on Cromwell), still his "sincerity" has little depth to it. Charles II is welcomed back in the hope that his coming will put an end to faction and fanaticism; the Restoration is thought of fundamentally, for all Dryden's pompous Augustan trappings, as an event entirely secular.

But there is always a timelag between the decisive event, which changes feeling, and the change in expression which it caused. The change to "commonsense", in the Restoration, was very far from complete; a great deal of the early exuberance still remained—but remained in degenerate forms, perpetually trying to do things which the true spirit of the age did not want it to do and did not allow it, therefore, to do with any success. The real soul of the Restoration was urging poetry towards that Augustan restatement or resettlement of its functions which might be summarized under three heads. First, the abandonment by real poetry of the poetic drama, at which the pitiful efforts of the eighteenth century need no elaborating. Behind this collapse of the poetic drama—and causing it—was the final loss of the tragic sense. Second, there was a similar abandonment of devotional poetry. That, broadly speaking, the eighteenth century was to relegate to hymn-writers and madmen. The modern reader, aware that Dr. Johnson was a man of great piety, is apt to be astounded at Johnson's opinion that sacred subjects are unsuited to poetry; we forget that Johnson's taste was formed overwhelmingly (as the *Lives of the Poets* show) on the poets *of his own century*, and for them his judgment was perfectly correct. The less "sacred" poetry *they* wrote,

[1] As he does in *Astraea Redux*.

the better for both sacredness and poetry. And thirdly, the Augustan settlement, unable to make real poetry out of the drama and religious themes, placed the bulk of its effort, and almost all of its real achievement, in the poetry of philosophical argument, of social comment, and of satire.

When the poetry of the Restoration is working on these lines, all goes well, and it is there that it finds its true bent. Such poems as Dryden's *Religio Laici*, *Absalom and Achitophel*, and *Macflecknoe*, such activities as the imitation or free translation of classical originals, then beginning, give us the best that the age can do in verse, and it *is* the best because truly in harmony with what the age was working to. Much of the wrongness of the rest can be ascribed to the opposite cause: it is trying to maintain the old order, to work in the old forms, when the essential quality which gave them life has been totally lost. It aims at magniloquence, and achieves bombast; at pathos, and attains sentimentality; at tragedy, and writes melodrama. Of all this, by far the most striking proof is the Restoration's effort at poetic drama. Here the failure is at once most obvious and most crucial, since that was the form most vital to the old order of poetry. What is called the "heroic" drama is the Restoration's most considerable effort at making a serious poetic drama of its own, and what it made of that form, as practised by Dryden, will show us how far such efforts could succeed.

The heroic drama, as a separate definable thing, was developed in the years after 1660 and hardly survived the century. There is no doubt that it hit the age's taste—or part of it—for it was immensely successful in spite of a good deal of well-aimed and well-deserved ridicule. To define it is not too easy, though once known, it is easily understood. Saintsbury's account of its origins is probably correct; it arose from "the Italian criticism of the renaissance, partly from the difficulty of accommodating ancient critical doctrines to the craving for romance"; hence comes "the idea of a 'heroic' fiction, which was not tragedy nor bound by the strict rules of drama, which was not Epic nor bound by the strict rules of the poem, but which loosened and at the same time adjusted both." On one hand, then, are the elements of the romances, forming the raw materials: heroes performing incredible feats of arms and exhibiting superhuman devotion to their ladies, and stories showing an endless series of surprising events. On the other hand, is the framework of classical drama, with its five acts, its formal rhetorical orations, its conventional similes, and its patches of "fine writing". It is probably this mixed origin—classical precepts, romantic content—which accounts for the pervading feeling of incongruity, between the formalism of the language and the wildness of the subjects. It was the former, perhaps, that allowed the Restoration to enjoy the heroic nonsense with a good conscience. In many ways, Restoration sophistication (like all sophistication?) was extremely superficial. It was purely verbal; if one said things in the right way (the up-to-date, Franco-classicist way), one could say the most arrant nonsense—and the most old-fashioned nonsense, too. As we shall see, the heroic drama, in some ways, was extremely old-fashioned; it reverted to the most primitive type of Elizabethan drama.

A heroic drama consists of virtually nothing but the dramatized adventures of a Hero: sometimes, for variety, two heroes, with one or two heroines in attendance. "The Hero" (says Saintsbury) "takes the place of the Action, and so supplies a more flexible unity of interest." ("More flexible" is a polite way of saying that one can put in any episode one likes, so long as it concerns the hero.) Consider Dryden's *Conquest of Granada*. This is a huge chronicle in two parts with five acts in each: a piece of magnifying ridiculed by Bayes' remark in *The Rehearsal* (Bayes, of course, is Dryden): "And therefore, Sir, whereas everyone makes five acts to one play, what do me I, but make five plays to one plot . . ." The *Conquest of Granada* consists of little but the mighty deeds of the hero Almanzor, who fights first on one side, then on the other, then reverts, like a spinning-top, and every time brings victory with him. The structure, if you call it that, is a frequent repetition of Aristotelian "reversals". Almanzor conquers on behalf of King No. 1, is treated with ingratitude (the king insists on pilfering the heroine, the beauteous Almahide), storms out to offer his services to King No. 2, conquers on *his* behalf, receives another dose of ingratitude very punctually, expresses horror and amazement, offers his services back to King No. 1, conquers again . . . and so on to the end of Part II, Act V. And this technique is repeated in all minor episodes. It becomes a mechanical sequence of *coups de théâtre*, which one soon learns to expect, though the hero remains astonished to the end. This martial simplicity of the heroic character is neatly commented on in *The Rehearsal:*

> *Smith.* But, Mr. Bayes, I thought your Heroes had ever been men of great humanity and justice.
> *Bayes.* Yes, they have been so; but, for my part, I prefer that one quality of singly beating of whole armies, above all your moral vertues put together, I gad.

We might take a look at this hero, Almanzor. (It is he who is the main original of *The Rehearsal's* Drawcansir.) First, he is the Superman, all alone against the world:

> *But know, that I alone am King of Me.*
> *I am as free as Nature first made Man,*
> *Ere the base Laws of Servitude began,*
> *When wild in woods the Noble Savage ran.*

(This seems to be one of the earliest appearances of the "Noble Savage".) He is the self-made man, carving his way to greatness on his own:

> *I am, but while I please, a private Man;*
> *I have that Soule, which Empires first began.*
> *From the dull Crowd, which every King doth lead,*
> *I will pick out, whom I will choose to lead.*
> *The best and bravest Souls I can select,*
> *And on their conquer'd necks my Throne erect.*

He is a very plain and simple fellow, as he confesses himself:

> *My heart's so plain,*
> *That men on ev'ry passing Thought may look,*
> *Like Fishes gliding in a crystal Brook;*
> *When troubled most, it does the Bottome show,*
> *'Tis weedless all above, and rockless all below.*

His style of speech is an unbroken fortissimo of rant:

> *He that dares love, and for that Love must die,*
> *And knowing this, dares yet love on, am I.*[1]

---

[1] That couplet is suitably dealt with in the invaluable *Rehearsal*:
> *He that dares drink, and for that drink must die,*
> *And knowing this, dares yet drink on, am I.*

This noble superman has but one weakness—Love. But this weakness is superhuman itself; he moves without gradation from the extreme of arrogance to the extreme of servitude. Of this, the most notorious specimen is Almanzor's speech when he falls in love with Almahide:

> *I'm pleas'd, and pain'd, since first her Eyes I saw,*
> *As I were stung with some Tarantula.*
> *Arms, and the dusty Field, I less admire,*
> *And soften strangely in some new Desire.*
> *Honour burns in me not so fiercely bright,*
> *But pale as Fires, when master'd by the Light.*
> *Ev'n while I speak and look, I change yet more;*
> *And now am nothing that I was before,*
> *I'm numb'd, and fix't, and scarce my Eye-balls move;*
> *I fear, it is the Lethargy of Love.*

The suddenness of this process is a standard symptom of the Hero.[1] Passion is thought of as a kind of irresistible disease—"love, like a *Lethargy*, has seiz'd my Will"—nobody succeeds in restraining it unless by the interposition of another passion of greater intensity. The Hero moves from one crisis straight to the next. The extreme crudity of the heroic psychology is notable; it is a black and white scheme of the utmost simplicity. The heroic drama abounds in quite unprepared conversions, reversals of character which are the parallels of the continual reversals of the action:

> *Yes, I am vanquish't: the fierce Conflict's past,*
> *And Shame it self is now orecome at last.*
> *'Twas long before my stubborn Mind was won,*
> *But melting once, I on the sudden run;*
> *Nor can I hold my headlong Kindness more,*
> *Than I could curb my cruel Rage before.*

"On the sudden" and "headlong" are entirely typical.

The heroic drama's handling of love is surprising, if one starts with the conviction that the Restoration was thoroughly worldly and sophisticated. It swallows without the smallest

---

[1] *The Rehearsal*, yet again, does not fail us:
 Why, did you not observe? He first resolves to go out of Town, and then, as he is pulling on his Boots, he falls in Love.

qualms the old romantic tradition of adoring, slavelike lover and haughty, cruel, adored lady. All the old conventions that we saw in Elizabethan sonnetteering are here still, and here without a hint of the irony that Donne and Marvell put into them. Killing with cruelty, dying for love, and so forth—

> *You are not in your killing mood today,*
> *Men brand, indeed, your Sex with Cruelty,*
> *But you're too good to see poor Lovers die.*
> *This god-like Pity in you I extol,*
> *And more because, like Heav'n's, 'tis general.*

This stuff, it would seem, was made acceptable because it was presented in the proper language. And it, is, perhaps, the natural reverse of the cynical materialism of Restoration comedy. Both are symptoms of the same radical defect in the age's sensibility; it cannot look the subject steadily in the face; it must either snigger or rant. And not unconnected is their handling of jealousy. The heroes of the heroic drama are for ever suffering agonies of jealousy for the smallest cause or no cause at all. Again, this seems the natural reverse of the mechanical joyless cuckolding which goes on through Restoration comedy.

Love, of course, comes into frequent conflict with Honour. "Honour's the only Idol of his Eye" is the motto for Almanzor. This honour-love contest (derived from Corneille, of course) is nicely parodied in *The Rehearsal*, when the hero struggles with his boots—one boot on (representing Honour) and the other off (representing Love)—

> *Sometimes, with stubborn Honour, like this Boot,*
> *My mind is guarded, and resolved to do 't;*
> *Sometimes again, that very Mind, by Love*
> *Disarmed, like this other Leg doth prove.*

Eventually "Exit, with one Boot on, and the other off".

It is clear that the essential stuff of the heroic drama is of positively childish simplicity. In any sense of the word deeper than the shallowest verbalism, it is far less, not more, sophisticated than mature Elizabethan and Jacobean drama. The artistic decline has been caused by some real deterioration of moral fibre and intellectual honesty. Provided—always provided—one does not make the Puritan error, and Jeremy Collier's error, of confusing frankness with immorality, one is justified in calling the Restoration's drama immoral, in the sense that it shirks handling moral issues in an honest and searching way, it takes refuge in the easy escapes of ribaldry in the comedies and rant in the serious drama. This is allied to—perhaps it is the same as—a comparative shallowness, a reluctance really to explore the recesses of the human soul, and a willingness to accept a readymade system to explain them. It seems paradoxical, at first sight—but then a great deal of the Restoration is paradoxical—for the age was certainly very interested in psychology; its literary criticism abounds in psychological jargon, in definitions of wit, imagination, understanding, etc. But the paradox can be resolved. All this talking *about* psychology, all these attempts to make schemes and definitions, may have been efforts to replace a lost ability to penetrate the soul, the ability which the Elizabethans had possessed in spite of (or because of?) their unscientific minds. The shallowness of the heroic drama comes out most noticeably when it attempts to be philosophical, to make profound moral remarks about Life. For example:

> *O Heav'n, how dark a Riddle's thy Decree,*
> *Which bounds our Wills, yet seems to leave them free;*
> *Since thy fore-knowledge cannot be in vain,*
> *Our Choice must be what thou didst first ordain.*
> *Thus, like a Captive in an Isle confin'd,*
> *Man walks at large, a Prisoner of the Mind.*

Put that against a not dissimilar passage by an Elizabethan who was by no means a great poet: Fulke Greville's stanza from *Mustapha*—

> *O wearisome Condition of Humanity!*
> *Borne under one Law, to another bound:*
> *Vainely begot, and yet forbidden vanity,*
> *Created sicke, commanded to be sound:*
> > *What meaneth Nature by these diverse Lawes?*
> > *Passion and Reason, selfe-division cause*

—and it is clear that though the Elizabethan does not, in fact, "say" anything more striking or more original than Dryden does, he says it in a way that hits incomparably harder, penetrates to depths that Dryden does not touch. Dryden's philosophical speeches in the plays have always a fatal air of being detachable, written in, as it were; they could always have come with equal force from another person's mouth at another point in the drama. They never give the feeling that Mr. Eliot describes as produced by Macbeth's "To-morrow and to-morrow and to-morrow . . .", the feeling that those words were inevitably forced out of Macbeth at just that point of his fortunes, when, on the edge of his own defeat, he hears of the death of the woman who had started his downfall.

The suggestion was made above that in some ways the heroic drama shows a reversal to immature Elizabethan drama. The resemblance between a play like the *Conquest of Granada* and *Tamburlaine* is astonishingly close: the same unwieldy size— two parts, ten acts; the same episodic structure, which might go on for ever, linked only by the hero's adventures; the same crude simplicity of the personages; the same long ranting tirades. Almanzor, and all his rivals, are in direct line of descent from Tamburlaine: self-made heroes, above the laws which govern common men, with love for their "divine Zenocrates" as their only weakness. The language shows similar resemblances: the insistent simple rhythms, for instance, and the taste for hyperbole in imagery, such as this conceit for tears:

> *What precious Drops are those*
> *Which silently each other's Track pursue,*
> *Bright as young Diamonds in their infant Dew?*

There is also the rant, often toppling into absurdity:

> *Her voice is like a* Syren's *of the Land,*
> *And bloody Hearts lie panting in her Hand.*

There is, too, a liking for "snip-snap" dialogue, almost Euphuistic in verbal ingenuity and playing with ideas:

> A. *Justice* distributes *to each man his right,*
> *But what she* gives *not, should I take by might?*
> B. *If Justice will* take *all and will not* give,
> *Justice methinks is not* distributive.

These are the resemblances: where there are differences, the advantage is all on the side of Marlowe. The crucial difference is that Marlowe's heroics do represent a genuine and considered (even if crude) attitude to life; his Tamburlaine, as we saw, is a critic as well as a conqueror, the dramatic embodiment of a radical mind. Nothing of the sort can be claimed of Dryden's heroics; there is no revolutionary feeling in them. They were written, after all, by a man whose real mind was thoroughly Tory. They are entertainment, and entertainment alone.

The Rehearsal alone is enough to show that the critical part of the Restoration mind—that part which was preparing for the Augustan settlement—perceived the absurdities of what the rest of it enjoyed so vastly. It is here that the heroic drama failed, and had to fail; it was not merely alien, it was totally opposed, to the real movement of the age. That was going to the acceptance of "Nature" (i.e., naturalness, commonsense) as the final standard; this drama is the apotheosis of the unnatural. This fact *The Rehearsal* duly takes note of. "I despise your Johnson" (says Bayes) "and Beaumont, that borrowed all they writ from Nature: I am for fetching it purely out of my own fancie, I." Dryden must have felt that as a palpable hit; for he himself (later) confessed his shame at the rant he had written— confessed that he had written it against his own judgment, purely to please the mob:

> I remember some Verses of my own *Maximin* and *Almanzor* which cry vengeance upon me for their extravagance, etc. All I can say for these passages, which are I hope not many, is that I knew they were bad enough to please, even when I writ them: But I repent of them among my sins.
> (Epistle dedicatory to the *Spanish Fryer*)

And it is not without significance that when his Almanzor describes the "hero's soul"—

> *One Loose, one Sallye of the Heroes Soul,*
> *Does all the Military Art controul . . .*
> *And, when th' Enthusiastique fit is spent,*
> *Looks back amaz'd at what he underwent*

he makes use of a word ("enthusiastic") which had, at the time, the invariable meaning of contemptibly fanatical and almost mad.

A drama written in this spirit of cynical contempt—written against the true convictions of its creator—is plainly disqualified from any real depth of meaning, since it comes from only part of its maker's mind. This, then, is the clue to its shallowness of philosophical reflection: what the drama's personages are doing and suffering has no relation to what the dramatist really feels and thinks about human life. Between the action and the comment there is no union. All through runs this fatal cleavage: the heroic militarism, the romantic Lady-worship, and all the rest of it, belong to a dead past. The true present, the seed of the future, holds them in dry contempt. As the seventeenth century passed into the eighteenth, these heroics came to seem more and more intolerable fustian; the military hero is thoroughly debunked. Debunked by Dryden himself (and this *is* his true self speaking):

He (Homer) forms and equips those ungodly mankillers whom we poets, when we flatter them, call heroes; a race of men who can never enjoy quiet in themselves till they have taken it from all mankind.

(Dedication of *Examen Poeticum*)

Pope's fancy was caught, as his mind agreed, with that sentence; it emerges in the lines from the *Essay on Man*:

> *Heroes are much the same, the point's agreed,*
> *From Macedonia's madman to the Swede;*
> *The one strange purpose of their lives, to find*
> *Or make, an enemy of all mankind!*

The point, in fact, *was* agreed: agreed by Prior—

Pray observe those miserable People whom you call heroes, how they go about roaring and crying like spoilèd Children for every thing they see, throwing away their own, and desiring other Peoples goods, never contented with the Common and easy use of things, and still drawing new troubles upon themselves from the inconsistency and Perverseness of their own Projects.

(*Dialogues of the Dead:* Cromwell and his Porter)

—agreed by Swift—

The very same principle that influences a bully to break the windows of a whore who has jilted him, naturally stirs up a great prince to raise mighty armies, and dream of nothing but sieges, battles, and victories

(Tale of a Tub)

—agreed by all the Augustans, till at last the very word "hero" has *ex hypothesi* a tinge of the ridiculous, the discreditable, and the unreal, so that Johnson can praise Shakespeare, in the Preface, because he "has no heroes, his scenes are occupied only by men". This is the true Augustan line of thought: looking at this, we can see the heroic drama in its proper perspective. It was not something new, with future possibilities; it was—and the facts were to prove it—the last and thoroughly decadent flicker of a living and popular poetic drama in England.

What happened to the poetic drama during the Restoration happened also, in essentials, to the poetry of religion. A cleavage appeared, and the result was a loss of total genuineness. Before the Civil War religious poetry (as the *Anniversaries* show) shared a great area of sensibility and expression with the poetry of secular love. Lines such as these—

> *The Phœnix builds the Phœnix's nest:*
> *Love's Architecture is his own*

might come from any metaphysical love-lyric; in fact, they come from Crashaw's poem on Christ's nativity. Conversely, these lines might come from any religious poem of the age—

> *But neither steele nor stony breast*
> *Are proofe against those lookes of thine,*
> *Nor can a Beauty less divine*
> *Of any heart be long possest,*
> *Where thou pretend'st an interest . . .*

—but they *are* from a love-poem by Aurelian Townshend. This union was never recovered. Religious writing after the Restoration shows a fatal self-consciousness; writers put on a special tone and adopt a special language when they deal with divine subjects. Symptomatic was a change in the sermon. The sermons of Jacobean and Caroline divines, such as Donne, Andrewes, Taylor, and so on, are full of wit and fancy, not infrequently variegated with puns. After the Restoration, sermons become sensible, plain, little varied in manner; in the name of decorum, all the elements of wit and fancy are excluded. Glanvil's *Essay concerning Preaching* (1678) insists on "plain-ness"—and plainness, he argues, is opposed to "hard words", to "deep and mysterious notions", to "affected Rhetorications", and to "Phantastical Phrases"; it is opposed also to pedantry, to "an affected use of scraps of Greek and Latin". The religious verse of the age changed in exactly the same direction. Dryden's *Religio Laici* discusses theology in a style deliberately prosaic and unemotional:

> *And this unpolisht, rugged Verse I chose,*
> *As fittest for Discourse, and nearest prose.*

"Discourse" gives it away. Religious verse has now become almost nothing but "discourse". The object is not to re-create a religious experience and to set it before the reader, but to persuade him, to convince him of the truth of something. This is no doubt symptomatic of an age in which scepticism is coming into the open as never before; the reader is no longer felt to be someone who may be assumed to have a common ground of religious experience with the writer, nor is it possible to write of religion (as Herbert and Vaughan do, for instances) in a tone of completely private absorption, a shutting-out of all things save the writer and his God. The reader is now someone probably or at least possibly hostile, who has to be convinced.[1] Hence, in religious poetry no less than in political, there enters the squinting look of the propagandist: both eyes never on the subject, for one must be always on its reception. And on religious verse this one-eyed manner produced the same kind of impoverishing. Take, for example, Dryden (in *The Hind and the Panther*) urging himself to sacrifice all things to God:

---

[1] Cf. Pepys's cynical, but no doubt correct, observation immediately after the Restoration:

. . . with him to the Abbey to see them (i.e., the King and Queen) at vespers. There I found but a thin congregation already. So I see that religion, be what it will, is but a humour, and so the esteem of it passeth as other things do. (2nd October, 1660.)

235

> . . . *And what thou didst and dost so dearly prize,*
> *That fame, that darling fame, make that thy sacrifice.*
> *'Tis nothing thou hast giv'n; then add thy tears*
> *For a long race of unrepenting years.*
> *'Tis nothing yet; yet all thou hast to give:*
> *Then add those may-be years thou hast to live.*

This is Dryden at his best; it would be ungenerous and untrue to
suggest that it is in any way insincere: but put it beside Donne
on the same theme—

> *Seale then this Bill of my Divorce to All*
> *On whom those fainter beames of love did fall.*
> *Marry those loves which in youth scatter'd bee*
> *On Fame, Wit, Hope (false mistresses) to thee . . .*

—and the drop in intensity is painfully clear. The way is being
prepared for that impoverishing of religious experience—except
in the regions of Dissent and eccentricity—which the eighteenth
century suffered from, and which, as has been said, thoroughly
justified Dr. Johnson's disapproval of religious poetry. Religion
in the Establishment will be reduced to something little more
than an ethical rationalism: the "Moral Virtues" which aroused
Blake's wrath, and which, as he pointed out, were really in no
way different from pagan ethics.

   Thus both in poetic drama and in religious verse, the
Restoration was still trying to do what could no longer be done.
But not really for long: it soon found what lay within its powers
and what was beyond them. It scrutinized with great care its
own achievement and that of the past, and the relationships
between them. It is now, for the first time, that literary criticism becomes a major part of literature, an important form in its
own right. "This very Critical age," Thomas Shadwell called
it: and he was right. Dryden's prologues and epilogues bear
witness to his rightness; they abound in nervous pleas to the
"Criticks", pleas usually jocular and jaunty in tone, but the tone
imperfectly concealing a real anxiety. Thus, the Epilogue to the
second part of the *Conquest of Granada* contrasts the freedom
from critical attention which the elder dramatists enjoyed with
the rigorous and malicious scrutiny which poor Dryden himself,
and his fellows, must endure:

> Fame *then was cheap, and the first commer sped;*
> *And they have kept it since, by being dead.*
> *But, were they now to write, where Critiques weigh*
> *Each Line, and ev'ry Word, throughout a Play,*
> *None of 'em, no, not* Jonson *in his height,*
> *Could pass, without allowing grains for weight.*

Of this critical activity the immediate literary influences—the classics and the French—need no expounding; but they are not the thing itself, they are only the material it found useful to borrow from. The thing itself is a passionate need to make order out of chaos, and this need, in the last analysis, is social and political. *No more Civil Wars!* is what it all comes down to. Pope perceived the connection:

> *Late, very late, correctness grew our care,*
> *When the tir'd Nation breath'd from civil war*

—and the spirit that inspires Dryden in his effort to put order and meaning into the literary past which he inherited is the same as induced Wren to plan a London of classical order from the ruins of the Fire and South to declare in a sermon that God had "changed Men's Tempers with the times, and made a Spirit of Building succeed a Spirit of *Pulling Down*".

The political motives which lay behind the longing for order were reinforced by the sudden leap of science into a position of more than modern prestige and veneration. (*"More* than modern" because unspoiled by fear and resentment.) The effect of this on English expression—its leading to a successful campaign for plainness and terseness—is too well known and too obvious to need elaboration. But perhaps even more important —for that would have come in any case—is an indirect effect. Now for the first time we get something that has since become familiar: literature feels uneasily inferior to science, it envies as well as admires the latter's undeniable achievements, it perceives that science has notably progressed and it feels that it can and should do likewise. Dryden is a spokesman for these feelings: the *Essay of Dramatick Poesy* expresses the man of letters' admiration for scientific achievement:

Is it not evident, in these last hundred years, when the study of philosophy has been the business of all the virtuosi in Christendom, that almost a new nature has been revealed to us? that more errors of the School have been detected, more useful experiments in philosophy made, more noble secrets in optics, medicine, anatomy, astronomy discovered, than in all those credulous and doting ages from Aristotle to us?—so true it is, that nothing spreads more fast than science, when rightly and generally cultivated.

And elsewhere he gives the corollary of that admiration, the feeling that poetry should go and do likewise:

. . . For we live in an age so sceptical, that as it determines little, so it takes nothing from antiquity on trust; and I profess to have no other ambition in this essay, than that poetry may not go backward, when all other arts and sciences are advancing.

(Defence of the Epilogue to the
Conquest of Granada)

Thus the prestige of science reinforced the purely literary ambition, derived from the classics and the contemporary French example, to reduce English literature to order. It is not only the beginning of fully-developed literary criticism that the Restoration witnesses; it is also the beginning of real literary history—an attempt, that is, to "place" the monuments of the past, to work out influences and trace descents, to come as near as may be to the logical cause-and-effect of a scientific theory. With what seems, at least, the utmost confidence, the course of true literature is traced and its limits marked out. Dryden's *Epistle to Roscommon* gives what became the accepted outline. First, the Ancients; then, decline to the Gothic barbarism of the Middle Ages—

> *Till barbarous Nations, and more barbarous Times,*
> *Debas'd the majesty of verse to rhymes*

—next, the revival in Italy—

> *But Italy, reviving from the trance*
> *Of Vandal, Goth, and monkish ignorance*

—finally, the French and English take it on—

> *The French pursued their steps; and Britain, last,*
> *In manly sweetness all the rest surpass'd.*

This is not new, except in its patness: it is the climax and the formulation of that contempt for the Middle Ages previously noted in Renaissance classicist and Puritan. And the bent for formulation, applied to English poetry in particular, is equally clear in Dryden's working-out of poetical "descents":

> Milton was the poetical son of Spenser, and Mr. Waller of Fairfax; for we have our lineal descents and clans as well as other families. Spenser more than once insinuates, that the poetical soul of Chaucer was transfused into his body; and that he was begotten by him two hundred years after his decease. Milton has acknowledged to me, that Spenser was his original. . . .
>
> (Preface to the *Fables*)

What it amounts to is a sense that English literature is by now considerable enough to be thought of as more than a haphazard collection of individuals, that it has a tradition and this tradition can and should be exactly formulated. There had been earlier attempts at such formulations—we have looked at one, in Drayton's epistle to Henry Reynolds—but not till the Restoration were they worked out with the conviction that they expressed a final, a "scientific" judgment, and the confidence which comes from feeling that they represented not merely the opinions of individuals but the settled taste of all men of good sense. From the Restoration, in fact, there comes into existence —what had hardly existed before—a definable orthodoxy in judgments on English literature. Moreover, this authoritative defining of the true direction of English poetry was accompanied by a great activity of classifying, of defining and distinguishing the various sorts of poetry, and their appropriate styles, limits, rules, and objectives. This had always been the bent of the Greco-Latin rhetorical tradition, with its inveterate addiction to the propagation of pigeon-holes; but it seems likely that the example of science, once again, gave it an extra stimulus in the years after 1660. The notion that literary criticism can be made "scientific" is an old recurring daydream, an immortal heresy: the men of the Restoration, in their own terms, suffered from it as much as any.

And then there was the desire to see progress. One's first impression from Restoration criticism is that it had an extraordinarily good conceit of itself, of the literary achievement of its own times. It seems at first sight to see the age as the grand climax of all that had gone before—a view seen at its most naïvely complacent in Bishop Sprat:

> Till the time of *King Henry the Eighth,* there was scarce any man regarded it [*sc.* the English language] but *Chaucer,* and nothing was written in it which one would be willing to read twice but some of his *Poetry.* But then it began to raise itself a little, and to sound tolerably well. From that Age down to the beginning of our late *Civil Wars,* it was still fashioning and beautifying itself. In the wars themselves . . . it received many fantastical terms . . . and withall it was inlarg'd by many sound and necessary Forms and Idioms which it before wanted. And now when men's minds are somewhat settled . . . if some sober and judicious Men would take the whole Mass of our Language into their hands as they find it . . . I dare pronounce that our Speech would quickly arrive at as much plenty as it is capable to receive, and at the greatest smoothness which its derivation from the rough *German* will allow it.
>
> *(History of the Royal Society)*

And Dryden on North's Elizabethan translation of Plutarch shows the same spirit:

> The *English* Language was then unpolish'd, and far from the perfection which it has since attain'd: So that the first Version is not only ungrammatical and ungraceful, but in many places almost unintelligible. For which Reasons, and lest so useful a piece of History, shou'd lie oppress'd under the rubbish of Antiquated Words, some ingenious and learned Gentlemen, have undertaken this task [*sc.* of making a new version].
>
> (Epistle Dedicatory to the Tonson translation of
> Plutarch's *Lives* "by several hands")

It is one of the oddities of classicist doctrine that this short-term conviction of recent progress was accompanied by a long-term certainty that all things had degenerated most dismally since the days of the Ancients: Dryden himself, in this same preface, argues with gloomy enjoyment that compared with them we "who succeeded them in after times" are but "Dwarfs of Wit and Learning". The men of the Restoration balanced their cocksureness—perhaps they excused it to themselves—by this dogma of an intellectual Fall of Man; and even when they deal with English poetry, their cocksureness, though real, is far from all-embracing. It does not represent the whole of the age's mind, and is found unqualified only in men of no literary distinction, like Sprat, or in the fanatics of classicist dogma, like Thomas Rymer. Rymer's notorious silliness, when he deals with Shakespeare, is not really typical of the Restoration; he has an old-fashioned air, he seems to belong rather to the early Renaissance, with his appeal to the Ancients as final court,[1] his inability to visualize any way of benefiting by them except the fatal way of literal imitation, and his heavily facetious worrying of Shakespearean plots by the standards of truth to "reality" and moral edification. Rymer, in fact, might be Sidney, as far as doctrine is concerned—the difference being that things had been written in the meantime which ought to have changed all that. But all those things, to Rymer, meant nothing at all; the extent of his mind's alienation from the realities of English poetry may be gauged by his wonderful proposals for an English tragedy based on Aeschylus' *Persae*: a scheme so splendidly ludicrous that it merits quotation in full:

But perhaps the memorable Adventure of the *Spaniards* in 88 against *England* may better resemble that of *Xerxes*. Suppose, then, a Tragedy call'd *The Invincible Armado*.

The *Place*, then, for the Action may be at *Madrid*, by some *Tomb* or solemn place of resort; or if we prefer a Turn in it from good to bad Fortune, then some *Drawing-Room* in the Palace near the King's Bed-chamber.

The *Time* to begin, Twelve at Night.

The Scene opening presents 15 Grandees of *Spain*, with their most solemn Beards and Accoutrements, met there (suppose) after some Ball or other publick occasion. They

[1] Cf. the title of his *magnum opus*: "The Tragedies of the last age considered and examined by the practice of the ancients and by the common sense of all ages." Rymer takes it for granted that the two are synonymous. So, of course, did Pope:

> *Learn hence for ancient Rules a just esteem,*
> *To copy Nature is to copy them*

—but Pope, in practice, made plenty of exceptions; Rymer did not.

talk of the state of Affairs, the greatness of their Power, the vastness of their Dominions, and prospect to be infallibly, ere long, Lords of all. With this prosperity and goodly thoughts transported, they at last form themselves into the *Chorus*, and walk such measures, with Musick, as may become the gravity of such a Chorus.

Then enter two or three of the Cabinet Councel, who now have leave to tell the Secret, That the Preparations and the Invincible Armado was to conquer *England*. These, with part of the *Chorus*, may communicate all the Particulars, the Provisions, and the Strength by Sea and Land, the certainty of success, the Advantages by that accession, and the many Tun of Tar-barrels for the Hereticks. These Topicks may afford matter enough, with the *Chorus*, for the Second Act.

In the Third Act, these Gentlemen of the Cabinet cannot agree about sharing the Preferments of *England*, and a mighty broil there is among them. One will not be content unless he is King of *Man*; another will be Duke of *Lancaster*. One, that had seen a Coronation in *England*, will by all means be Duke of *Aquitayn*, or else Duke of *Normandy*. (And on this occasion two Competitors have a juster occasion to work up and shew the Muscles of their Passion than *Shakespear's Cassius* and *Brutus*.) After, the *Chorus*.

The Fourth Act may, instead of *Atossa*, present some old Dames of the Court, us'd to dream Dreams and to see Sprights, in their Night-Rails and Forhead-Cloaths, to alarm our Gentlemen with new apprehensions, which make distraction and disorders sufficient to furnish out this Act.

In the last Act the King enters, and wisely discourses against Dreams and Hobgoblins, to quiet their minds. And the more to satisfy them and take off their fright, he lets them to know that St. *Loyola* had appeared to him and assured him that all is well. This said, comes a Messenger of the ill News; his Account is lame, suspected, he sent to Prison. A second Messenger, that came away long after but had a speedier Passage, his account is distinct, and all their loss credited. So, in fine, one of the *Chorus* concludes with that of *Euripides*: *Thus you see the Gods bring things to pass often otherwise than was by man proposed.*

(A Short View of Tragedy, chap. 1)

Rymer was kind enough to suggest that "Mr. Dryden might try his Pen on this Subject". Mr. Dryden, however, had too much sense. For Dryden, the one critic of first-rate quality in the age and the true maker of the Augustan settlement, soon abandoned the rigid idiocies of pure classicism, if he had ever held them at all; and by allowing in practice a steady stream of exceptions, he reduced the classical dogmas, which he honoured, like everyone else, with the most duteous of lip-service, to a status not much better than that of commandments revered no doubt, but regularly (and beneficially) broken. By so doing, he preserved his integrity and life as a critic; but at the cost of imposing on himself and on those who were to follow him a fine assortment of radical contradictions, a deep cleavage between the principles according to which men thought they *ought* to judge and admire, and their real spontaneous admirations.

One of the most central of these contradictions is that of which one side can be seen in the above-cited passages of Sprat on the progress of the language and of Dryden on North's prose. The Restoration held firmly this dogma that the *language* of the past was inferior to that of the present—not only in prose, of course, but also in verse, ever since Mr. Waller had "refin'd English numbers."[1] At the same time, Dryden recognized with great honesty—and obviously felt with the deepest possible appreciation, as his noble eulogies of Shakespeare and Chaucer prove—that much of the actual *poetry* which the past had produced, using this inferior medium, was superior to that of his own times. It never seems to have occurred to him to wonder how a superior poetry could possibly be produced with an inferior language, poetry being made out of language; his theory, perhaps, went wrong partly because it was bedevilled by that science-inspired ambition to see progress, and partly through an inadequately analytical attitude to language: he did not see that changes which were improvements in the direction of producing a good clear expository prose may have been thoroughly retrograde where poetry was concerned. Especially dramatic poetry: for it was there, as he recognized himself, that his own age was undeniably inferior. As he puts it in the dedication of *Examen Poeticum*—he is talking of Chapman's Homer, and observes (as he did of North's Plutarch) that the original would appear to much better advantage

[1] This dogma receives its absurdest expression in Rymer's summary: "Chaucer refin'd our English. Which in perfection by Waller."

in the harmonious version of one of the best writers, living in a much better age than was the last. I mean for versification and the art of numbers; for in the drama we have not arrived to the pitch of Shakespeare and Ben Jonson.

There this radically false distinction appears again: "versification" and "the art of numbers" are thought of as something quite distinct from "the drama"—even the poetic drama. This false distinction seems always to be haunting classicist criticism—we have seen it earlier in Sidney's observation that *Chevy Chace* would be a much better thing if dressed up *à la* Pindar, and it is analysed later in Coleridge's remarks on the æsthetic effects of "Latin Verses":[1] "language" is one thing, "poetry" another. It haunts the criticism of the eighteenth century with dire effects on all its verse but the very greatest. It seems to be due, in the last resort, to the forming of ideal models to which reality must somehow or other be made to conform; thus, one may suspect that the over-valuing of Waller, and the particular role assigned to him, were largely due to the need for finding the English equivalent of *enfin Malherbe vint.* . . . The facts that the models were of alien extraction and the whole attitude strongly pedagogical widened the gap still farther; that the "art of numbers" is something which can be taught and learned is a notion which may work with Latin and French (*"faire de beaux vers"* is natural, "make good verses" is pedantic and affected), but it never has worked with English.

When the line of English poetry had been settled to the Restoration's satisfaction and the direction of its progress agreed on, when the Middle Ages, save for Chaucer, had been handed over to those dusty antiquarians whom Pope and Swift find so comic, when the metaphysicals had received their sentences of dismissal as "unnatural" and "harsh" (great wits, if you like, but not good poets), when the minor Elizabethan dramatists had been consigned to that virtually total oblivion in which they were to rest until the Romantics resurrected them, when, in fact,

---

[1] "I was, at that early period, led to a conjecture . . . that this style of poetry, which I have characterized above, as translations of prose thoughts into poetic language, had been kept up by, if it did not wholly arise from, the custom of writing Latin verses, and the great importance attached to these exercises, in our public schools." (*Biographia Literaria*, chap. I.)

the whole rich chaos of English poetry had been brought to an order and decency comprehensible and even enjoyable to an English gentleman well-grounded in his Virgil and Horace, one great problem remained. And that, of course, was William Shakespeare. He has always been, virtually since his lifetime, both the central fact and the central problem of English criticism. No theory which does not account for him is worth the making; but he seems to upset all theories. The bewilderment which one can see his contemporaries already expressing—how to reconcile his greatness with his lack of learning, lack of art, lack of "personality" ("a handsome, well shap't man: very good company"), lack of everything, indeed, except greatness—this bewilderment forms the beginning of a debate which tormented English criticism for some two hundred years. His existence, and the fact that nobody save Rymerish cranks could seriously dispute his supremacy, was *the* stumbling-block in the way of any real victory in England of classicist doctrine. One can estimate his power by imagining what would have happened if France had produced, about the time of Montaigne, let us say, a dramatist of equal genius, working in the native, medieval tradition and breaking all the rules. Had such a genius existed, French classicism could never have won the total victory which, in the absence of any major achievement from the opposition, it did win. That the English classicists did thoroughly recognize the supremacy of Shakespeare—it is a complete error to suppose that the Restoration and early eighteenth century in any way "neglected" or depreciated him—may be briefly proved by two quotations: one from Dryden, the founder of Augustanism, and one from Addison, a leading consolidator:

> . . . *But spite of all his* [*i.e., the author's*] *pride, a secret shame*
> *Invades his Breast at* Shakespear's *sacred name:*
> *Aw'd when he hears his* Godlike Romans *rage,*
> *He in a just despair would quit the Stage;*
> *And to an Age less polish'd, more unskill'd,*
> *Does with disdain the foremost Honours yield.*
>
> (Prologue to *Aureng-zebe*)

Our inimitable Shakespeare is a stumbling-block to the whole tribe of these rigid critics. Who would not rather read one of his plays, where there is not a single rule of the stage observed, than any production of a modern critic, where there is not one of them violated?

(Spectator, No. 592)

Shakespeare, then, had to be accommodated. But accommodated in some way which would not compromise the general thesis, that literature—and especially the language—had progressed. Dryden and Addison, as quoted above, hint how it was done. It was done by representing him as the grand Exception and the great In Spite Of. The general thesis required that good poetry could be produced only by those who knew and obeyed the rules, and only in ages of good sense and good taste; but the loophole was available (luckily provided by Horace himself[1]) for the irregular genius who could "snatch a grace beyond the rules of art", and the English classicists so widened that loophole, for the particular benefit of Shakespeare, that it more or less eliminated the wall. The thesis of progress was maintained by seeing the Elizabethan age as astounding-but-barbarous, as ignorant in literary matters, with Shakespeare supremely great *in spite of it*—in spite of his age, in spite of his audience, in spite of his language. This view picks up and elaborates on that contemporary view of Shakespeare which saw him as the untaught natural genius contrasted with the learned art of Jonson. It becomes the accepted commonplace that what is bad in Shakespeare can be put down to his audience's ignorance and bad taste; the "clenches" and bombast which were reprehended *in toto* in a poet like Donne, are excused as partial blots on Shakespeare.

Once found, this formula served the eighteenth century to perfection. One can see it operating both in Pope and Johnson:

One cannot therefore, wonder, if Shakespeare having at his first appearance no other aim in his writings than to procure a subsistence, directed his endeavours solely to hit the taste and humour that then prevailed. The Audience was generally composed of the meaner sort of people. . . . Not only the common Audience had no notion of the rules of

---

[1] Verum ubi plura nitent in carmine, non ego paucis
offendar maculis. (*Ars Poetica*, 351.)

writing, but few even of the better sort piqu'd themselves upon any great degree of knowledge or nicety that way.

(Pope: Preface to S.)

Shakespeare engaged in dramatick poetry with the world open before him; the rules of the ancients were then known to few; the publick judgment was unformed; he had no example of such fame as might force him upon imitation, nor criticks of such authority as might restrain his extravagance: He therefore indulged his natural disposition. . . .

(Johnson: do.)

The formula was based on ignorance of the Elizabethan literary scene: there were in fact plenty of persons who could—and would—have taught Shakespeare "the rules" if he had cared to learn them; but for all that it was hardly questioned till Coleridge. "Shakespeare's judgment equal to his genius" is its classic refutation. Though even Coleridge—and still more the Victorians—continued to cling to it in one respect: they were still inclined, with a sigh of thankful relief, to hand over their Shakespeare's bawdy to the audience of the Globe.[1] The notions that he might have been bawdy because he liked it, and that his bawdy might sometimes have a positive and essential value in his poetry, were far too alien to romantic and Victorian concepts of poetry to be entertained for a moment.

By this means the classicist doctrine provided its own solution of what is, after all, still and always the central problem that the critic of Shakespeare must deal with: how to keep the balance between the two undeniable facts which make up the fact of Shakespeare—the popular and successful dramatist serving a particular audience and the most universal of poets. The taste of the Restoration and the Augustans did it, in effect, by accepting Shakespeare and rejecting the Shakespearean moment, by admiring his poetry and deprecating the way of life and hence of language in which such poetry can be written. It amounted to a final recognition of what had happened to English poetry over the century, of the gulf between the Shakespearean moment and the England of after the Civil War. They were quite right to recognize that gulf, to admit that they could no longer write—that it was no longer possible for anyone to write—in the

[1] E.g., Coleridge's remarks on the "low soliloquy" of the Porter in *Macbeth*.

Shakespearean manner. The way in which they saw the fact was not our way—why should it have been?—for not being in the least addicted to that modern literary masochism which always sees the past as superior to the present (and by so doing, it may be, considerably assists in making the latter genuinely inferior), they congratulated themselves on the changes that had taken place, saw the one undeniable exception as an unaccountable accident, and were thereby set free to work in their own ways at what they *could* do with real success. Their critical formulations were nonsense: Shakespeare was far more helped than hindered by the age and public he wrote for, and a critical attitude which accepts mature Shakespeare but can make nothing of Donne is indefensible. But the self-confidence with which the Restoration could make its erroneous formulations was far more beneficial to its own creation than our desperate efforts to appreciate everything and account for everything. Ours is that "catholic" taste which in truth is no taste at all.

Chapter 10

CONCLUSION

THIS book makes no pretence of being a history of seventeenth century poetry. The most it might claim is that it suggests a theory of its course. Like all theories, where literature is concerned, it leaves itself open to all manner of criticisms, and could guard itself only by a lavish admission of exceptions. Excuse may be found, if needed, by pleading that of all the periods of our literature the seventeenth century is not only the richest but also the most intricate—as the age itself was, whose real meaning was the infinitely confused and painful transition from medieval to modern. Because that *was* the real meaning of the age as a whole, it will often be found—it has often been found in this book—that the most reliable index to the nature of any particular work is its relationship, or lack of it, to the medieval heritage.

In the opening years of the century, there occurred a moment of convergence. Church and State, in the Anglican settlement and Stuart monarchy; courtly and popular; the traditional ethos of the countryside and the critical alertness of the capital city—these, for that moment, came together to a degree far greater than they, or their equivalents, ever achieved in any other time. What is claimed for this moment is not that it was morally better, socially more enlightened, or politically more intelligent, than other moments, but simply that its qualities and its defects alike had a oneness which is more than a delusion caused by the passing of time—for neither the Restoration after it, nor the sixteenth century before it, yields us that quality. This feeling of unusual oneness in a society is perhaps the only reliable constant common to all those ages which posterity has agreed to single out as "great". They are no better than other times; take their qualities one by one, and they may be found, in many of their features, demonstrably worse; but the unity they possess seems to give them the power of bestowing significance and beauty on activities which at other times would have neither—or have them in lesser degree. The unity of the great age we have been examining can be seen under preparation in the closing

S

years of Elizabeth's reign: in itself a time of uneasiness and disillusion, but bearing the seeds of the later achievement. For those years were doing one work of crucial importance; they were bringing to maturity, to intellectual and social prestige, the poetic drama. This was to be the central expression of the moment of convergence—made by it and making it—for this in itself reached greatness by being a centre for converging elements; it was both vulgar and intellectual, traditional and modernist, religious in essence but secular in form. Moreover, it was literally, geographically, centred, as the medieval drama —its predecessor and in many ways its true ancestor—was not; the latter, scattered over the provincial towns of the country, outside the interest or before the time of the new machine of printing, making no contact with the world of courtliness and the new spirit of the Renaissance, could never be a focussing-point for an intellectual life, as the new professional drama, centred in London, could be and was. In this lies the justification for calling the great moment the Shakespearean moment; for its centre was the drama, and of it he was not merely the supreme exponent, he was also as typical as supreme greatness can ever be typical. His quality is that of the dramatic moment he worked for. He has it in greater purity, with more intensity, with wider scope, than any other man: but not differently.

Hence the poetic drama could spread its power beyond the theatres. It became a magnet of such strength that it attracted a whole school of non-theatrical poetry into its field, and filled it with the dramatic attitude. The vital link, the particular person through whom this spreading was accomplished, was Donne; his youthful visits to the London theatres may be seen as events of the first importance to English poetry. Important too, not quite so vital, was Ben Jonson, throwing a bridge, temporary but genuine, between classicist and popular. From these two, but especially the former, the dramatic attitude spreads through two generations of English poets and into the domains of love-lyric and devotional verse. And farther than verse; for it went, too, into the sermon.

This was how it worked: but it could not have worked at all unless the society it worked in had satisfied certain conditions. The society itself had to be "dramatic" if the dramatic attitude was to spread through all its expression. It had to be hierarchical, sensuous, magnificent, and imbued with a tragic philosophy of life—and that meant, then, an orthodox Christian philosophy, since that alone, for that age, could yield the tragic sense. This is not to say that Shakespeare himself—or any writer of the time—had to hold as a private individual, opinions always in agreement with such a society; what *was* essential—and what did happen—was that such a view of life could impose itself so powerfully that no tragic art could be so much as thought of outside those terms: and this is the sense in which it can be truly said that Shakespeare's personal, individual opinions are irrelevant to his drama. Whether he entirely agreed with, say, the sentiments regarding kingship expressed by the "good" characters in *Macbeth*, is undiscoverable and would be unimportant if discovered: the point is that without those sentiments the drama would not exist. When he makes his drama, he makes it in collaboration with his age; for the drama, and the dramatist, are now, as it were, "comfortable" in their society. (In the 1590's (and before) they were not; the evidence, for Shakespeare, is in the Sonnets.) Comfortable, but not uncritical; the stress and tension around them make sure of that.

The tension was inherent in the society itself. But it was reinforced by the presence and growing strength of elements contemporary, intermingled, yet essentially alien: the classicist and the Puritan, both of whom, for reasons some similar, some different, were hostile to the native tradition in drama or to the whole dramatic attitude. The classicist's hostility was veiled, insidious, for in social environment and political alignment he was usually in the midst of the Shakespearean society itself. But it was a real hostility for all that; when it triumphed, it would mean the decadence and end of the native poetic drama. Parallels with other arts are always risky; but it has at least a symbolic value, if not a cause-and-effect connection, that the first completely classical building in England—Inigo Jones's Banqueting House—was built in 1629, when the drama's decline was beginning: Elizabethan and Jacobean architecture, with its surprises and variety, its rule-less blending of borrowings and nativeness, has a true affinity to the contemporary drama.[1]

[1] Cf. Marcus Whiffen: *Elizabethan and Jacobean Architecture* (Chap. V):
In short, an Elizabethan house resembles an Elizabethan play:

The Puritan hostility, being open and being linked with political, religious, and to some extent social differences, was more obviously effective. And in the wings, so to speak, waiting his turn to appear, was the rationalist, the man of commonsense. These two, and the classicist, each from his own viewpoint, all stood for a way of life which was tidier, more categorical and dividing, more progressive perhaps—certainly more successful in influencing the future: but as far as dramatic and especially tragic poetry was concerned, impoverished.

If one tries to arrive at some scheme whereby to put order into the rich confusion of the seventeenth century, one may find that the age was divided between two great types of mind. Call them A and B, and they might be defined like this:

A	B
1. Puritanism	Anglo-catholicism
2. New science	Traditional medieval theology
3. Renaissance classicism	Native popular art
4. Iconoclasm (i.e., hatred of the sensuous, especially in spiritual matters)	Sensuousness, allowed to permeate all things
5. Austerity (i.e., hatred of courtliness and magnificence)	Courtly splendour
6. Insularity: distrust of Continental influence, especially baroque and Catholic, and tendency to look on the English as a new Chosen People	Attempt to preserve what remained of the medieval Continental unity
7. Parliamentary sympathies, tendencies towards egalitarianism	Monarchist sympathies, hierarchical view of society
8. Optimism: belief in progress	Pessimism: scepticism about possibility of human improvement
9. Introspectiveness, alienation from the dramatic attitude	Dramatic and tragic sense

it contains some fine scenes and a good many digressions—not necessarily without their own charm.

The parallel might be extended to the other end of the century—could it not be said that the formalized heroics of Vanbrugh's Blenheim have an affinity to those of Dryden's dramas?

To which might be added (to be taken with a grain of salt):

A	B
10. Cambridge	Oxford

Such a scheme is of course nothing *but* a scheme: it is not to be supposed—human nature in general, and the seventeenth century in particular, being as complex as they are—that many men will be found to answer to all the qualities of one and to none of the other. But the scheme does work: it will always be found that the dominant part of a man's mind can be placed decisively on one side, even if a lesser part of him goes on the other. Milton, for example, shows little or no interest in the new science; his insularity shows itself only in the old-fashionedness (early Renaissance) of his Continental affinities and in his feeling for the English as Chosen People: but otherwise he seems to fulfil all the conditions of *A* and none of those of *B*. George Herbert will respond to all the qualities of *B* except the trivial last—he went to Cambridge. Even in the comparatively few men whom one feels to be balanced between the two, there is usually something that makes the verdict finally clear. Falkland's doubts about the King's cause, his sympathy for the Parliament's, and his lukewarm regard for the Church hierarchy, may seem to incline him towards *A*; but the background of his Catholic family and his friendships with men like Chillingworth and Jonson make his final decision to fight for the King seem the only decision he could have made. Marvell is an even more doubtful case: the one writer of the age, perhaps, in whom elements of real Puritanism, of a deep feeling for the Latin (including the Epicurean) heritage, and of the metaphysical way of writing, contrived to exist together—for a time, at any rate—without jarring. But even in him, even in his best verse, there is a certain coolness, an air as of not being completely committed, which prepare one both for his choice of the Parliament's cause and for his later collapse into thoroughgoing anti-monarchist propaganda. And such doubtful cases as Falkland and Marvell are rare.

If these, then, are the two great types of seventeenth century mind (the rationalist has been excluded as a rare bird before 1660, and as belonging in spirit rather to the following age), there seems no doubt that when the crisis of the century—

which was the Civil War, but was also wider than the war—brought the tension between them to breaking-point, it was A which came out on top and A which therefore bequeathed its heritage in full to the eighteenth century. If one takes one by one the qualities of A, their descendants can be seen flourishing and multiplying; they have changed, of course, from their fathers, in accordance with the changing age, but the paternity is unmistakable. Puritanism continues in the forms of nonconformity and methodism. The new science goes from strength to strength. Renaissance classicism bequeaths its dogmas, though interpreted more sensibly, to the classicism of the Augustans. The iconoclasm continues in the increasing alienation of great sections of the community from the arts, in the almost total decay of religious art through the eighteenth century, and in the nonconformist middle classes' detestation of the drama. The austerity is witnessed at both ends of the social scale; at the lower end, in the decay of the folk-festivals which had been a vital part of the seventeenth century world: at the upper end, in the degeneration of magnificence into mere ostentation, incapable of evoking any but a hostile response from men of fine spirit and intelligence—hence Pope on Timon's villa, and hence the Chesterfieldian ideal of the Man of Breeding as one who avoids all display. Insularity develops into a reversal of what had been the invariable order of things before the eighteenth century: England now becomes an exporter, not merely an importer, of ideas and attitudes; and what it exports are the qualities of A—science, rationalism, introspective sentiment. Parliamentary sympathies go into Whiggery and radicalism. Optimism continues as deism and rationalism. Introspectiveness gives birth to the analytical sentiment of Richardson and Sterne. The poetic drama collapses into meaningless mediocrity; the tragic sense expires. And deplorable as the conditions of both universities become in the eighteenth century, the state of Cambridge seems a trifle more respectable than that of Oxford.

Against this, it seems that most of the qualities of B died or went into a prolonged state of hibernation. There is no need to go through them all; but the general impression, that this type of mind comes to an end, is confirmed if one considers those few figures of the eighteenth century who do have some affinity to it. They seem in essentials isolated, against the current of their age, whenever they betray that affinity. Dr. Johnson, for instance. His terror of death and hell was felt to be unbalanced and morbid even by those who admired him; Boswell is always explaining it away as "constitutional melancholia". But for Donne it needed no explaining away; it lay within his natural way of thinking. And because he and his age thought it natural and proper, and expressed it freely, it emerged into great art; it was more than a private terror. Blake on this has one of those remarks of his which, though completely wrong-headed, show an extraordinary gift for seeing something which right-headed persons did not see. "Was Johnson hired to Pretend to Religious Terrors while he was an Infidel, or how was it?" There *is*, as Blake felt, an impression of real discrepancy between the "robust commonsense" which was Johnson's outward face to the world and the dark terrors which lay beneath it.

So, from the Restoration onward—for the eighteenth century is really born in 1660—the second type of mind, that above called *B*, goes swiftly towards extinction. And this was the mind which nourished the Shakespearean moment, and which created the kind of society in which such a moment was possible. Its extinction means the end of the conditions in which a Shakespearean poetry, even granted the supreme individual genius—which no society can "create"—could ever be established on anything like the terms on which Shakespeare's poetry was established—as a form, that is, which combined the highest spiritual and intellectual distinction with a living dramatic function and a popular appeal. Thereafter, even if a writer should appear with anything like the Shakespearean gifts, he would never be able to give full expression to them all: some at least must be frustrated or debased.

Perhaps there was one later writer in English who did have a cluster of gifts not utterly dissimilar from Shakespeare's: a writer who possessed a poetic sensibility, a range of human sympathy which extended through all ranks and types of men and all moods from farcical to tragic, a sense of tradition and history vital if not always "accurate", a freedom from any kind of narrowing dogmatism but a deep underlying Christian Toryism, immense fertility and inventiveness, and a careless indifference to the pedantries of form and the niceties of polish. That writer was Walter Scott. What he found possible to do with his

255

gifts will enforce the general argument more powerfully than any abstractions. His poetry and his vision of human life—this is the vital contrast—instead of being so totally fused that the former was the only possible expression for the latter, were separate things. His verse could express little more than romantic tushery; the humour and tragedy had to wait for his prose. He lived in an age without a centre: a moment not of convergence, but of flying apart.

INDEX